Kimberly's Hmmmings

My Journey through Breast Cancer
Encouragement for Walking through
Life's Difficult Seasons and Circumstances

Kimberly McGary

WestBow Press
A DIVISION OF THOMAS NELSON
& ZONDERVAN

Copyright © 2015 Kimberly McGary.

All rights reserved. No part of this book may be used or reproduced by any means, graphic, electronic, or mechanical, including photocopying, recording, taping or by any information storage retrieval system without the written permission of the publisher except in the case of brief quotations embodied in critical articles and reviews.

Scripture taken from the Holy Bible, NEW INTERNATIONAL VERSION®. Copyright © 1973, 1978, 1984 by Biblica, Inc. All rights reserved worldwide. Used by permission. NEW INTERNATIONAL VERSION® and NIV® are registered trademarks of Biblica, Inc. Use of either trademark for the offering of goods or services requires the prior written consent of Biblica US, Inc.

Cover photographs provided by Valerie Holifield Photography
P.O. Box 523, Crystal City, MO

"Carpe Diem" by Ron Johnson as sung by Christian musician,
Dan Smith on his Not Ashamed album, 1996.

WestBow Press books may be ordered through booksellers or by contacting:

WestBow Press
A Division of Thomas Nelson & Zondervan
1663 Liberty Drive
Bloomington, IN 47403
www.westbowpress.com
1 (866) 928-1240

Because of the dynamic nature of the Internet, any web addresses or links contained in this book may have changed since publication and may no longer be valid. The views expressed in this work are solely those of the author and do not necessarily reflect the views of the publisher, and the publisher hereby disclaims any responsibility for them.

ISBN: 978-1-4908-8008-2 (sc)
ISBN: 978-1-4908-8006-8 (hc)
ISBN: 978-1-4908-8007-5 (e)

Library of Congress Control Number: 2015907289

Print information available on the last page.

WestBow Press rev. date: 07/08/2015

Contents

Dedication vii
Acknowledgments ix
Foreword by Dr. Curtis T. Porter xi
Statement of Faith by Kimberly xiii

1. The Beginning of My Story 1
   (June 2012 – January 2013)

2. Pain, Biopsy and Diagnosis 6
   (February 2013)

Chemotherapy I
First Round of Chemo Treatments (4)
One every other Week

3. Hair Today and Gone Tomorrow 13
   (March 7, 2013 – April 6, 2013)

4. Life with Chemo Side Effects 48
   (April 7, 2013 – May 1, 2013)

5. Ellie Mae 77
   Kimberly's Rottweiler

Chemotherapy II
Second Round of Chemo Treatments
12 Weekly Treatments

6. Chemo is Working 81
   (May 2, 2013 – May 31, 2013)

7. Fatigue is a Daily Companion 111
   (June 1, 2013 – June 30, 2013)

8. Countdown to Finish Chemo 136
   (July 1, 2013 – August 2, 2013)

   Photographs 171

9. Surgery 181
   (August 3, 2013 – August 14, 2013)

10. Days of Recovery 196
    (August 15, 2013 – September 3, 2013)

11. Radiation Treatments 219
    Five days a Week for 6 Weeks
    (September 4, 2013 – October 17, 2013)

12. The End of Cancer Treatments 259
    Final Days - The Port Comes Out
    (October 18, 2013 – October 23, 2013)

Final Chapter in Kimberly's Life by Linnie G. Porter 269

Dedication

I would have never had the courage to have undertaken this project without the support, teaching, counsel, prayers, and regular encouragement of my pastor and friend, Dr. Curtis Porter. His encouragement was the nudge I needed to share my story in print. I am grateful for his willingness to share his love for people, passion for God's Word, dedication to follow Holy Spirit's leading, and devotion to Jesus Christ with me. God used him to forever change my life.

Acknowledgments

I want to thank my parents, Paul and Shirma Laughlin, for their love, care, and provision. Without their daily help, I would not have had the energy or ability to share my story and the Lord's daily encouragement with others. I also want to thank Linnie Porter for the many hours she spent praying, typing, formatting, editing, and navigating the process of publishing, in order to bring this project to print. Her help was indispensable. Additionally, I want to thank Dodi Osborn for her tireless efforts editing and praying throughout the whole process.

My acknowledgements would be incomplete without thanking all the wonderful hospital staff who took care of me throughout the whole cancer treatment process. The staffs from St. Luke's Hospital and St. Anthony's Medical Center were absolutely phenomenal. I am forever grateful for their tender, loving care. The Lord placed a wonderful support system around me. I cannot begin to name all who supported, encouraged, and prayed me through this season of life.

I am greatly blessed and thankful for each and every one.

Foreword

In my fifty-nine years as a senior pastor, I have never met any other woman like Kimberly McGary. Beaten down by feelings of inferiority, low self-esteem, self-rejection and worthlessness, she discovered the Biblical secret of Father God's love and deliverance from Satan's strongholds and control.

After twenty years of marriage her husband decided he wanted a divorce. Becoming bankrupt had cost them their lovely home, and left her with no credit to start over. She moved back home with her parents. Then, the doctor informed her of stage two breast cancer. But Kimberly, now free from multiple debilitating strongholds, rested and relied on Christ's healing power. He assured her He would remove the cancer.

The ugliest chemo available was administered every two weeks rather than the normal three weeks, followed by another regimen of a different kind of chemo, which was administered on a weekly basis. Surgery and radiation followed. After nine months of treatment, God's good news was heard: "No Cancer!"

In the two years since I completed the twelve months as Transitional Senior Pastor of First Baptist Church, Festus/Crystal City, Kimberly has continued to encourage others to experience the Spirit-filled life and deliverance taught in II Corinthians 10:4-7. She fills three days of appointments at First Baptist Church of Festus/Crystal City every three weeks for people wanting Father to set them free from spiritual bondage. She and I work together, counseling those three days. In the meantime, she, having learned stronghold counseling by counseling with me, has become an effective and successful counselor in my absence.

Everywhere Kimberly goes, most people immediately realize that there is a contagious spirit about her that draws them to her. During treatment and on many return visits to see her oncology doctor, her infectious laughter, positive attitude, and genuine love for everyone turns the twenty-four chemo stations into a party atmosphere. Candy was added to the visit, blessing doctors, nurses and patients alike. When Kimberly appears in the ward, many nurses and her doctor all insist on warm hugs. Some cancer patients ask for her hugs as well.

While she was having her nails done, one serving her said, "Kimberly, you are special. You are different from anyone else we serve." Dr. Gill commented in my presence, "You have done better than any of my other cancer patients." Customers at the grocery store chain where she works often tell her what an inspiration she is to them.

Kimberly is a walking miracle who reveals Christ's love to every person she meets, including waitresses in restaurants. Her prayers for them are powerful missiles sent to Heaven for their needs.

This book is a compilation of daily emails she sent to people who were asking regularly about how she was doing. After giving an update of her physical and mental condition, Kimberly shared Scriptures explaining that she could be radiant and joyful because of the promises of Heavenly Father. Close to 300 people asked to be included in the emails. Then, some would forward her emails to many others. Some even asked for a copy of all the emails from the nine months of writing. One woman told her she had given up her regular daily devotions and used her emails each day to know God more perfectly. Before writing anything, or in making important decisions, Kimberly would "hmmm" them over in her heart. Some call this "thinking, considering, deliberating, or exploring possible answers from the Lord."

As I read Kimberly's emails, I must admit that God gave me new insights, which go beyond my college, seminary, and doctoral degree work. Open your heart to the Lord and His Holy Spirit as you read these words which have come from the heart of Father God. You are on a spiritual journey that can change your life, just as He changed Kimberly's! All you must do is open your mind, heart and will to Holy Spirit's teaching. He is the great teacher of us all.

Dr. Curtis T. Porter,
Marriage and Family Counselor,
Transitional Senior Pastor

Kimberly speaks of her faith in Jesus Christ.

Jesus is the reason I have joy and contentment as I walk through
this season of life containing bankruptcy, divorce,
the loss of my home, and cancer.
My joy and contentment are not dependent on my circumstances.
They depend on the Lord, His love, and His faithfulness to me.
I have them each and every second of every day!
Nothing can change that!
Not only do I have joy and contentment, but a grateful heart
for the many blessings He continually bestows upon me.

Chapter 1

The Beginning of My Story

June 2012 – January 2013

June 2012

As I begin sharing my story and this season of my life with you, I find myself wishing I could share with you from the beginning of my walk with the Lord. But, I know it would not be practical or necessary.

I will start by sharing with you a few of the events that transpired a short time prior to my getting the cancer diagnosis. Bankruptcy was the first major event in the nine months preceding the diagnosis. The bankruptcy process started in June 2012 and was finalized in court by the middle of July. Then, on the Thursday before Labor Day of that same year, my husband expressed his desire for a divorce. Sometime later he filed for it. By the end of October, the decision was made to no longer make house payments. My paycheck alone was not nearly enough to make house payments and live so as my husband moved out and separated from me on November 17. I moved in with my parents. I searched for an apartment but was unable to find any complexes willing to rent to me while allowing me to keep my dog, Ellie Mae. Because Ellie Mae is a Rottweiler, she was labeled as an aggressive, large breed dog, making her unacceptable to all the apartment complexes that I inquired to rent from. Little did I know at that time, but the Lord had used the rejection of Ellie Mae to place me right where I needed to be for the coming months…with my parents.

I began to sort through the mixture of emotions I was feeling and worked to settle myself to the realities of the new life I was facing. Bankruptcy, divorce, and losing my home were never things I had believed nor desired to be a part of my life, but they came anyway. As I finished the month of November, worked my way through Christmas time, began the new year, I did my best to give all of the hurt and pain to the Lord. All the while, I asked Him to keep me from anger, bitterness, resentment, and unforgiveness towards my husband. The Lord was faithful to do so.

The pain of the rejection was deep, but what I believe hurt the most was the loss of "the dream" of a healed marriage. I had persistently prayed, asking the Lord to heal my broken marriage. The marriage had been broken for a very long time, but I knew deep in my heart the Lord had the ability to heal it. I clung to that hope for many years. Truthfully, it was for most of the almost twenty-year marriage. I had continually worked and prayed for a prosperous marriage and believed that one day, the Lord would work it all out. And He is, just not in the way I had imagined. Because my dream had been for the Lord to heal the marriage, I felt as if something inside me had died. And, I suppose, it had. The dream of the healed marriage died.

January 2013

By the middle of January, I began to feel pain in my breast. I did not think much of the pain in the beginning, because it was simply a dull ache. My initial thought was that I had bumped it, without realizing I had done so. I ignored the pain, assuming it would go away with time as it healed. I have always had a high pain tolerance. So, what was a little pain? After three to four weeks of pain, I began to realize there were occasional sharp pangs of pain added to the ache, which was getting worse rather than better. At this point I reached up and felt the spot where the pain was centered and discovered a large knot had developed in that area. Wisdom told me to call the doctor and make an appointment to have it checked out. I did, and my journey with cancer began.

As I think back on the time leading up to the beginning of my awareness of something not being right in my body, I remember the words the Lord spoke to me in one of my quiet times with Him. I had been pouring out my heart to Him concerning the things I was facing and thanking Him for taking such good care of me. He placed a fabulous support system of family, friends, and church family around me. I asked Him about my future and reminded Him that I trusted Him with it.

As I sat before Him to hear what He would speak to my heart, He told me, "There are harder days ahead, but there are days ahead filled with more joy and happiness than you have ever known. Trust Me, My child. I am with you, walking with you each and every day. My sustaining hand upholds you. You are fully sheltered under My mighty wing."

All I could do was to sit and wonder. Harder? How much *harder* would the days be? I was already dealing with bankruptcy, divorce, and losing my home. I had difficulty imagining things getting worse. Of course, I knew they could, but I could not get a vision of what would come to make things more troublesome than they already were.

Then, I chose to focus on the brighter parts of His Words…"More joy and happiness than you have ever known." That sounded great! I wanted to get to that part! His promises to sustain and shelter me were also a great comfort. I was blessed to already know the truth of God's Word, which taught me to focus on the positive things in my life and not the negatives, so that, is what I chose to do.

The Lord is all of those things. My focus must be on Him and His truth. I knew, whatever was to come, God would give me His grace to walk through it. It is His promise. His grace is always sufficient, no matter the circumstance.

As I think back, I have to acknowledge how much the Lord had grown and taught me, especially in recent years. The stronghold counseling I had done with Dr. Porter had been a key to opening the door to Holy Spirit's fullness in my life. Before that time, I rarely had heard God's voice in a very real and consistent way. I had also been virtually unaware of the differences among Holy Spirit's voice, Satan's voice, and my own thoughts. I was bound by fears and insecurity that had a stranglehold on my life. I had learned to "manage" the strongholds fairly well, but was not "free" of them. There is a *big* difference between managing and free!

I praise the Lord because I now have a clearer understanding of who He is and how He sees and loves me, as well as a better understanding of my value and worth to Him. I have the realization of a life vastly different from what I knew before, a life with the ability to say *no* to fear rather than just hiding it, the ability to feel comfortable in my own skin in a way I had *never* experienced before. I could walk in true peace in a way I had never previously perceived possible, and had the ability to walk in God's strength and not my own. I had the capability to wait and trust the Lord when all that could be seen were awful circumstances. I know there is more the Lord desires to do in me and teach me. There is positively much more I desire for Him to do as well. But, now I have a brighter hope than I have ever known before. I am not exempt from the pain of life, but I have learned how to allow Holy Spirit to walk me through the difficult seasons and continue to stand as the waves of pain and difficulty crash onto me. I still have pain and tears, but they are accompanied with His peace which truly passes all understanding. His comfort is always there for me as I spend time working through the emotions with Him. I haven't done it perfectly, but learning to allow Holy Spirit to deal with the emotions and hurts inside me has been a vastly better approach than trying to work through them on my own, or worse yet, hiding or burying them.

As I think back even further, I remember the time just prior to all the dominoes of difficulty in my life beginning to fall in rapid succession. During these months, I'd spent many hours walking and jogging for exercise. As I exercised, I would pray and listen to my iPod, which was filled with worship and praise music as well as podcasts of sermons and Biblical teaching. I would sing, worship, devour the teaching, and spend time listening for Holy Spirit to speak to my heart as I prayed. Little did I know at the time, but the Lord was preparing me for the season of storms ahead.

I had recently begun to hear God's voice more clearly than I had ever experienced before and began keeping a written record of the things He spoke to me. During this time, the Lord blessed me with approximately three months of what I will call "mountain top" time with Him. It was the sweetest, most uplifting, and most empowering time I had ever known in my relationship with the Lord. Near the end of the "mountain top" season, as I listened to the Lord speak to my heart; I remember Him telling me, "The seasons are changing. The storms are coming. Trust Me. I will carry you through." I sensed in my heart the storms were strong, even though I had no idea what kind of hardship they would bring. I also distinctly remember the lack of fear I felt. Lacking the feeling of fear was a relatively new experience for me since I had previously been bound by strongholds of fear for as long as I could remember. I rejoiced in the truth that I was free from the fear which had restrained me. God gave me the ability to know pain and problems were coming and to decide, before they arrived, that I would trust Him to carry me through.

Having said this, I still needed His regular encouragement, which He readily provided as He continued to prepare me for the coming days. On another day the Lord asked me, "As I allow the storms, dear one, will you trust Me? Will you let Me be God and place you deeper in Me so that you may learn from Me in this darker time?" He continued by saying, "The place of abiding is where you must be in order to weather the storms and dark places. Come and abide, dear one, under the shelter of My wing." Another day he reminded me, "I will sustain you in each and every storm. I am the anchor that holds. You are held safely in Me." The Lord knew I was a lady who needed much encouragement. He not only provided it directly, but also through others during these difficult months.

As you begin reading my story and the daily encouragement the Lord gave me, keep in mind that it was originally written in daily emails and sent to those who desired updates on me and my medical condition. I will add bits and pieces to what I had originally written so that it will flow better and make more sense to those of you who do not know me.

It is my prayer, that as you read my story, you will be encouraged to get to know the Lord if you don't already know Him, and to grow deeper in your relationship with Him if you do. There is nothing more precious or important in your life than the relationship you have with Jesus, your Creator and Lover of your soul, and your ability to allow His Spirit to guide, teach, and flow through you.

Chapter 2

Pain, Biopsy and Diagnosis

February 2013

Thursday, February 14, 2013

I have my doctor's appointment tomorrow at 10 a.m., to be checked out in order to see what is causing the pain. The nurse said they will send me down to mammography after my appointment. It will be good to have that done tomorrow.

Friday, February 15, 2013

I spent quite a bit of time at the hospital and doctor's office, but I'm glad I was able to do it all in one day. First, I was seen by the gynecologist. She sent me down to mammography. From there, I was sent directly over to have an ultrasound. It was kind of funny. Well, funny might not be the right word, but all of the nurses and technicians I came across expected me to be worried and upset. But, God gave me His perfect peace. The last nurse, who was scheduling my biopsy, was very surprised. I could tell by the way she looked at me. She said that I looked like I had a lot of peace about it all. I assured her I did, and told her that God had given me His perfect peace. I told her that He had taken care of me for 44 years and He would take care of me for the rest of my years. She told me she thought that was a great philosophy. I told her it was not a great philosophy, but great truth.

Saturday, February 16, 2013

The pain is greater today, more so now than this morning. I even feel sharper pangs. How much of that is due to all the poking, prodding, squashing, and mashing of yesterday, I don't know. Father God will work it all out I am sure.

Thursday, February 21, 2013

He is the God of my hope, my need, my pain, my healing, and my strength. He is the God of everything I have and all that I am. He will collect the pieces of my broken life to bring complete healing as I let Him. He is teaching me this wonderful truth as I allow him to gather the pieces and make His masterpiece with them. He gives me tears of joy and thankfulness as I contemplate it all. He is so good and loves me so much more than I can comprehend.

Thursday, February 28, 2013

The biopsy went smoothly. Holy Spirit covered me with His peace through the whole day. Jesus says, "Peace I leave with you, My peace I give you. Not as the world gives…" His peace is perfect peace, which "passes all understanding." The results may be back on Friday, but more likely Monday. I am very sore today. After the biopsy, they did another mammogram. I am sure that has added to the discomfort. A small titanium clip was placed in the breast as a marker for the exact spot of the biopsy.

Sunday, March 3, 2013

My mind is more interested in hurrying the test results than it has been. I still have much peace about it, but look forward to the resolution of it all. I am grateful Holy Spirit taught me how to walk in the Lord's peace and to be diligent in guarding my mind. I know how easy it would be not to walk in His peace. I have been very aware, as I talk with others, how Satan could use their words and worries, no matter how well intentioned, to cause me to step off into worry. I am grateful for the encouragement to guard my heart and mind diligently and the reminder of how important it is to "take every thought captive, making it obedient to Christ." Satan is a sneaky, sly, and crafty adversary. Holy Spirit is so good to give me His discernment. "Greater is He that is in me than he that is in the world."

The lump had to have developed quickly since I was just at the gynecologist's office near the end of last year and nothing was detectable at that time. The lump feels much bigger now than it did before the biopsy. I think part of the difference may be due to inflammation. We shall see soon enough. It would be my desire to move as quickly as possible to resolve the problem. I plan to do so as I have further information. I know there will always be challenges ahead to face, but this season has been loaded with them. It seems like before I can get one fully behind me, the next is already upon me. I am reminding myself, "He is my shelter, my shield, my strong tower, my God in whom I trust." He positively is. He has been so faithful to me. I am also reminded that He tells us in His Word, "In this life, you will have trials and tribulations." I have made a conscious decision: I will praise Him in this storm, or season of storms, and in any others as they come my way.

Monday, March 4, 2013
Diagnosis: Infiltrating (Invasive) Ductile Carcinoma

The call from the gynecologist, giving me the diagnosis, came as I was working. I had just finished waiting on a customer when my phone began to ring. I stepped off the sales floor to answer it. The doctor gave me the cancer diagnosis and told me he hoped we had caught it in time. I did not know one type of cancer from another, so the diagnosis of Infiltrating or Invasive Ductile Carcinoma meant nothing but "cancer" to me. This particular type of cancer, as I was later to discover, is a variety known to throw radical cells throughout the body, starting multiple colonies all over the body, very early on. I was diagnosed as having stage two cancer. The amazing thing about this particular cancer is how fast growing and aggressive it is. I had been to the gynecologist in October and showed no signs of anything abnormal. By the middle or end of January, I already had a sizeable knot in my breast. The pain was caused by the rapid growth of the cancer. The cancer cells were dividing so quickly that it caused the displacement of the normal cells around them, bringing pain. Praise the Lord for pain! I have never been one to do the home breast exams, so without the pain; it would have been a much longer time before I realized I had cancer.

My gynecologist gave me the name and number of the doctor who he considered to be the best breast care specialist at St. Luke's Hospital and told me he wanted me to be seen right away. As soon as I ended my conversation with him, I called. When I reached the breast care specialist's office, they initially told me I would have to wait until Thursday for a first appointment. I told the nurse scheduling the appointment that my gynecologist told me he wanted me seen right away. I was asked my name and who my doctor was and put on hold. In less than two minutes, I was given an appointment for the next day. My gynecologist had already called and talked to the specialist.

My diagnosis came on Monday. The specialist's appointment was on Tuesday. My port to receive the chemo therapy was put in on Wednesday, as well as my first oncologist's appointment, blood tests, and a CT scan. Thursday, I had my first round of chemo as well as a bone scan and an echocardiogram. It was a whirlwind week! As I think back on it, the only time I had tears was when I was lying in the hospital bed awaiting the surgery for the placement of the port. As I lay there thinking about it, I had peace, but I really did not want to have to go through all I was facing. As I was praying and pouring my heart out to the Lord, He reminded me to trust Him. I agreed with Him that He was trustworthy and set my heart to do so. I dried the tears and thanked Him for His faithfulness to me and all the promises He had given me in His Word. I thanked Him for His love for me and His peace as well as His assurance that all would be well because He was in control. It is amazing how much peace we can have when we know the Lord is in control and truly believe it. Did I always stay in the center of His perfect peace? No, but most of the time I did. When I took my eyes off the Lord and His truth is when I could feel the peace begin to slip. Holy Spirit faithfully reminded me to put my focus on the Lord. As I did so, perfect peace was restored.

The only other time I felt the possibility of tears was during the first visit with Dr. Julie Gill, my oncologist. She told me that I would be losing my hair because of the chemo. That felt like a hard blow. As I took that information in, I looked over at Dr. Porter who was sitting in the examining room with my parents and me. The Lord used him to help me see my own value, not only to the Lord, but to others. Through my counseling time with the Lord and him, I had begun to be "more comfortable in my own skin" than I had ever been in my life. The Lord reminded me of the many things I now knew and had learned to walk in. My value did not lie in the hair on my head. My value was in the Lord and all He had created in me. I was loved by Him, hair or no hair. I could feel Holy Spirit again reminding me, it would be okay and to trust Him.

Looking back on those days:

Looking back, Holy Spirit's voice was a calm and constant reassurance and encouragement. Each day He would remind me to trust the Lord and know that I was loved completely, cared and provided for perfectly. His encouragement was continuous. It never left me. Even as I write to you now, I hear His voice gently and comfortingly speaking to my heart, "Trust me. I love you, my child, more than you know. I will never leave you nor forsake you."

Chemotherapy I

First Round of Chemo Treatments (4)
One every other Week

Chapter 3

Hair Today and Gone Tomorrow

March 7, 2013 – April 6, 2013

Chemo Day 1... Thursday, March 7, 2013

I know I am just on the first day of chemo, but the chemo treatment itself was actually a pleasurable time. I know it sounds a bit crazy, but we laughed and talked our way through it. We had great fellowship among my parents, Dr. Porter, my nurse, and me. We prayed before the chemo started and the nurse stepped in and asked if she could take part in our prayer time as well. She asked if we would pray with her about a relative who was recently diagnosed with cancer. The Lord knew she needed us today, and we needed her, too.

A couple of hours ago I began feeling flu-like symptoms: a good-sized headache, body aches, weakness, lightheadedness, and unsteadiness. There is no nausea. I would much rather have the other symptoms than that! The Lord continues to give me His peace, His joy, His strength, His comfort, His wisdom, and His provision for every need, and many of my wants, too. Our God is good all the time!

I pray that the Lord would work in me and through me whatever He desires in this season. He has taught me the truth of His Word which says all things work together for good for those who love the Lord, and are called according to His purpose (Romans 8:28). Now, that is a promise to take to the bank. He does not mean some things, a few things or even most things. He means *all things!* It is in the hardest, ugliest, and most difficult times in my life when He grows me the most.

I must be at the hospital again in the morning for a bone scan, an echocardiogram, and a shot to boost the white cells. I will also stop in again at the cancer counseling area. They have already given me lots of information, shown me wigs, hats, and scarves, along with different options of wearing them when I lose my hair. The doctor tells me hair loss is a side effect somewhere around day 14 to day 21. The countdown starts with today's treatment. I pray that I do not lose my eyebrows and eyelashes. They tell me, some folks do and some don't.

Friday at the Hospital... March 8, 2013

My body does not feel exceptionally well today, but I did not expect it to. I have flu-like symptoms that seem to come in waves. They will come crashing in, and then recede, just like ocean waves hitting the beach. I had some nausea off and on, but Father was good to keep everything in the stomach. I praise and thank Him that the weakness, headaches, body aches, and shakiness are only intermittent.

Today started at the hospital with a shot to start dye circulating through my system for the bone scan a couple of hours later. From there I went to get an echocardiogram for a baseline of where my heart is at the beginning of chemo. Sometimes chemo harms the heart muscle. I pray Father will protect my heart from any damage. Janet was my technician for the heart test. We had a great time bragging on the Lord, sharing how He has blessed each of us, and how good He is. I asked if there was anything I could pray for her. Her mother has health issues and is out of state. That was heavy on her heart. I prayed over her, for her mother, and thanked Father for His goodness to her. When I finished, she asked to pray for me. What an encouraging time!

Next, I went to the cancer resource center and spent time with the counselor there. Dr. Porter convinced me to take one of the free wigs they had. I am still not so sure about it, but he encouraged me to pray about it, so I may like it in the long run. The resource center gave me some other head coverings for free, too. Volunteers make them and donate them. My Mom does some sewing and is planning to make some so I will have more variety to match whatever I am wearing.

It is such a blessing to be with my parents at this time. What a support they are to me. The Lord told me the timing for what He has allowed in my life is no accident. I see it!

I plan to work tomorrow. I doubt I will be up to full steam, but I am asking the Lord to give me the ability to make it through the workday. It is important for me to work enough hours to keep my health insurance.

The plan for chemo is four treatments, biweekly followed by twelve weekly treatments for a total of twenty weeks. The rest of the treatment will depend on the test results and how well the cancer responds to the chemotherapy. I have one test scheduled for genetic testing. It is my prayer that I am negative for the genetic factor. If I test positive, a double mastectomy and hysterectomy is almost a given. Radiation is not off the table either. I will just have to take it one day at a time. The Lord's grace is sufficient for my every need and He will walk with me every step of the way.

Saturday and Sunday Update ... March 10, 2013

The Lord gave me a good day on Saturday. Praise the Lord; I made it through the full workday. I was pooped by the end, but I made it. I did need a bag of pretzels and a Coke to take the edge off the nausea.

Today is Sunday, my favorite day of the week. It is a great joy to spend time in worship with my church family. Their outpouring of hugs, love, gifts, cards, prayer, words of care, concern, and encouragement are wind in my sails. I do not know how anyone goes through the valleys of life without the Lord and the support of their church family.

Each day I thank Him for those who love and care for me and pray on my behalf. I am humbled by the number of folks who are diligently praying for me. "Thank you" does not begin to convey the depth of what I feel in my heart.

I learned a valuable lesson today. Always take my medicine with me! I thought I would get home sooner this evening than I did, so I did not put any in my purse. Wrong assumption! I stayed way too late visiting after the evening worship service. I began feeling so lousy that I will be certain medicine goes with me wherever I go. Lesson learned!

Morning and late evening are the toughest, but each day gets better. The medicine is kicking in and I feel the improvement. Last night I slept much better and was able to go back to sleep after waking up in the night without lying there for two hours as I had the two prior nights. The nurse forewarned me sleeping problems could be a side effect. She spoke the truth!

Monday, Made it... March 11, 2013

Father is always so good and gracious. He gave me the energy to make it through the workday again. I was tuckered out at the end, but made it all the same! He sent lots of my favorite customers to encourage me. Several of my customers had tears in their eyes as I shared my news with them. I hated to tell them, but did not want them to be shocked in a week or two when they come in and I am hairless.

One of my regular customers who is just finishing her chemo gave me some tips, and another customer who is battling cancer did as well. I asked him what he suggested for getting through chemo. He quickly answered, *"Prayer!"* I told him I agreed and had that one covered. The Lord also sent Mary, another customer to me to encourage. She is having a lumpectomy tomorrow and has had to put her husband in a nursing home within the last month. My heart breaks for her, but I am grateful for the opportunity to love and encourage her. Then, there was Carla, a breast cancer survivor who came in today to find out about my diagnosis and was a great encouragement, too.

The store manager brought two buckets of roses to give to senior customers as a token of appreciation. I loved giving them to the ladies and watching the smiles light up their faces. I know it may seem like a small thing, but what fun that was!

My coworkers are very supportive and continued to check on me to make sure that I was okay and not too tired. I am grateful for their love and concern. I am thanking and praising Father for where He has placed me at this moment in time. He knows what we need before we even have any idea what we will need. He told me to keep my focus on Him and the next obedient step He is asking me to take. He reminded me that He is already there, in the future, and knows everything it holds for me. What a comfort that is!

Tomorrow is the genetic testing appointment. It takes a week to ten days for the results to come back. I trust Father with the results. He has it all in His hands. He is sovereign and will show Himself strong when I am at my weakest. I do not have the strength to face all I am facing, but He does. Greater is He that is in me than he that is in the world (I John 4:4). He already knows the outcome and is working it for my good. The enemy tries to lie and tell me otherwise, but I am so grateful Father has taught me to trust Him and to listen as Holy Spirit reveals the lies Satan tries to plant in my heart and mind. I continually ask Holy Spirit to keep me sensitive to His truth so I will not be deceived as the enemy tries to sneak his destructive thoughts into my mind. I am aware that the battlefield is in the mind.

Genetic Testing Day... Tuesday, March 12, 2013

You have no idea how nice it is to receive the love, care, prayers, hugs, cards, gifts, texts, emails, calls, offers of help, and words of encouragement. I am humbled at the outpouring of love. My heart is full to overflowing. "Thank you" seems like a couple of small words, but my gratitude is heartfelt and sincere just the same.

I can tell that the whirlwind of the past week is starting to catch up with me. The last hour and a half of work was a challenge. I was pooping out fast and a headache pounded in. But, the Lord gave me His strength. My Dad took me to work this morning so that he and my Mom could also take me to the genetic testing appointment. At first, I did not think it was necessary. They have done so much running me around this last week. But, I am glad that I let "Hoke"(my dad) drive "Miss Daisy"(me) today. (For those of you who saw the movie "Driving Miss Daisy" that will make sense.) I rested on the drive to the hospital from work and then fell asleep in the waiting room as I waited for my appointment. The tiredness really hit me today. I am, again, feeling very grateful to Father for placing me with my parents for this particular valley in my life. I see His hand of provision for me so clearly, especially since I was not really thrilled to have to make the move back home. I know it was pride as well as the desire not to burden my parents. The Lord is good to use each life situation to grow in us a humble heart. The process is not particularly pleasant, but good all the same.

At the genetic testing appointment, I gained some general information. They drew blood and took an extensive history of my family's medical background. The genetic testing results will help the doctors determine my treatment plan. Both the oncologist and the breast care specialist are interested in the results. I can see Satan trying to slip his worries into my mind through the genetic counselor's words. She kept telling me she knew I would be worrying about the test results. I refuse to worry. I am trusting Father to take care of me. He has been so faithful to take care of me for 44 years. He is the same yesterday, today, and forever, so I know He will continue to take care of me.

I lost quite a bit of weight in the last year. I have kept it off for a year, but the steroids they are giving me are making me ravenously hungry. I feel like eating like a hog! I know I will need the help of Holy Spirit to produce His fruit of self-control. I need wisdom about what to eat and how much to eat to help the body with all its needs without adding the weight back on.

Blessings of the Day... Wednesday, March 13, 2013

I am enjoying thinking over the blessings of the day. If I don't stop and think about them, I will fail to appreciate them or be grateful. The first and foremost praise is that I made it through the workday. This was an extra blessing because I was up much of last night with digestive tract issues and throwing up. Praise the Lord! The digestive tract is now happier.

My workday was again filled with lots of love, hugs, and encouraging words from my coworkers and customers. I am blessed. My pastor friend, taught me, when we give love and it is returned to us, it is called "reciprocal living." There is nothing like it. Both parties giving and receiving are equally blessed and encouraged.

I had a special visit from Shruthi, a little girl who was adopted by friends. I was blessed to travel to India with her new Mom and help bring her home. What a highlight to the day. This little one has a very special place in my heart and always brings joy to any place she graces with her presence.

The doctor's office called with the results of the bone scan, CT scan, echocardiogram and other tests. They were all good. The only thing found that was a bit out of the ordinary was in my MRI. It showed a spot by the initial tumor that might or might not be cancer. They are not particularly concerned about it, but want to implant another "marker clip," so when surgery is done, that area will be attended to as well, just in case. It should be a simple procedure that consists of an ultrasound and then implanting the clip. It will be another opportunity for "Hoke" to drive "Miss Daisy" to the hospital. My Dad is a great chauffeur. I could get used to that. Speaking of driving, Holy Spirit impressed someone I don't even know to bless me with a gas card to help with all the trips to the hospital. The love of Jesus shines as He loves and blesses me through others and their generosity.

I took about a half hour nap in the driveway in the car after I arrived home from work. The sun felt so good and I was so tired. After coming in the house, I ate and then crawled onto the bed. I was so tired I didn't even take my coat off. I was soon fast asleep and slept until about a half hour before time to head to church for evening Bible study and prayer time. The nap rejuvenated me enough to get up and go. What an inspiring, middle of the week pick-me-up my church family is. Their love, hugs, prayers, and encouragement put me right up in the clouds.

Father reminded me again that He is my strength and reassured me that what I am facing, He will use for my good and His glory. Though I do not see the "whys," I trust Him. I think Job said, "Though He slay me, yet will I trust Him." I don't have a sense that this is what He will use to take me home to heaven, but whatever the case, I am His to use as He chooses. He is the potter; I am the clay (Isaiah 64:8). Several times in the last few days, the Lord pointed me to the truth of the trials and difficulties of life. He will use this time to conform me to the image of Jesus. I am reminded of the verse (Hebrews 5:8) that tells me Jesus learned obedience through what He suffered. This is part of the perfecting process, growing me to be "mature and complete, lacking nothing." That is His promise.

My prayer requests are for energy to face the tasks of the day, and relief from the frequent headaches and hurting skin. My skin feels like what you feel when you have the flu and a high fever. I am not sure how to describe the feeling other than that.

Another Good Day... Thursday, March 14, 2013

Hello again! I look forward to this time each day as I share my heart with you. A smile lights my face and warmth overflows in my heart as I think of Father's love and care for me. Love is a precious thing. It gives the same wonderful warmth whether it is experienced face to face or from a distance. When love is given, the person giving receives as much of the blessing as the one receiving. As I sit here soaking in the remembrances of the acts of love shown me, my heart cries out to the Lord to reveal to your hearts the deep love He has given me for all of you.

The Lord answered prayers for energy to make it through the workday. I did it with flying colors. The day was difficult starting. I had a hard time keeping awake during my prayer and study time this morning. The eyes just did not want to cooperate. Then as I went to work, the headache was strong. But, as the day wore on, I felt a renewed energy and a softening in the headache. I felt better at quitting time than I did at starting time. What a praise that is!

Father answered the prayer for energy to attend my divorce recovery group. The care and concern each member has for the others in the group is a blessing. I am reminded, the enemy wants us all to think that we are the only one who has faced or is facing our specific mix of trials and challenges in life. He does his best to try to isolate us from the encouragement of others. We all face trials in life and bear pain despite how "have it all together" we look on the outside. By sharing our burdens with others and allowing them to walk with us in the valleys of life, the weight of the burden is cut in half because of sharing it with another.

Beautiful and Warm Spring Day... Friday, March 15, 2013

It is again that time of evening when I contemplate the experiences and blessings of the day. My quiet time with the Lord is the favorite, but my time with you rates pretty high on the list, too.

My digestive tract started working in a happy and consistent way again. It has not been overly cooperative since the first chemo treatment and caused me to feel pretty miserable. When the alarm went off, I enjoyed an extra special quiet and prayer time. God reminded me of His great love for me and for all His children. We love Him because He first loved us. It gave me a lot to *hmmm* (contemplate, ponder, think about) about this morning as He spoke to me about His love and the power love has to open hearts and change lives.

The procedure at the hospital went well. The gentleman checking me in had a radiant smile. We talked of how great it was to use the smile the Lord had given us and how sad that so many do not.

I slept most of the way home from the hospital. Naps are becoming a necessity and not just a treat. On the way, we stopped and picked up food for Ellie Mae. Dad went with me to get the dog food and would not let me lift the bag. Wow! I have never been so spoiled in my life. I am used to being self-sufficient. It is taking a little bit of getting used to, but it is nice to be pampered just the same. Mom spent the afternoon working on a head covering for me. My Mom and Dad are the best.

My scalp is beginning to ache and I wonder if that is the precursor to the hair falling out. I have not noticed any excess hair leaving its roots yet and am still contemplating when I should get a really short haircut to avoid long chunks of hair falling as the process begins.

I developed a mildly sore throat last night. Dr. Gill, the oncologist, told me if I were to develop a fever of 101 degrees, I needed to be immediately on the phone with her or on the way to the emergency room. Because of the way chemo affects the immune system, waiting to address a fever could be potentially fatal. I have always been one to tough things out. I suppose I will have to change my way of doing things. Mom and Dad found a really cool digital thermometer. All I have to do is stick it in my ear, push the button and wait a second or two for the reading. Wow! If only they had those when I was a kid. I remember sitting for what seemed like hours with the thermometer hanging out of my mouth, rolling my eyes and mumbling, "Is it done yet?" from between clenched lips. With this fancy thermometer, I know I will be more willing to check my temperature. I usually check it a time or two every day simply because I don't feel perfectly healthy. I am still learning what is "normal" while taking chemo treatments.

Dr. Gill asked me what I did for a living. When I shared with her I was an assistant customer service manager for Schnucks Markets and that I dealt with the public face to face on a daily basis, and handled money all day, she told me, having done that would be a good thing. These things have strengthened my immune system because I came in contact with lots of germs on a daily basis. I smile as I tell you this part. She also said the fact that Ellie Mae, my sweet, loving Rottweiler who loves to give kisses and has been consistently and very affectionately slathering me with them, would also help my immune system. Yeah! I love her kisses. Mom cringes every time she delivers them to my face, but she cannot begrudge the fact that Ellie Mae has done good things for my immune system.

Mom and Dad found a great deal on some undergarments for me. I needed a few more that did not have the strap placement where it would rub against the port for the chemo treatments. The prayer request here is that at the end of all the treatments I would still have something to put in those new undergarments. I will not entertain that thought unless it is necessary. "Do not worry about tomorrow. Tomorrow will worry about itself. Each day has enough trouble of its own." (Matthew 6:34).

Hello, again! Saturday, March 16, 2013

As I sit across the screen from you this evening, thinking of the blessings of the day, I am reminded of my pastor friend, Dr. Porter. He often asks those with whom he is talking, "What is your greatest blessing of the last seven days?" I am sad to say, when he first started asking me this question a couple of years ago, I would have to really think to come up with one. I did not realize it at the time, but I had allowed Satan to keep my mind focused on the negative things in my life. Hmmm... how long would we continue to keep blessing someone if they never bothered to notice and thank us? Fortunately, our God is extremely patient and loves us enough to keep working with us, blessing us, and encouraging us to see His blessings in our lives. Now, when Dr. Porter asks me what my greatest blessing of the last seven days is, I have so many that I do not know where to start. A favorite verse reminds me to keep my focus on good things.

> Finally, brothers, whatever is true, whatever is noble, whatever is right, whatever is pure, whatever is lovely, whatever is admirable, if anything is excellent or praiseworthy, think about such things. (Philippians 4:8)

Several of you have asked me how I can be so calm and at peace with all that I am going through. The simple answer is I trust the Lord.

When I am giving Him all my cares, concerns, and burdens, trusting Him to take care of them, I have peace. I spent many years of my life not trusting Him and worrying what might happen. What good did all that worry do? How far did it get me? None and nowhere. God has shown that He is faithful to me. I cannot help but trust Him in light of His faithfulness.

On to the blessings of the day, the morning was warm and beautiful. I had sufficient energy for the workday. I continue to be blessed with the love, care and concern of many of my coworkers and customers. Father keeps blessing me with fuel money for trips back and forth to the hospital, too. He knows all I will need and continues to provide. I was also given a very useful gift by one of my customer friends today. I went too long without my medicine and felt ill last Sunday because I did not bring any to church. Well, I received a handy pill container that will hook right onto my key chain, so that I will not have an excuse to let that happen again.

I gained some information from folks concerning the timing of hair loss. One tidbit I learned is that the aching scalp is not a precursor, but an itching scalp is. Another source gave me this bit of information. It is a little more delicate in nature. This source informed me, when I start losing the hair on the more private parts of my body, then my head is soon to follow. I think I have decided to wait until my hair starts to fall out, and then have my Mom to give me a really short cut. Everyone I talked to who has faced it said that even though they thought they were ready, it was still a big shock. I speculate it will be for me, too. The last time I was bald, I was a whole lot cuter than I am now. I had my "baby face" charm to rely on.

I have a constant headache now and plagued by a sore throat. Sometimes the headache makes it a bit hard to focus on the task at hand. As of now, I do not have any visits to the hospital or doctors planned until my chemo treatment. Yea! I have felt almost like a semi-permanent resident of St. Luke's these last few weeks. I used to get easily turned around in a hospital, but now, I can change from building to building in the hospital and to the doctor's building on either side and not get lost. For those of you who know me and directions, this is another big praise.

Top of the Evening... Sunday, March 17, 2013

Top of the evening to you on this St. Patty's day! I was reminded today was St. Patrick's Day by the chocolate covered pretzels decorated with little green shamrocks I am nibbling on as I write to you.

My first praise of the day, I woke up before the alarm went off and realized I had slept all night without getting up. This might have been a first since starting chemo. Most nights I have been up two or three times during the night.

Today, being Sunday, means it was a fabulous day. I suspect just the thought of worshiping and sharing love with my church family was much of the reason I felt so good. I always know my "Hugs and Love" bank is going to receive rich deposits when I get in among my brothers and sisters in Christ. They make me feel like a million bucks with their love for me. After Sunday school class I had a special opportunity to sit and chat with one of my Christian sisters who has walked the road with breast cancer. She told me her scalp hurt before she started to lose the hair. This was different from another cancer survivor, who said his itched. Well, the thing is, my scalp hurts and now has begun to itch. I just don't know.

This evening, I had the opportunity to pray with another special sister in Christ, who is awaiting a diagnosis on a suspicious spot in her breast. I am praying it is not cancer. I teased her and said that if it is, we could both be bald together. Hey, maybe we could start a new fashion trend. However, I am not sure I can convince the rest of you ladies about this strategy.

Prayer is one of the most precious gifts we can give to each other. Lately, the Lord has been speaking to me about the importance of prayer and its power. I give my cares to the Lord in prayer and trust Him to care for them.

> Therefore confess your sins to each other and pray for each other so that you may be healed. The prayer of a righteous man is powerful and effective. (James 5:16)

This verse shows us how important it is that we pray for one another and reminds us of the power of prayer. There are conditions which make the prayer powerful, healing, freeing and effective. God tells us it is important to confess our sins to each other and to pray for each other. There is power in Jesus' name and it is He who gives us the spiritual weapons, the authority, and the strength when we pray (II Corinthians 10:40). He reminds us "we can do all things through Christ who gives us strength." (Philippians 4:13). He can and will bring freedom to us as we pray, confess and use the authority He has given us.

My battle with cancer has opened the hearts of a few folks and allowed them to draw closer to the Lord. It brings tears of joy as I think of the wonder of the Lord working in their lives.

The Hair begins to fall...Monday, March 18, 2013

With a deep sigh, I start my time with you tonight. I just brushed my teeth and ran the comb through my hair. The comb filled with loosed hair with each run through the locks currently residing on my head. Hmmm... I am left to wonder. Should I buzz it off short before going to work tomorrow? Can I wait a day or two yet? How quick will it fall out now that it has started? Working in the grocery store, I surely do not want to be shedding like a shaggy dog. There are food safety and health department issues to consider. Fortunately I do not work in any of the food preparation areas.

I gave my Mom fair warning that I might be getting her up in the morning to help me with a "buzz job" before I go to work. I suppose you will have to wait on the edge of your seats till tomorrow to find out if the "buzz job" happened in the morning or not. I will see how much I lose overnight and how much I seem to be losing in the morning. If I don't cut it in the morning, I am sure that I will be taking a hat to work with me, just in case. One of my coworkers was teasing me today, telling me that she couldn't wait to draw pictures on my bald head. She always makes me smile. I love a little bit of good natured harassment.

I pray that the loss of hair will not be too traumatic. I am really okay with it. I just don't want to have to go through it. Keep reminding myself how much less time it will take me to get ready for work or anywhere else I happen to be going. I must look at the positives. Another is I won't have to shave the legs or armpits either. That hair could stay gone and I would not mind. I will start a list; it will be my Philippians 4:8 of losing hair list.

As I think about "not wanting" to go through the hair loss, I am reminded of how the Lord sometimes asks me to do things that I really do not want to do. It tests our love for Him. The Bible tells us that if we love Him, we will obey His commandments. Obedience is how we show our love for Him. Often times, as He asks me to do something that I do not want to do, and I have to bow my knees and say, "Okay, Lord. You know that I do not want to do what you are asking, but, I want to be obedient. I need your help to bring me to the place where I truly want to do what you are asking." Sometimes it takes longer to bring my heart in line with His will, but He is always faithful to give me the ability to "want to" as long as I am "willing to be willing."

Remember, God knows your heart. He knows your every thought. Don't try to hide from Him the fact that you don't want to do what He has asked or commanded. Hmmm... He even knows the very number of hairs on your head, or lack thereof! Isn't that a comforting thought? He has each and every hair on our heads numbered.

Jesus laid down His life for us so that we would not have to pay the penalty for our sin, which is spiritual death and eternal separation from God and His love (John 15:13). Isn't it hard to imagine, as imperfect, and as much of a pain in the neck we are sometimes, that He would love us that deeply?

> For God so loved the world that he gave his one and only Son, that whoever believes in him shall not perish but have eternal life. (John 3:16)

What love! And then He made it so simple for us to have a relationship with Him and secure our place in heaven. All we must do is to acknowledge that we are sinners. If we are truthful with ourselves, we all know that we are. Who has never told a lie, never stolen anything, disrespected a parent, or taken the Lord's name in vain? As you realize you are sinner, and then confess with your mouth that Jesus is Lord, believing in your heart God raised Him from the dead, He saves you (Romans 10:9-10).

Jesus covers our sin with His perfection and righteousness when we put our faith and trust in Him. I don't know about the rest of you, but that truth always makes me want to shout from the mountain tops, because I see how very much He loves me by His great sacrifice for me. He loves you that much, too.

Did she buzz it all off or Didn't she? Tuesday, March 19, 2013

I know many of you are on the edge of your seats. Did she buzz it off this morning or not? Drum roll, please... No, she did not buzz the hair off this morning. I am positively shedding, but as yet, it is not coming out in clumps. I talked with two ladies at the store today. Both have been through breast cancer. Their advice to me was to wait until it started coming out in clumps. To be honest, I am a bit relieved. I have a bit more time to prepare myself.

Alecia, my niece has offered to have her hair cut and made into a wig for me to wear. What a sweet gesture! I am not yet sold on the idea of wearing a wig, so don't get any hair cut yet.

I got a great suggestion to add fun when the time comes and I buzz the hair. It was to cut myself a Mohawk and play with it a bit before I remove it totally. It was also suggested to make sure I take pictures. These would be a fun remembrance of a less than pleasant task. As I think about fun, my coworkers and I had a ball laughing and joking about the loss of my hair. I appreciate their hearts as they bring fun and merriment to the situation. They positively did! I also got a "tickle" out of those of you that came to see me at the store or hunted me up to see if I buzzed it or not. Your loving curiosity blesses me.

As I think about the blessings of the day, I realized that part of yesterday and most of today, was minus the headache which has consistently plagued me since the first chemo treatment. I know I am fast approaching the next treatment, but a few days reprieve from feeling like I have the flu is a blessing. The pain which initially caused me to find the lump in my breast has disappeared for several days. I will have to ask the doctor about that.

But at the very least, I would think it might mean the tumor has stopped growing as rapidly.

I spent many years living in fear and frustration. Jesus tells us that He came so we could have life and have it in abundantly (John 10:10b). Fear is not a part of the abundance He talks about, but His peace most certainly is.

> Peace I leave with you; my peace I give you. I do not give to you as the world gives. Do not let your hearts be troubled and do not be afraid! (John 14:27)

There is no place I would rather be than with the Lord, waiting upon Him, trusting Him, and resting in His perfect peace.

Entering His Rest... Wednesday, March 20, 2013

Good evening! Today has been another really good day. I had plenty of energy and very little headache. I received a special blessing today when one of the ladies I used to work with brought me two wigs she used when she went through breast cancer treatments. I now have the option to be a short haired blonde, a medium length blonde, or a longer-haired curly brunette. I still have not decided if I'm going to wear wigs, scarves, hats, or what. Who knows, maybe I will do a little bit of all of the above. It is comical, but the men seem to think I need to purchase a red wig. Very few of the women think I need red, but a lot of the men do. Hmmm... I wonder why that is?

I have received wonderful ideas, reminding me of the advantages of having no hair. An email I received had a list showing me how much money I would be saving on shampoo, conditioner, razor blades, and band aids when I might cut myself shaving and electricity because I wouldn't be using my curling iron and hair dryer. Then, there was also money saved on trips to the beauty shop.

The Lord guides us to rest in Him. In Him is where we find ultimate rest for our spirits and souls. Peace, comfort and the ability to do all He asks of us is found by placing our complete trust in Him, resting in Him and allowing him to work in us and through us.

> So there remains a Sabbath rest for the people of God. For the one who has entered His rest has himself also rested from his works,

> as God did from His. Therefore, let us be diligent to enter that rest, so that no one will fall, through following the same example of disobedience. (Hebrews 4:9-11)

It is important to remember, obedience is always a condition of entering His rest. *No* Obedience, *No* Rest! There will also be *No* receiving of the abundant happiness and joy found in Christ Jesus if we are disobedient.

Chemo 2...Awesome Day of Praises... Thursday, March 21, 2013

As I sit down with you across the computer screen tonight, I can hardly keep my booty in the seat. I have so many praises and blessings to share, that I can hardly contain my joy and praise to the Lord for blessing me and giving me the opportunity to watch Him work. He is awesome!

My morning started early, with an inspiring time of prayer and study. Father reminded me of how essential obedience is in allowing Him to do all He desires in our lives, even if what He is asking of me does not make sense. The power of prayer does not so much reside in the one offering the prayer, but in the one hearing and answering. The Lord is "The One" who ultimately brings the power to our prayers.

> The eyes of the Lord are on the righteous and His ears are attentive to their cry. (Psalm 34:15)

Join me in praise, adoration, and thanksgiving for who He is and for the many ways He blesses us (Psalm 34:1-4). I will start by sharing the biggest praises relating to cancer first. I had my second chemo treatment today. My oncologist, Dr. Gill is a wonderful woman and excellent doctor. I shared with her that the pain was gone from the cancerous area and she told me it was a great sign! As we continued the visit, she told me that I was doing better than 99% of her other cancer patients. Praise the Lord, and thank you, Jesus!

As a side note, Dr. Gill speculated my hair would fall out in 14-21 days, start to finish. So, unless I see chunks begin to fall, I need not buzz the hair yet. I am glad for a few more days with hair. She also advised me not to have any hard pulls or tugs on the hair or use any harsh chemicals. Doing so would expedite the balding process.

As the chemo was being administered, my parents and Dr. Porter, who had accompanied me, enjoyed great time of fellowship. We talked, laughed and prayed together. What a blessing those three are! I could not ask for better companions.

In the afternoon, Dr. Porter and I did counseling. It is always great to see the Lord releasing people from their strongholds and giving them His great freedom.

Now I will share with you the best news for the day. The genetic testing office called with the results of my blood tests for the BRCHA1 and BRCHA2 genetic abnormalities. The news is great. I tested negative for both genetic abnormalities. This means that the suggestion to do a double mastectomy and hysterectomy is not an automatic one.

> Now to Him who is able to do immeasurably more than all we ask or imagine, according to His power that is at work within us. (Ephesians 3:20-21)

God is able and often does so much more than we can think or ask. I see His great hand of mercy and love today. There were many more blessings from today that I would love to share but my head is bobbing and the energy for more is just not here this evening.

Little Piggies and a Hair Cut... Friday, March 22, 2013

Father has given me another great day. It started off at the hospital getting the shot to boost my blood counts. I had a super nurse who gave me a great idea for getting my hair cut. I wanted to save a few locks of hair for a memento. She told me just how to do it.

As the Lord would plan it, I ran into DiAnna, one of the ladies from my Sunday school class. She told me she knew just how to do what I wanted done. She created little "piggies" which were small braids of hair banded at both ends so the hair would not slip out when they were cut from my head. I looked very much like the little black boy on the television show "The Little Rascals" when she got the little "piggies" braided and ready to be cut off. The "piggies" stuck straight out from my head! Needless to say, we were having so much fun, we had to take pictures. After cutting off all the "piggies," DiAnna gave me a great, short haircut which will help me ease into having the rest of the hair fall out. She said she could see a few spots where the hair was already thinning. I am not surprised. I have been filling the trash can with hair each morning as I comb and style it. The back of my head is shaved pretty close, while I still have a bit of length in the front and sides. I am glad I had DiAnna cut my hair. We had a great time laughing and joking our way through it.

I felt better today than I did the first day after my last chemo treatment, but as the day wore on I developed a whopper of a headache and grew tired. Another effect I noticed is that I no longer walk quite as fast as my normal "speed walk." With the diminished energy, I become light-headed when I walk too fast. The good news is I had enough energy and ability to do all the things I shared above. God has promised to use things that do not look or feel like blessings at the time for our good (Romans 8:28).

> For I know the plans I have for you, declares the Lord, plans to prosper you and not to harm you, plans to give you hope and a future. Then you will call upon Me and come and pray to Me, and I will listen to you. You will seek Me and find Me when you seek Me with all your heart. I will be found by you, declares the Lord. (Jeremiah 29:11-14a)

He has great plans for us and will listen as we pour out our hearts to Him. The question is will you seek Him with all your heart, so that you may allow Him to give you hope and a future? Even though I am not excited that the Lord has allowed cancer to be a part of my life, I trust Him to use it for my good and His glory.

Joy, Strength… Saturday, March 23, 2013

Yesterday was more difficult. I had to work and snow is in the forecast. I work in the grocery business, and you all know what happens in the grocery stores when snow is forecast. The store was swamped and I was on my feet all day. Chemo surely takes the "sap out of me." But, the Lord gave me the ability to make it through the day. The best I can describe how I feel is similar to the feeling of having the flu, weak, headache, body aches, light headedness, a stomach that is not quite happy, skin that aches, and a pervasive feeling of diminished energy.

My new hair cut opened the door for me to share with a few more of my customers that I have been diagnosed with breast cancer and am going through chemotherapy. I am doing my best to break it to as many of them as possible before they come in and see me completely bald and are shocked by it. I want them to still feel comfortable chatting and visiting with me. I know for some, it is difficult to know what to say. I seek to reassure them that I am fine and the Lord has me in His hands.

When I tell them that I need them to do me a big favor, they listen in closely. Then, I tell them that when I am bald, they need to tell me I am still beautiful. It lightens the mood and they smile and promise to do so. It will give them something to say and to feel like they are encouraging me and take away the burden of wondering what to say.

One of my regulars came in a couple of days ago and told me that he had decided I was going to be like Demi Moore in G.I. Jane, the movie. He said when I lost my hair; I would be just like she was, "sexy as all get out." He made me smile and laugh. I told him to keep telling me that. He promised he would, and left with a smile. Whether I am dealing with the effects of cancer or just dealing with everyday life, a smile and a joyful attitude is the only way to face them. Smiling and joy are contagious. It is hard for people to resist a smile and genuine joy, especially when you combine it with heartfelt love and care for them. As I think about the "Joy of the Lord," Holy Spirit reminded me of the chorus, "The Joy of the Lord is My Strength." Its sweet melody danced through my mind as I lay in bed pondering the weakness I have felt. Then I considered the joy the Lord has given me, even though many days have been challenging. As I lay and pondered the words to another song, reminding me that when I feel weak, God is the one who makes me strong. It is the power of Christ that gives me strength. I cannot get by living on my own abilities. I know that it is not my strength I am to walk in, but His. Mine will never get me there.

It is His joy that gives me strength. But, where do I get His joy? "Do not grieve, for the joy of the Lord is your strength." (Nehemiah 8:10b). In His presence is where I find my joy. I need His strength. I am inherently weak, even more so in my physical body now than ever before.

It is in my weakness that He shows Himself strong. His grace truly is sufficient for every difficulty we have faced, are facing, or will face. He offers joy, strength, grace, and power to me and to you. Will you take Him at His Word and seek Him to provide them for you today? I sigh contentedly, knowing He is the one who gives the victory.

Sleep... Encouragement... Obedience... Sunday, March 24, 2013

Happy snowy Sunday! Since the snow had not started falling when I got up this morning, I thought I would enjoy my time with you and the Lord, and then go to church. But, when I stepped out of the house into a shower of snow and ice pellets, got into my Blazer, and started down the road, I decided it was probably slick enough that the better part of wisdom would be to stay home. I returned home and listened when Holy Spirit told me to go back to bed for rest. I felt so much better after sleeping most of the day. I went to church for the evening service.

After the service, I had time to "love on" and hug my church family. As I think of how I am encouraged by the love, hugs, prayers, and thoughtful words of others, I pause to think of how the Lord encourages and speaks to us through His Spirit, too.

I spent much of my life not hearing Holy Spirit's voice. I would hear Satan's voice loud and clear as he told me I was not good enough, had many things to fear, and that God could never love me quite like the Bible said He did. Satan lied and deceived me so much that I could not even tell it was his voice discouraging me. I believed the voice I heard to be my own. And worst of all, I believed the lies. The Bible tells us that in the heart of who he is, Satan is a liar (John 8:44b).

Praise the Lord, I have since learned the voice of God's Spirit will never discourage or put me down. His Words will always lift us and encourage us. He places Holy Spirit in those who receive and accept Jesus as Lord, Savior, and Master; sealing us for the day of salvation

Something that was instrumental in helping me to make the deliberate choice to ask Him to change me transpired approximately a year ago as I heard my pastor, Dr. McLain teach Psalm 139. As I listened, Holy Spirit prompted me to highlight, underline, and then sign my name to verses 23 and 24. I consciously made these verses my prayer, asking Him do this work in my life. I prayed these verses daily for several weeks. The Lord heard and answered. I have never been the same since.

> Search me, O God, and know my heart; test me and know my anxious thoughts. See if there is any offensive way in me, and lead me in the way everlasting. (Psalm 139:23-24)

Needless to say, there is still much the Lord desires to do in me, and much that I desire Him to do. He reminds us in Philippians 1:6 that He will complete the work in us that He starts at the time of our salvation. Will you trust Him, opening your heart and life to Him, allowing Him to do the completing work that He desires in you? He loves us and wants what is best for us, but, it is up to us whether or not we will receive it.

New Symptoms and Prayer... Monday, March 25, 2013

Hello! I breathe a deep breath and sigh thinking how very tired I am. I was able to make it through the workday. Some days are harder than others. I think yesterday's naps were key to the energy level today. My ankles have positively increased in size, and as I get up in the mornings, I can see that my face is a bit swollen, too. I suppose this is par for the course because the nurse asked me if I had noticed any swelling when she gave me the shot to boost the white blood cell production.

I am beginning tell a difference in the taste of food. It does not taste nearly as good as normal. Some of my favorites do not even sound appealing. This might not be too bad except for the fact that I still want and need to eat. I have gained a few pounds and am not particularly happy about it. But, I know that it is important that I eat. Hmmm...eat the right things, and plenty of them, but not too much. The diet I was eating has been hard to maintain as I go through chemo because now I always want to eat when I am tired, and chemo makes me tired. I know that my body is the temple of Holy Spirit and that I should treat it that way, but dealing with cancer and the effects of the treatments puts a crimp in many of the things I was doing to keep the body in better condition.

One of my customers, who is a golfer, brought me a Pebble Beach golf hat to wear when the hair is completely gone. I also gained a bag of "tummy drops" which another customer brought me for the time after each chemo treatment when the tummy is not quite happy. They are an all-natural peppermint drop. I am blessed the medicine keeps the nausea under control, but the stomach never seems truly happy for several days after chemo. The love, care, compassion, encouragement from my customers is daily a blessing to me and I have the same from friends, family, and church family. I am truly a blessed woman.

As I contemplate the love of others, I cannot help but contemplate God's great love. He continues to show me on a daily basis how much He loves me. He does it in many different ways, with His Peace, His Presence, His Provision, His Comfort, His Rest, His Power, His Wisdom, His Protection, and with the awesome opportunity He gives me to come before Him and lift all my cares to Him in prayer. I am grateful that I have the ability to come to Him in prayer. All throughout His Word, He promises us when we call to Him, He will answer. Knowing Jesus as our Savior is what opens the door to prayer. Jesus tells us that He is the Way, the Truth and the Life, and no one comes to the Father except through Him (John 14:6).

> Ask and it will be given to you; seek and you will find; knock and the door will be opened unto you. For everyone who asks receives; he who seeks finds; and to him who knocks the door will be opened. (Matthew 7:7-8)

The original language is literally translated to seek and keep on seeking, ask and keep on asking, knock and keep on knocking. Persistence is what the Lord is encouraging in us as we seek Him in prayer. In Luke 18:1, Jesus shows us we should always pray and not give up. But, the best thing about prayer is that the Lord hears and answers when we come to Him with a pure and clean heart and mind.

Isaiah 65:24 takes it up a notch, letting us know He is already in the process of answering before our hearts cry out. Nothing is hidden from the Lord. What a great comfort that is. The Lord truly understands how we feel and what we are going through. His heart is touched because He understands our pain and suffering.

Daily, I realize a greater and greater need to come before Him in prayer. I almost feel like shouting because of the joy He put in my heart by reminding me of the gift He has given us in prayer. "Oh, thank you Father for the joy and the privilege you have given us to approach your throne boldly, in our time of need."

Swelling Feet and Legs, Falling Hair…
Wednesday, March 27, 2013

The last hour and a half was a struggle for energy at work, but Father gave me what I needed. Since one of the things that still taste good is salad with Ranch dressing, I picked up things to make a salad. After coming home,

I made some pre-portioned salads. Now I will have some quick and easy pre-made meals to grab when I get hungry.

By the time I finished preparing the food, my legs, ankles, and calves were so swollen they felt like balloons. They looked like it, too. I called the oncologist's office to ask about it and lay down with my feet propped up on pillows to take a quick nap. Propping the feet up helped and relieved a bit of the swelling. They at least felt better. The doctor's office called back and told me to see if they are any better today. At the moment, they are. I slept with them elevated on pillows all night. We shall see how they do tomorrow as I am on my feet all day. When they are swollen, they are so puffy that they do not even look like my legs.

Yesterday, I noticed my hair falling out more than the day before. I looked at the bathroom floor and could not figure out who was shedding more, me or Ellie Mae. I also noticed, as I took off my Bluetooth when I got to church last night, that a big chunk of hair accompanied it. Sigh… I am wondering what it will be like as I prepare for work this morning.

As I sit and wonder what the day will hold, I realize that wondering is really of no value. I must live it, trusting the Lord with each step. The Lord encourages us always to live by faith and not by sight (II Corinthians 5:7). It is my prayer for Father to continue to teach me how to walk in faith in a deeper, more consistent way. Each day of life is filled with opportunities, disguised as situations that may seem impossible or just incredibly difficult. We must not lose heart, but allow Him to work in and through us (II Corinthians 4:16-18). Everything we have here is temporary and will soon to pass away. What the Lord has for us in eternity is permanent. That is good news!

As I continue to think about the challenges and struggles I face, I will not be destroyed as I walk through the hard times. His grace and power are sufficient to keep me standing firm. My own will never sustain me.

> We are hard pressed on every side, but not crushed; perplexed, but not in despair; persecuted, but not abandoned; struck down, but not destroyed. (II Corinthians 4:8)

What a great promise! God will never grow weak or tire as we do. We can trust Him to renew our strength as we hope in Him. I thank and praise Him. He is so faithful!

Fatigue and Expectations... Thursday, March 28, 2013

I am quite tired tonight. Today was one of the hardest days I've faced thus far. The fatigue was more than usual. But, I praise the Lord that I made it through the workday. All eight hours!

I started the day with the Lord and reminders of His strength. It was the perfect way to begin. He knew I would need the reminders. At work, I felt light-headed and weak most of the day, and the swelling was no better. The doctor's office called in a "water pill" prescription to help alleviate the puffiness in my feet and ankles. I was also given a potassium supplement to help replenish the potassium the water pill removes from the body. To help alleviate the fatigue, I took a nap as soon as I got home this afternoon.

After rising from the nap, Mom and I got out the hair clippers and she gave me a buzz cut all over. It was time. My hair began falling out in clumps today and I knew it was no longer reasonable to wait. Tomorrow will be my first official "hat day". It may seem odd to you, but, it is a relief to have taken the next step by shaving the hair down to a buzz cut. Each day, I would look and evaluate and decide if that was the day. Now, I no longer have to contemplate it. It is done! All in all, it is not as bad as I thought it might be. It might be different when it is all gone. Who knows? It may be easier than I expect.

I realize the Lord has made the whole process much easier than expected. Not that it is easy, because it isn't. But, He has been so very faithful and loving each and every step of the way. He removed much of the sting from many of the more painful parts of this journey.

We, as His children can be such "knuckle heads" sometimes. We know how good He is and that He loves us completely, yet we act surprised when He blesses us and answers our prayers.

> If any of you lacks wisdom, he should ask God, who gives generously to all without finding fault, and it will be given to him. But when he asks, he must believe and not doubt, because he who doubts is like a wave of the sea, blown and tossed by the wind. That man should not think he will receive anything from the Lord; he is a double-minded man, unstable in all he does. (James 1:5-7)

This truth hits me between the eyes today, because I know my expectancy of the Lord has not been up to the level it should be. I may not have been "way off" from where I should be, but I know there is still room for more improvement on my part. The Lord reminds me, no matter what He is doing in my life, there is "more, always so much more."

In Philippians 1:20 He reminds me that not only am I to expect His wisdom when I ask, but I am also to expect His courage. Then in John 21:27, Jesus tells Thomas, "Stop doubting and believe." God has given us all we need to believe and expect great things from Him.

Some of you know I am a thinker and I love to contemplate things. As I tell a friend of mine, I like to hmmm a lot. As a last thought, I want to encourage you to hmmm on the Lord's faithfulness to you and expect Him to answer as you call on Him. Expect Him to do great things on your behalf. He loves you so very much. Never doubt it!

Gypsy, Pirate or maybe Harley Momma…
Friday, March 29, 2013

I arrived home from work, ate dinner, then lay down for a nap, which turned out to be "down for the night." Because of fatigue, I needed it, though. The medicine to get rid of the extra swelling keeps me "hot footing" it across the hall to the smallest room in the house at least once an hour all night long. But, the praise is, the swelling is much improved. My feet, ankles, and calves no longer look quite so much like elephant feet. In the mornings, my feet and ankles feel pretty good, but by the end of the workday of eight hours on my feet, I can tell an uncomfortable difference. With the medicine and the night hours off of them, they return to a manageable sense of normalcy.

I continue to search for foods that still taste good to me. The salads with ranch dressing still hit the spot. Salad, along with some chicken and dumplings was dinner last night. The jazz variety of apples and pretzels taste pretty good, too. I think it will be a trial and error process to see where the taste buds are. Bananas have become a bit bland tasting, but I continue putting them into my diet because of the potassium. I may fix some greens today to help as well. I normally love greens and maybe I will find a way to flavor them so they will not taste like cardboard. Cardboard is the best way I know to describe how many foods taste. Mom teases me and tells me that cardboard would be cheaper than groceries. And it would be. Hmmm… maybe cardboard with a little ranch dressing.

Yesterday, I had lots more energy and made it through the workday. The last hour and half I could feel my body winding down, but, I made it through with flying colors. The love, hugs, caring words, and encouragement of my coworkers and customers always helps give me the boost I need to keep one foot in front of the other. I am humbled by the love and concern the customers give to me. It amazes me. I am just an employee in their grocery store. But, I have developed friendships with many of them and am blessed each time they come in and I see their faces, hear how they are, and what is happening in their lives. Life really is meant to be lived in community. We all need the support and encouragement of others. I am saddened when I see those that refuse to step out of their shell and allow others the joy and privilege of getting to know them. I know it is hard to do sometimes, because I have been there.

The fear of rejection can be a formidable enemy. It was one of the fears that used to plague me until the Lord set me free. God loves us, just as we are. You may reject God, but in this lifetime, He will never reject you if you come to Him with a sincere heart.

That means that we do not have to be good enough, pretty enough, strong enough, rich enough, obedient enough, or any other "enough" you want to think up. Jesus died for us in our worst condition because of God's great love for us (Romans 5:8).

God's heart is a Father heart above anything else, and He longs to gather us as His children if we will let Him. He created you and me for relationship with Himself. If you will answer His call to you, He will come to you (Revelation 3:20).

For those of you who were wondering what kind of head covering I went with yesterday...drum roll please. It was a red and black patterned scarf tied at the back. Mom said I looked like a gypsy because I had paired it with big silver hoop earrings. Brett and Bob, two of the guys I work with, thought I was a bit more pirate-like. Brett told me that I needed bigger gold earrings to complete the look. A few others told me I had a "Harley Momma" look.

Preparation and Perspective... Saturday, March 30, 2013

Today, I did not leave the house all day. It was wonderful. I had some extra nap time, when the phone wasn't ringing. I spent time talking to folks and catching up a bit, and did some computer work and paperwork.

I straightened up my living quarters, and even got to spend a little time in the fresh air and sunshine. Did you know that a scalp that never sees the sun feels a bit tender when it sees sun for the first time? I did not burn it, but as I enjoyed the fresh air and sunshine, I could feel the heated rays of the sun on the almost bare scalp. I will positively have to watch myself when the warmer weather comes. I am an outdoor girl, love the sunshine, and rarely use sunscreen.

The swelling has been less today. Praise the Lord for that. As I climbed on the scale, I could see I had come down about 15 pounds and was back in the normal range of weight. Whew! I stayed off my feet most of the day and I am sure that helped, too. Hopefully, my feet and legs will be ready for tomorrow. It is the Saturday before Easter Sunday in the grocery store. We will be busy. I will need the Lord's strength to get through it.

Before retiring for the evening, I want to leave you with a spiritual truth to hmmm on. It is one I gleaned from my "African Momma and Daddy." They are one of the couples I went to Africa with on my first international mission trip. They unofficially adopted me while we were there. And I adopted them right back.

The spiritual truth they shared with me is this: "God does not punish His people, He prepares them." Hmmm… as I thought on this, I can see how Father prepared me for this season of my life. I have faced bankruptcy, divorce, losing my home as well as all the ugliness that goes with those things, and now cancer and its treatments. I have had several folks wonder how I can believe God is good, loving, and faithful when He has allowed me such heartache and pain. But, as I look back over the last two years of my life, I can see God's hand preparing me. Father blessed me with the ability to counsel with Dr. Porter and gain freedom from strongholds that would have allowed these life events to devastate me. And, as I exercised, walking and jogging, last spring and summer, spending hours each week worshiping Him, listening to teachings on my iPod, praying, and listening to Him speak to my heart, He taught me how to trust Him in a deeper way. He taught me how to rely on Him, His strength and provision. For over a year now, He has been teaching me how to more clearly hear His voice and follow His direction as He speaks.

It is in the hardest and most painful times of life that the Lord grows me the most. That is, only if I let Him. I would not ask to go through all I have and am going through, but neither would I give up the growth and closeness with Him I have gained through this season of storms. The way

He prepared me boggles my mind sometimes, yet my heart understands. Because He loves me and has a Father's heart toward me, He has made available provision, support and supply for every need, every step of the way.

I know, as I continue walking through this season with the Lord, He is using this time to prepare me for what He has yet ahead for me. That is exciting! In no way do I see the things that have come my way as punishment. They are opportunities to allow God to work in and through me. It is a matter of perspective. There is the world's perspective and God's perspective. I know which perspective I choose. What about you?

Easter…Joy…Gifts…Blessings… Sunday, March 31, 2013

Good Morning to you all! I have decided to join you this morning rather than last night because I know that my clarity of thought will be much better. If I wait too late, my brain becomes a bit fuzzy and muddled. What better way to start my day, than with loved ones, recounting the blessings of yesterday and looking forward to the blessings of today.

Yesterday was a really good day. The store was busy, but the day was one of delightful fellowship with my customers and coworkers. The morning started with a show of support from one of my coworkers. Soon after I walked into work, the grinning face and now "bald" head of Brett greeted me. He had shaved his head to encourage me in my battle with cancer. Needless to say, I had to hug him and make him stand still so I could take a picture of us together. I received lots of hugs, words of encouragement from others, too. There were even tears shed by some of my customers as they learned of the cancer. I am amazed by the number of others who have faced cancer. Many customers, who were not even my "regulars" came and shared that they are or a family member has or is, facing it as well. It makes a special connection between us as that burden is shared. It always amazes me how shared pain causes hearts to connect in a special way. Hmmm… the ability to share burdens is a special gift and blessing.

> Praise be to the God and Father of our Lord Jesus Christ, the Father of compassion and the God of all comfort, who comforts us in all our troubles, so that we can comfort those in any trouble with the comfort we ourselves have received from God. For just as the

> sufferings of Christ flow over into our lives, so also through Christ our comfort overflows. (II Corinthians 1:3-5)

Isn't that great! He comforts us and then gives us the blessing of allowing His comfort to flow through us to others. That is just like God to give joy through pain. Hmmm... joy through pain. There has been no greater joy brought to earth than through the pain and suffering of Jesus Christ. Hebrews 12:2 reminds us that Jesus chose to suffer and die for our sins because of the joy set before Him.

Do you know what that joy was? It was the opportunity to redeem you and me from our sinful condition so that we might have a relationship with Him and spend eternity in heaven with Him. I am always humbled and amazed that He loves me that much. He loves you that much, too.

Today, we have the distinct joy and pleasure to celebrate that fact. Today is the day that we celebrate His death, burial, and most importantly His resurrection. He did it all for us. And, amazingly, as He gives His life for us, He pays for the consequences of our sin. It is a gift, a free gift! There is nothing we can do to earn it. All we have to do is believe and accept it.

> For it is by grace that you have been saved, through faith, and this is not from yourselves, it is the gift of God, not by works, so that no one can boast. (Ephesians 2:8-9)

Amazing isn't it? But remember, a gift is not truly yours till you reach out and take it from the hands of the giver. The free gift God offers us of salvation, heaven and eternal life is gained exactly the same way. If you have that gift, rejoice in it. If you do not yet have it, accept it today. There has never been a more precious or valuable gift given. God's gift of salvation and eternal life is the greatest blessing, ever.

As I got home from work today and started looking for more scarves to cover the "hair evacuation zone," I found several that I had kept for years in a box in the closet. I am glad that I did not get rid of them. My Mom had some, too. As of now, I like the scarf and hat idea much better than the wig idea. Now, my head is not only starting to look like a mangy dog, but it is starting to itch like one, too. I suppose that is because the hair is shedding out at a faster rate. So, if you see me scratching or rubbing it, I do not have fleas! Neither does Ellie Mae.

Another Great Day and God's Provision ... Monday, April 1, 2013

Hey, all! It is me again. As I think back over my Easter Sunday, I see a day overflowing with blessings. Sunday is my favorite day of the week. There is nothing I enjoy more than time spent worshiping, learning, and fellowshipping with my church family. Their encouragement always lifts me. It is no wonder Father tells us in His Word "not to give up meeting together" (Hebrews 10:5). He also knows the power of corporate prayer and worship. Anything He tells us to do is clearly for our benefit, as is abstaining from the things He tells us not to do. He knows the blessing that comes from obedience and the negative consequences that come from disobedience. He wants nothing but the best for us, which is why He gave us the Bible, which shows us the way to receive His very best.

Two sweet ladies from my church family blessed me with hats today. The Lord continues to grow my "head covering" collection. In Philippians 4:19, He promises to supply all our needs through Jesus and reminds us not to worry as He assures us He will meet all our needs.

Even better, not only does He promise to supply all our needs, but, as we delight ourselves in Him, He promises to give us the desires of our heart, too (Psalm 37:4). As I walk through this difficult time of life, and look back over other times in my life, I can clearly see how the Lord has supplied and is supplying all I need and more. His ability and willingness to meet our needs is limitless.

Feeling Great! Ready to Exercise!... Tuesday, April 2, 2013

Yesterday was a fabulous day. I felt so good, I almost felt normal. Praise the Lord for that! The farther I get from the last chemo treatment, the better I feel. I am beginning to feel a bit of reluctance about going to the treatments. I know it is because I am aware of how the chemo is going to make me feel. The feeling will not stop me from doing the treatments and what the doctors recommend.

There are many things in life we all have learned to do what we may not necessarily feel like, but do them anyway, because we know they are beneficial for us. Hmmm... exercise is one of the things we do not always want to do, but know it is good for our bodies. The more we exercise and make it a part or our routine, the more we want to do it. Spiritual exercise works the same way.

The more we read God's Word, pray, seek His face and step out in obedience, the more we see, feel and know the results of a close and intimate relationship with the Lord. As a result, we want to continue those disciplines because we want more growth and closeness with the Lord. Hmmm... what blessings and eternal benefits are we forfeiting by our spiritual laziness?

Think about this. If I were to reject the treatments the doctors are giving me, it would result in death for my body because the cancer would continue to grow, unchecked, eventually killing my physical body. It is the same with our spirit and soul. If we do not accept Jesus and the salvation He offers us, we will continue to be ravaged by the effects of sin and its consequences.

> For the wages of sin is death; but the gift of God is eternal life in Christ Jesus our Lord. (Romans 6:23)

Only Jesus Christ can give spiritual life and the promise of eternal life. Apart from Him, we are spiritually dead and have no hope for eternity.

A Buzz Cut and Encouragement...Wednesday, April 2, 2013

I felt good most of the day but began to tire about an hour and a half before the workday was through. I think that was mainly caused by a lack of sleep. I worked a late shift last night and then had to be back early this morning. I had an intense headache today. Plus, I also have a sore throat. That could be from the chemo. My throat was sore after the last treatment, too. I increased my ice eating during the last treatment to try to help. Eating ice during the chemo treatment is to stop sores from forming in my mouth. The mouth has greater blood flow than other parts of the body as well as rapidly dividing cells which allows the chemo more quickly affect that area. The cold temperature in the mouth caused by eating ice slows down the blood flow, prohibiting the development of mouth sores. I have cold-sensitive teeth, so eating the ice is not pleasant.

As I was working, one of my coworkers asked me how I was feeling because she could see that I did not feel well. I shared with her about the headache and one of my customers, overheard and asked if he could lay his hand on me and pray. I told him absolutely. He did so and the headache eased. Praise the Lord! The connection Father gives to brothers and sisters in Christ is absolutely wonderful. They do not even have to know each other.

With each day, the hair on my head is becoming more and more "patchy." And, my head is itching like crazy. Yet, all I can do is to rub it rather than scratch it because the scalp has become quite tender. I want to share with you the special thing my Mom did. My Mom went to the beauty shop and had the beautician give her a "buzz cut" similar to the one she gave me when my hair started to come out in clumps. Was that not too sweet or what! I am blessed with great parents. I cannot imagine walking through this season in life without their support. The Lord knew how important their support would be for me at this time. I have no doubt that is why I am here living with them and not in an apartment somewhere by myself.

As I think of my Mom's encouraging gesture, I am reminded of how important encouragement is in each of our lives and how God calls us to encourage one another (I Thessalonians 5:11). Harsh words can cut emotionally just like a knife would physically (Proverbs 12:18a). Encouraging words can be a balm, bring healing and an internal boost to the receiver. What kind of words do you use with others? Are they words of encouragement? Or are they words of criticism?

> Above all, love each other deeply, because love covers over a multitude of sins. (I Peter 4:8)

As I do a little hmmm along this line of thought, I am reminded of Barnabas, who was known as the "son of encouragement." I think of Holy Spirit and how He strengthened and encouraged the early Christians and today He is our indwelling encourager. I want to be just like Him. How about you?

Faith, Hope, and Chemo 3... Thursday, April 4, 2013

Yesterday I had plenty of energy and felt good all day. My day was filled with the love and encouragement of many friends, family, church family, coworkers, and customers. How blessed I am! As I think about support and going to my chemo treatment, I realize how grateful I am for my parents and Dr. Porter accompanying me. Their presence, support, and encouragement are a fantastic boost. Thinking about chemo treatment makes me realize that my feelings of "not being eager" to take it have increased. I know how it is going to make me feel. "Yucky" is putting it mildly. I know I will choose to go and complete the treatment. Why? Because I have the hope the treatments are killing the cancer, and I will return to full health and strength. Hmmm... hope.

Hope is a wonderful thing. I have not only the hope of healing, but even greater, the hope and faith I have in the Lord. Ultimately, He is the one who gives healing; not only physical healing of our bodies and healing of our wounded emotions, but also spiritual healing.

Why do I have hope and faith in God? It is because of His great love and compassion, and His many promises and His faithfulness. (Read Lamentations 3:22-23). Even though God has allowed suffering and grief into my life, I trust His compassion for me. I know He loves me with an unfailing love. I see it, feel it and experience it daily.

The Lord gives us the ability to "Faith Him" because He is continually faithful to His Word and the promises. The Bible is full of them. He places within each of us the ability to trust Him if we choose to do so. When we choose Jesus as Savior and Lord, He places His Holy Spirit in us, thereby giving us His indwelling power and even greater hope and faith in Him. We are anchored securely when we put our faith and hope in Him and His unfailing love for us (Psalm 33:28). In this world of craziness and turmoil, as we place our faith and hope in Him, our souls find rest (Psalm 62:5). Isn't that awesome?

Needing More Rest... Friday, April 5, 2013

I feel the chemo taking more effect on the energy level than I have had prior to now. My nurse, Jessica, told me yesterday that it often has that effect. She was a wealth of information as I asked questions. What a blessing she was to me.

Dad, Mom, and Dr. Porter accompanied me to have my treatment. We had a great time talking, laughing, praying and visiting with those that passed our way. I am amazed by how many folks Father sends us every time we go for my treatments. I am always blessed each and every time I set foot in the oncology office and treatment center. Isn't that just like God to take something I feel reluctance about and then bless my "socks off" in the process of experiencing it? God is so good to do that for me.

This is just my imagination talking, but in my mind's eye, I can see Father sitting on His throne, thinking. Hmmm... who can I send to encourage, bless, and love on Kimberly today? Tears run down my cheeks as I share this thought with you. He really does love each and every one of us that much. More, really! As imperfect, sinful, hard-hearted, and rebellious as we can be, He loves us all the same. Wow! What love!

After the chemo treatment and lunch, I spent time counseling folks with Dr. Porter. One person we talked with shared a fear of not being loved unconditionally. We often give love, but give it in a way that says, "I love you, but if you cross me or do something I don't like, you are off my list and I withdraw my love from you." That type of love is friendship love, also known as *phileo* love. God's kind of love is *agape* love and means, "No matter what you do, good or bad, I will love you. There is nothing you can do that will cause me to withdraw my love from you." *Agape* love is what He desires us to give everyone. We cannot produce *agape* love, only Holy Spirit living in us can.

Love is one of four essential needs for each one of us. We all need love, affirmation, security and significance in our lives. Love, I believe is the greatest. Why else would we go such extravagant lengths to gain it? "And now these three remain: faith, hope and love. But the greatest of these is love." (I Corinthians 13:13).

Each Unique and Wonderfully Made! ... Saturday, April 6, 2013

Happy Morning. I was able to take my lunch to the park and sit at one of the picnic tables and enjoy God's creation and breathe deeply of the fragrances of fresh outdoor air. And, great news, I could taste the pizza I had for lunch. It almost tasted normal. Not quite, but almost.

I even noticed daffodils and hyacinth blooming in the neighbors' yards. All are different, each beautiful in its own way. As I think about it, He made each of us the same way. No two people are exactly alike. We each look different, sound different, walk different, like and dislike different things, and have different talents and abilities. He created each of us to complement the others around us and to work together in unison as one great big family. That is, if we cooperate and walk in love with Him and each other.

Just think about the wonderful uniqueness God gave you. He loved you so much that He created no one else, now or ever, exactly like you. You are one of a kind (Psalm 139:13-16a). Isn't that awesome! He created you specifically, with attention to intricate detail, when He knit you together in your mother's womb. He had a specific plan for you and for me. Yet, He gave us free will to either cooperate with Him and His will for our lives or to reject it. He allows us choices. But in His great love for us, He gives us the answers to the way to live a blessed and abundant life. He placed all we need to know for direction in our lives in His instruction and letter of love to us, the Bible. Have you spent time there today?

After the shot at the hospital yesterday, the rest of my day was spent counseling with folks with Dr. Porter. I love listening as he shares wisdom from God's Word. Most of all, I love seeing Holy Spirit work in folks' lives, setting them free from strongholds and bringing freedom and joy.

This is usually one of the hardest days to make it through a full eight hour workday due to the fatigue caused by the chemo. As I reach up to feel the tumor, I can positively feel it shrinking. Praise the Lord! That means the chemo is doing exactly what it is supposed to be doing.

Chapter 4

Life with Chemo Side Effects

April 7, 2013 – May 1, 2013

Secure in My Father's Hand...Sunday, April 7, 2013

Yesterday was the first day I did not have an appetite. For me, that is a first. I think it might have been because I felt so lousy. Yesterday was the hardest day I have faced so far. Fatigue was much greater than after the last treatments. I did make it through the workday, though it was not easy. After I arrived home, I took a nap and lay on the couch until it was time to go to bed. I did not have energy for anything else. A scratchy throat and draining sinuses persist, now a minor cough has added itself to the mix. The medicines are working to keep the digestive tract running smoothly and the swelling under control. I think I will have the energy to attend church this morning. That is the best praise! I am grateful for the continued prayers, love, hugs, emails, cards, calls, and expressions of support and care.

> Now to Him who is able to do immeasurably more than all we ask or imagine, according to His power that is at work within us. (Ephesians 3:20)

God is able to, and often does so much "more than we ask or can even imagine." How awesome is that? His power at work within us who know Him as Savior and Lord is through His Holy Spirit, who is given to us at the time we decide to follow Him (Ephesians 1:13). Nothing can take away our salvation once we have given ourselves to the Lord. We are totally secure as we are resting in our Father's hand. That is why I can walk through the valley I am in with His peace. No matter what comes, I am secure.

Patience, Perseverance, Joy, and Peace...Monday, April 8, 2013

Good morning! I am still in need of more rest, so the longer time in bed today was a blessing. I rested so much last night that my eyes are swollen this morning. That is another one of the side effects. My eyes will swell overnight when I rest, sometimes even when I take a nap. The praise is that the swelling goes away

I am still keeping an eye on my temperature, because of all the congestion, scratchy throat and cough. These are the most annoying of the symptoms I am dealing with right now, along with the fatigue. I am an "on the go" kind of lady. I like to do what I want to do, when I want to do it. Fatigue does not allow me that option. It feels frustrating, but I have learned, and am still learning to decide what is most important and doing those things while letting others go.

The Lord is teaching me more patience. Patience is like a muscle, you have to use it to develop it. It is one of the most difficult things in life for many of us, especially Americans. We are constantly inundated with messages from our media telling us that we need it "Now!"... "Our Way!"..."Why Wait!"... "We make it Easy!"... "Buy Now, Pay Later!" Our society tells us that we deserve what we want, when we want it. These thoughts cause me to hmmm a little on patience.

> Consider it pure joy, my brothers, whenever you face trials of many kinds, because you know that the testing of your faith develops perseverance. Perseverance must finish its work so that you may be mature and complete, not lacking anything. (James 1:2-4)

Perseverance and patience are closely related. We must operate in patience to persevere and to become mature and complete, "Perseverance must finish its work" in us (James 1:12).

Isn't it easier to withstand a trial or be patient waiting when you know good things will come because of your obedience? We must focus there. That is exactly what Jesus did as He faced the cross for us. He endured the insults, being spat upon, questioning, scourging, beatings, being viciously crowned with thorns, as well as carrying the cross, and then horrifically dying on it, all for the blessing and joy of reconciling us to God. When we look at our lives in the scope of all He had to endure for us, whatever trial or difficulty we are facing today is minuscule in comparison. It is not always easy to see things with God's perspective, but it is always worth the time and effort spent to do so. How are we to face life's difficulties? He tells us how to bear our trials and afflictions. Hope in Him, wait upon Him, and pray. His Holy Spirit will give us the ability. The best part is, we can be joyful as we wait when trust is in Him (Romans 12:12). Is it easy? No, but He never promised us easy.

> I have told you these things, so that in Me you may have peace. In this life, you will have trouble. But take heart! I have overcome the world. (John 16:33)

That is more good news. Not only can we be joyful as we wait and persevere, but we can also have peace. As I have walked these last few months of life, I can only bow my head in thanksgiving for all that Father has done to prepare me. He taught me how to trust Him, thank Him, rest in His love and presence, walk in His peace, be filled with His joy and allow His Spirit to work in and through me. I do not have it perfect by any means, but I am grateful for the patience He has worked in me. It keeps me focused on Him and not my circumstances. Focusing on my circumstances would undoubtedly swirl me into a pit of despair.

We have the great privilege and ability to draw near to God, who will in turn draw near to us. That is my favorite hmmm of the morning. Nearness to God... there is no greater peace, no greater joy, no greater comfort, no greater fulfillment.

His Creation, You, and Worship...Tuesday, April 9, 2013

It's that time of morning again for me. Yesterday was still a bit rough for me. Fatigue was really strong. And, the way I feel right now, I suspect it will be today, too. I called Dr. Gill, and she said that it might be due to a virus I have contracted in addition to the chemo. The congestion, scratchy throat, and cough caused by the virus may be what is causing me to feel "slammed" extra hard by fatigue. I have done very little except work the last few days... well, work and go to church, but church is always a refresher. As I think about going to church and how it refreshes me, a devotional I read comes to mind.

> Come, let us bow down in worship, let us kneel before the Lord our Maker; for He is our God and we are the people of His pasture, the flock under His care. (Psalm 95:6-7)

God created us. We are under His ever watchful eye and ever caring hand. Those things alone should be enough to cause our hearts to respond in worship. He is the One who gave us life and sustains it. It is His breath, breathed into us, that gives life (Genesis 2:7).

Just knowing that it is His breath giving us life and sustaining us should be enough for our hearts to worship Him. However, He gives us many more reasons. The book of Psalms is full of words of worship for the Lord. Each Psalm comes from a different perspective and focuses on the various aspects of God that are worthy of worship. Today, I want to focus on God as Creator. Psalm 8 really speaks to my heart this morning.

I am always amazed and awed as I look at all God has created in nature. The intricacies and details He wove into everything He created is awesome when you open your mind to consider them from the lily of the valley and the ant, to the redwood trees and elephants, the wonders of the earth with the snow peaked mountains and mighty rivers, grassy plains, wide canyons, and smoking volcanoes, and finally, the heavens with stars, moons, comets, planets, suns and galaxies.

To top it off, we are mankind, the part of His creation He "crowned with glory and honor." Consider the intricate detail He put into each of us: hair color, eye color, shape of face and body, the way all our organs work together to function as one complete unit, our minds with the capacity to think, our eyes and how they see, our ears with the ability to hear, our tongue and the diverse flavors of taste. His creation is but one part of what makes Him worthy of worship.

We cannot worship in truth unless we worship Him for who He is and not just who we want Him to be. As humans, we have a tendency to want to form God into the image of what we want Him to be, to confirm our desires. But to worship Him in truth, we must see and know Him for who He really is. The Bible will reveal Him to us as we study it and ask His Spirit to teach and guide us. Worship Him for all that He has created, including most importantly: You!

Comfort ... Hmmm ... Wednesday, April 10, 2013

Hello, friends and family. What a gorgeous day God has given us. It feels like June in April. I have not been able to taste anything, no matter what it was. I am still as hungry as a horse and want to eat, but just can't taste it. Today is also one of the days my skin and body aches, and I have had a nagging headache all day. I managed to function relatively well, but the combination of chemo and the suspected virus has been challenging. I coughed and blew my nose most of the day.

Today, I decided I would shorten the workday to a half day and come home to rest. The fatigue is kicking my tail. I called work and had them cover me for tomorrow. I want to give my body every chance to recover to be ready for the next treatment. Needless to say, I am not looking forward to the next one. But, I am looking forward to getting through them just as fast as the Lord will allow.

My Mom came in to tell me goodnight before she went to bed, she kissed me on the forehead and hugged me. I wrapped my arms around her and left them there. I had the feeling of being a little girl again and wanting Mom to hold me and make it all better. As we hugged, a few tears ran down my cheeks because my mother's love and comfort was just what I needed in that moment. As always, the Lord is good to provide what I need through others and through Himself. Hmmm...God comforts us. "As a mother comforts her child, so I will comfort you." (Isaiah 66:13a).

The Lord is a great comforter. Often, I will close my eyes and feel myself crawling up into His lap and laying my head on His chest, relaxing and giving Him all the tensions and hurts that weigh heavy on me. I allow Him to wrap His arms of love around me, covering me with comfort as only He can. He truly is the God of all comfort. He has compassion on us and covers us with His comfort. He does this because He loves us and His heart desires to comfort us. He also gives us comfort so that we may comfort others (II Corinthians 1:3-5).

God gives us comfort in different ways, some directly from Himself and some through others. One of the ways He gives comfort is through His Word, but the main way Father delivers comfort is through Holy Spirit, our constant indwelling companion. God's presence gives us joy and comfort. It is wonderful for me to know His presence is constant and forever. Jesus reminds us of this when He tells His disciples that He is asking the Father to send Holy Spirit to them.

And I will ask the Father, and He will give you another Counselor to be with you forever…the Spirit of truth. The world cannot accept Him, because it neither sees Him nor knows Him. But you know Him, for He lives with you and will be in you. (John 14:16-17)

Hmmm… that is great news. I think I will hmmm myself to sleep on that wonderful truth and allow His comfort to sooth all that ails me tonight.

Contented and Grateful…Thursday, April 11, 2013

Good Afternoon! It feels like summer. I am ready for lots of outdoor time. This year, I may be just sitting on the deck and reading and not enjoying my usual jogging or walking. Whatever the case, I will be very happy to enjoy the fresh air! I am resting and working on paperwork today. I opened my bedroom window and have lots of fresh air blowing through. I have been feeling "cooped up" lately, so even though I am not outside, the fresh air makes me feel almost like I am.

    A great praise for the day is that I can taste some things today. Yea! Breakfast was somewhat tasty. I had eggs, sausage, grapefruit, and grape juice. I could taste the grape juice best and the sausage next best. Then, later, as a snack, I had some dip that my Dad makes and corn chips. My Dad makes the best dip. It was so good, I ate it all. Then, my parents brought me a burger. I could positively taste the dill pickle chips, onions, and ketchup. It is great to taste at least some things. It is sad to say, but we take so many things for granted that God has given us. Our sense of taste is just one.

    Children were asked to describe what they thought the greatest wonders in the world were. All kinds of answers were given, from statues and buildings to inventions and technology. One little girl mentioned the five senses of sight, touch, taste, hearing, and smell. The Lord made our bodies in such a way as to be blessed by even the everyday things of life. I have never been as grateful to taste things as I am now. I can only ask Father to forgive me for taking His gift of taste for granted. Think of sight and hearing. Do we take time to be grateful for those precious gifts, too?

    We can always find things that are not as we would like them to be. When we look at our life and I mean really look at our life. Most of us have all of our senses, in addition to the abilities to walk and talk, work and play, sing and dance, to think and learn, as well as to worship and pray. Most of us have food on the table, clothes on our backs and a roof over our head. We are very blessed and should be grateful and content with what we have.

The Apostle Paul learned to be content, no matter his circumstances in Philippians 4:11-12. How did he do it? And, how can we? Our connection and union with the Lord gives us the strength and ability to be content. He is truly all we need. He is the reason I have joy and contentment as I walk through this season of life, which includes bankruptcy, divorce, the loss of my home, and cancer. My joy and contentment are not dependent on my circumstances, but on Him and His love and faithfulness.

God promises to meet our needs. I can testify to the fact that He has and continues to do that for me constantly. As I continue to hmmm, I not only think of my blessings and how grateful I am for them, but for all the simple things that are often taken for granted. I have been given so much more than what it takes to be content. Most all of us have, especially those of us living in the United States of America.

I Timothy 6:9-10 gives us fair warning that greed and the love of money will lead us into destruction. It is not wrong to desire nice things, but to love "things" and not the "Giver of all things" will lead us into ruin (Hebrews 13:5). Father loves to provide for us and supply all of our needs. Are we content? Are we grateful? Or, are we still looking for that next thing that we think will make us happy and fulfilled? He promises never to leave us or forsake us. There is no greater fulfillment than what we find in Him.

As my mind returns to the many blessings of the day, I think of Ellie Mae and tasting things. I cannot help but chuckle to myself. As I have eaten lately, I am regularly finding little hairs in my food. If that happened before, I could blame it on Ellie Mae, even though I hardly ever found one of her hairs in my food. (Those of you with house dogs understand what I am saying here.) But, lately, I have found lots of short, dishwater blonde hairs in my food even though I have my head covered any time I am eating. I suppose there will be one more positive to being bald. No more hair in my food.

Today, I noticed a lot more hair in the shower drain than the last two days. And, before I tied a bandana on, I noticed that my "buzzed off" stand of hairs is now much thinner. It is kind of odd how the hair has fallen out. I thought it would fall out evenly all over. It hasn't. It "balded up" the sides above my ears first, then unevenly up the back of my head, leaving a thinning stand across the crown and top of my head holding fairly firm. I am now beginning see the top and crown hair letting loose. I just hmmm on the oddness of it all. Most of the leg hairs have gone, but I still have a few stubborn ones that won't let go. That seems odd, too. I am sure, however; that both the stubborn leg hairs and the rest of the hair on top of the head will eventually release. The leg ones could go anytime and I would not be offended. For that matter, they could stay gone even when the rest of the hair grows back and I would be content. No shaving! Well, that is enough about hair. It is likely more than you wanted to know. It is just where my thoughts took me. Thank you for humoring me as my mind wandered.

Dear friends and loved ones, may your heart be content and grateful for your many blessings, both large and small. You will find joy and true contentment when you realize, the Lord truly is all you need.

Burdens, Prayer, Peace, and tender feet...Friday, April 12, 2013

Hey there! It's me again. I do not have to work until this afternoon. I had the ability to sleep in and took full advantage of it. I made it through the workday yesterday with flying colors and then even made it through a bridal shower after work. However, by the time I got home from that, all energy was gone. After taking Ellie Mae out for her last sniff over the yard, I hit the bed. The need for extra rest has been one of the hardest things for me to accept. I am an "on the go" type of lady and stopping to rest is just not easy.

He reminds me that I am only responsible for what He tells me I am responsible for, not everything that I want to be responsible for. That gives things a whole new perspective. We often take on more responsibilities than are truly ours, physically, spiritually, and emotionally. The Lord reminds me, when I am doing as He instructs, I am not responsible for the results. He is. I am only responsible to be obedient. That eliminates a huge amount of stress. God did not make us to carry large amounts of internal stress and strain.

Hmmm... He wants to be the one to carry our burdens for us (Psalm 68:19). But, in order for Him to bear them for us, we must give them to Him. When we give our burdens to Him in prayer, and I mean truly give them to Him, He will carry the weight of them for us. How do we know if we have "unwrapped" the fingers of our heart and mind from around what we are laying before Him in prayer? How do we know that we have truly given Him our burden?

When we have truly given Him what burdens our hearts and minds, we will have His peace (Philippians 4:7). His peace is so wonderful we cannot fully understand it. The peace we have is "in" Jesus. It is Jesus' peace that is beyond all understanding. It is different from anything else you might find and consider to be peace without knowing Jesus as Savior and Lord. Not only is it different and so great that it is beyond comprehension, but when we have it, our hearts will not be troubled and we will not be afraid. Wow! That is good news. For me, this is something to shout, sing, and dance about. For many years of my life, I was consumed by fear. Fear was my constant companion and, to a great degree, controlled every part of my life. I had learned to "manage" it, but was not free from it by any means. Jesus' power has now freed me from fear and His Holy Spirit taught me how to continue to walk in freedom from it, trusting the Lord as I lay my burdens before Him in prayer.

I feel even better now than when I first got up. Praise the Lord! I still have some cough and congestion, but the sore throat is gone. I still have the constant headache, but it is mild this morning. The eyebrows and eyelashes are holding firm to my face. More praises!

I have a new side effect to share with you. The pads of my feet are quite tender and a bit sore. It feels like I have been walking around on rough concrete and rocks without shoes on and with feet that have not been toughened enough to take it. Hmmm... that is an odd one to me. The praise is that it is bearable and I do not experience the discomfort all the time.

Spring, Growth, Renewal, Transformation...
Saturday, April 13, 2013

Happy Beautiful Day! The first thing I heard this morning was the melodic chorus of several birds singing a cheerful song in the morning sunlight. I love to see new growth springing forth after the harshness of winter. I saw a long row of daffodils standing tall and bright, gently swaying in the cool breeze. The grass below is beginning to develop a deep rich green color as new tufts begin to replace the dried brown carpet of winter. The ornamental cherry trees are popping with gorgeous pink blooms. The cherry trees are my favorite because I love the color pink. Spring is here! Hmmm... spring...new life...new growth...renewal.

The Lord has me thinking about how He gives us new life and then continues to grow us after we accept Jesus as Savior and Lord. Before accepting Him, we were dead in our sins.

> But because of His great love for us, God who is rich in mercy, made us alive with Christ even when we were dead in transgressions. It is by grace you have been saved. (Ephesians 2:4-5)

As we receive Jesus Christ, trusting Him and the sacrifice He made for us on the cross, we are made spiritually alive. We leave the death of winter and enter the new life and growth of spring. The ultimate goal of growth is to become like God's Son, Jesus Christ. II Corinthians 8:29b tells us we are "to be conformed to the likeness of His Son."

We are to be transformed and conformed to the image and likeness of our Savior. This process takes place internally. It is not dependent on our physical bodies. Our bodies are, in all reality, deteriorating as we age or as sickness and disease ravages them (II Corinthians 4:16). The great news is that our spiritual growth and renewal is not determined by the condition of our physical bodies. In my current weakened state, I find that to be especially good news. When we read and study the Bible, we are "renewing our minds" with His truth. We are replacing the false thinking of the world with truth.

As you spend time reading and studying, pray and ask Him to guide you into truth. Holy Spirit, who comes to live in you at the time of salvation, is there to help teach you and give you a deeper understanding (John 16:13a).

Holy Spirit is your guide as you read, study, and seek to walk out your faith. You will hear His voice as you get quiet before the Lord asking for wisdom, revelation and direction (Colossians 1:9b-12). The reason He wants to give us knowledge of His will, spiritual wisdom and understanding, is so we may please Him in everything and to be able to endure this life with patience. I want Him to grow, renew and transform me. Don't you? Are you spending time with Him in His Word and prayer? I know, as I do my part, He will be pleased with me, allowing me to bear fruit, giving me endurance and patience.

I took advantage of not having to work by taking a leisurely pace today. The slower pace is a blessing. I am sure Father knew I would still be fighting the virus and planned for me to have today and tomorrow off for extra rest in preparation for the next chemo treatment. I am grateful. I think the congestion and cough are less even though they are still with me. The only symptom that seems to be worse is the pain on the bottom of my feet, especially the left one. Why one hurts worse than the other is a mystery to me, but it does. The feeling is now like that of having walked across hot concrete which not only made them raw because they were not tough enough to handle it, but burned them in the process. As you can tell, I have done some crazy things in my lifetime by walking across rocks, pavement, and hot concrete with bare feet; otherwise I would not know how to compare the pain. When I am off of my feet, I do not feel the pain. But, the longer I am on my feet the more the pain intensifies.

Geese, Guarding, Thinking, Truth, the Mind…Sunday, April 14, 2013

Yesterday was a day of rest for me. I enjoyed a walk with Mom, Dad, A.J., my great nephew, and Ellie Mae. We walked over to the pond in my parents' subdivision and fed a goose, some fish and turtles. As we finished our walk around the pond, we found a second goose sitting on a nest. We must have gotten a little too close, because the first goose, its mate, quickly swam across the pond and ran out of the water toward us and began hissing at us. The goose was very serious about guarding its mate and the nest. We gave them a wide berth as we passed by. I did not want to be chased by an aggressive goose.

Hmmm… guarding…thinking. It is important for us to guard our thoughts. It reminds me of how important "what we think" is to "who we are." An insightful quote from Albert Einstein reads: "The world we have created is a product of our thinking; it cannot be changed without changing our thinking."

Hmmm… how are you and I changing as a result of our thinking? Are we changing for better or worse? What we think shapes our attitudes. Our attitudes determine our actions. Then, our actions form our habits. In the long run, our habits determine our future. Where our future leads starts in our mind with our thoughts. God's Word is full of scriptures encouraging us to think properly. My favorite is:

> Finally, brothers, whatever is true, whatever is noble, whatever is right, whatever is pure, whatever is lovely, whatever is admirable,

> if anything is excellent or praiseworthy, think about such things. (Philippians 4:8)

If we choose to think and live according to God's Word and the leading of Holy Spirit, we obtain spiritual life, peace, and the ability to please God. I know which I want. How about you? God knows what is in our hearts and minds. He knows the motive and attitude behind each thought (I Chronicles 28:9b).

Satan has been trying to sell me his lies in this season of life. He told me the cancer is because of something I did wrong and that God is punishing me. He told me that God doesn't love me or He wouldn't have allowed it, and lots of other lies. Can you imagine where I would be if I allowed myself to feed on Satan's lies? I would be a mess. Fortunately, I have learned enough of God's Word to know these were lies. I rejected them, with Holy Spirit's help, and continue to focus on the truth of God's faithfulness and unfailing love for me. Satan knows, if he can control our minds, he can control us. Our minds are a much greater battle ground than we often realize. It is of utmost importance that we win this battle with Holy Spirit's help.

What are you feeding your mind? What kind of Music? Movies? Television programs? Conversations with friends? Reading material? Pictures? Do they line up with the truth of God's Word? You have heard the old adage, "You are what you eat." When it comes to the mind and your way of thinking, you truly will be a product of what you feed your mind. As you think, so are you. My encouragement is to hmmm on the things you are feeding your mind and make any adjustments necessary to renew your thinking, and attitudes.

Fear and Trust ... Monday, April 15, 2013

The best praise for the day is that my left foot, which has been giving me much discomfort when I stand on it, was almost fine today. Thank you, Lord! My energy level stayed good all through the workday. The headache was mild and I could taste everything I put in my mouth. There were no body aches or skin aches. The stinging I had on my tongue is gone, too. My only real concerns are the continued cough and stuffed up sinuses.

As I continue to watch my hair evacuating my head, I realize I am beyond the 14-21 days the doctor said it normally takes for it to all fall out.

It is now about 28 days since the beginning of the hair loss. I still have some spots with hair. I know I said I looked like a mangy dog before, but I really do now. Most of my head is almost bald or bald, but then, I still have spots and streaks that have a decent stand of hair. Mom volunteered to buzz them shorter for me. I thought about it, but I noticed that having a few spots of hair helps hold the scarves I am wearing in place. It works kind of like Velcro. Several have teased me about using double faced tape. What they don't realize is that I am allergic to some of the adhesives found in tapes. I would end up with red welts wherever the tape touched my skin that would itch like crazy. Between the patches of hair and red welts, I would look even mangier. I speculate all the hair will soon be gone. The shower drain strainer is now always full after my showers. I am glad to have kept my eyebrows and eyelashes. I am praising the Lord for that.

As the Lord was preparing me for all the storms and difficulties of these last months, He spent much time teaching me not to fear and to trust Him. "Fear and trust" are my hmmms today. Fear and trust cannot co-exist where God is concerned.

> When I am afraid, I will trust you. In God, whose word I praise, in God I trust; I will not be afraid. (Psalm 56:3-4a)

This Psalm tells us that when we feel fear, and we will feel fear from time to time; our response is to reject it and put our trust in God. As we do, we will not be afraid. Isaiah 12:2b reminds us of the same truth and then gives us the additional truth that the Lord is our strength. We are not to trust our own strength, but His. Jesus told His disciples not to fear or allow their hearts to be troubled.

Jesus did not give his disciples an option to fear. His command was point blank. Don't do it! It is a firm command, not a suggestion. How do we do it? The first step is to receive Jesus as your Savior and Lord. At that point, Jesus gives you His Spirit to live in you. He enables you to trust and not to fear.

> For God did not give us a spirit of timidity (*fear*), but a spirit of power, of love and of self-discipline. (II Timothy 1:7)

Another step in following Jesus' command to trust and not fear is meditating on God's Word and obeying it as Joshua 1:7-9 instructs us. My favorite promise is that He will be with me wherever I go. (See also, Jeremiah 1:8 and Acts 18:9b-10a.) If He is with me, what is there to fear? God is my refuge, my fortress, my shield, and my help.

As I ponder and hmmm on these truths, I know my trust in God is the only reason I do not have fear. I have peace as I walk through this challenging period of time. Without trusting in Him, I would be a fearful, shaking, quaking mess. Because He is my Savior and Lord, He is with me always. No matter the problems or difficulties I face, He gives me His courage and strength. Mine would never sustain me. He showed Himself faithful in the past, He continues to show Himself faithful in the present; which leaves me no doubt He will continue to show Himself faithful in the future.

Witnesses to the Good News!...Tuesday, April 16, 2013

Good Evening! I felt fairly well most all day and had enough energy to work without struggling to make it to the end of my shift. The only negatives I could speak of are a headache, cough and runny nose. I talked and prayed with a friend at lunch time. The headache eased back into a dull ache instead of the sharper pain I had been experiencing. What a blessing it is to have praying friends.

I was also blessed by an abundance of sweet customers who loved and encouraged me today. Several have even added me to their church prayer lists. It is no wonder I am doing so well. The prayers of my own family, friends, and church family are being lifted before Father's throne for me as well as my customers and their church families' prayers. I truly am one blessed lady.

Father gave me many opportunities today to tell others how good He is and how faithful He is to me. Hmmm... when we tell others of how faithful the Lord has been to us, we are His witnesses. A simple definition of a *witness* is one who bears testimony. Christians are to give testimony of Jesus, Father and Holy Spirit (Acts 1:8). When Jesus was talking to His disciples before ascending into heaven, He told them they would be His witnesses. Not only does this pertain to Jesus' disciples, but, to all Christians.

The "good news" is that Jesus came and died on the cross; thereby, paying the penalty for your sins and mine. He took the punishment we deserve and gave us the opportunity to be redeemed and saved from spiritual death and hell, which is the gift of salvation. A Christian has the promise of heaven because Jesus paid the full penalty for our sins. We are forgiven. That is good news, indeed. If we, who are Christians, do not tell others about Jesus, who will?

If you already know Jesus as your Savior and Lord, think about where you would be if no one had shared with you. If you don't know Jesus as Savior and Lord, what is keeping you from Him? Is it worth the loss of your soul and eternity in heaven? (Matthew 16:26).

Hmmm... Who am I?... Wednesday, April 17, 2013

Happy beautiful afternoon! I was surprised by the warm temperatures as I stepped out of work today. Maybe I will get a half hour or so outdoors before I head to church this evening for Bible Study and prayer time. I had sufficient energy for work; the headache was not too strong most of the day. Part of the day, I had sharp pain behind one eye. I speculate it is sinus related, because I still have the draining sinuses and cough. There were minimal body aches, and my feet were fine. More praises! I did notice a new side effect. Across the knuckles on the back of my left hand, the skin is discolored and a rash is beginning to develop. Well, at least the chemo side effects keep it interesting. There always seems to be something different. But, if these are the worst of it, then that is great. It could always be worse. Even if it was, God's grace would still be sufficient.

Mom and Dad just came in from working their church re-sell-it sale. For me, they brought in a bag of scarves that are all different colors. I think there were ten of them. Yea! I have more choices to cover the "mangy dog" look. As I think about the loss of my hair, I realize, as much as I would prefer to have my hair, it really hasn't been traumatic for me to lose it. The Lord has been so good to continue to help me stay focused on Him and to realize that my hair does not define who I am. Hmmm... who am I?

Father has been teaching me that I am who He says I am and not who anyone else says I am or even who I think I am. I am spiritually alive and a new creation in Christ because He set me free from my sin (II Corinthians 5:1). Why did God do this? It is because He chose me and loves me. That's why. I am not only chosen and loved, but I am valuable to God because the price paid for me was the highest price possible. Jesus suffered and died to buy me and pardon me from sin. When I gave my life to Him, I became a member of His family and an heir of His kingdom. Nothing will ever be able to separate me from Him.

> The Lord your God is with you, He is mighty to save. He will take great delight in you, He will quiet you with His love, He will rejoice over you with singing. (Zephaniah 3:17)

Isn't that wonderful? Can you picture it? God delights in us and rejoices over us with singing. Wow! My mind's eye loves trying to conjure up that image. My heart swells just to think about it.

Chemo 4…Thursday, April 18, 2013
Laughter, Joy, Medicine, Smiles, Many Praises, Friday, April 19, 2013

Happy morning! Happy day! I have lots of praises. My appointment for chemo therapy was yesterday. The first praise is that all my blood counts were great, even the platelet count, so the treatment proceeded on schedule.

This was the last of the first type of chemo treatments which consisted of two different chemo drugs that normally produce heavier side effects than the drug they will be using for the next twelve treatments. The side effects are what make it difficult to want to walk through the hospital doors to receive the treatments. The next twelve treatments will be every week and not every other week as the first four have been. I will not have to make the return trip to the hospital to get a shot the following day after chemo for the next twelve. This particular drug does not require that. Yea!

Here is the biggest praise. When Dr. Gill checked the tumor and its size, she told me that it shrank a lot. Praise the Lord! I felt certain it had, but it is always great to have the expert confirm your observations. Dr. Gill gave me a prescription for an antibiotic to help with the sinus infection which developed as a result of the virus. That is where the persistent cough and sharp headaches I have been experiencing are coming from.

"Hoke" (my Daddy) again drove "Miss Daisy" (me) and her mother (my Mom) to the appointment. My Dad is so good to always drive me to the appointments. It is such a blessing to me. He, my Mom, and Dr. Porter have been a great threesome to have as my cheering section for the treatments. And as you know, taking care of me is "a big job." He and Mom do a great job taking care of me.

The treatment time was happy as it usually is, filled with good fellowship and laughter. Father is so good to provide merriment, especially, when the situation could be a somber one. At one point I was laughing so hard several nurses came over to check and see if they could "get in on the party." Because of all the fun, the part I dislike the most, eating ice as they administer the one chemo drug, was not nearly as difficult to bear. I tried a different approach this time, holding the ice in my mouth longer and not eating so much. It should have the same desired effect. Keeping the inside of my mouth cold was the objective and that was accomplished. I think about the laughter and the joy shared. Hmmm…"A cheerful heart is good medicine, but a crushed spirit dries up the bones." (Proverbs 17:22)

The joy I allow the Lord to put in my heart is like "good medicine" to my body. I have heard several times that the attitude I have chosen as I face dealing with cancer and its treatments is of utmost importance. As the doctors and nurses do their part, working to heal my body, I am to do my part by not only following the doctor's instructions, but most importantly, by following Father's instruction. Ultimately God does the healing, but He works wonderfully through the folks in the medical profession. Faith, trust, obedience, and the refusal to fear are all key ingredients, as well as prayer, worship and spending time in His Word.

As we immerse ourselves in God's truth and step out in obedience, He grows our faith. As we walk in faith, we are able to deflect the lies the devil throws our way and choose the Lord's way (Ephesians 6:16b). When joy is in your heart, your face shows it. Then, as your face radiates the joy you allowed the Lord to give you, you can share it with others.

When you share the joy you have by allowing others to see it on your face and in your life, Father multiplies it by allowing others to benefit from the joy overflowing from you. Isn't it awesome how God works? Hmmm… are you doing what it takes to have true joy and peace in your heart?

I cannot begin to tell you the difference it has made in my life since I deliberately began choosing to be obedient to the things I knew God was calling me to do. My encouragement to you is to take that next step of obedience. The steps are not always easy and there is often sacrifice involved, but the profit gained is always exponentially greater than the price paid.

As I sat down to the computer last evening, the effects of the chemo had my eye lids so heavy that I could not keep them open. I knew that my thoughts would be far from coherent. I will also spend today counseling with folks. As you know, it is a favorite time for me. Watching the power of Jesus work to set folks free from their strongholds is a great joy

Thought for the Morning...Saturday, April 20, 2013

My words will be short, because I have to work early today. As you all know, I hmmm and think a lot! As I was reading in the Psalms, this small phrase caught my attention and made me think. "The Lord knows the thoughts of man..." (Psalm 94:11a).

God knows my every thought and my every hmmm. Are they honoring to Him? Would He be pleased with what I have in my mind? What about you? Where is your focus today?

When He is the center of our focus and we are seeking to know Him and His truth, as well as seeking to know His will in order to do it, our thoughts will always be pleasing to Him. Hmmm...join me in that thought.

Rest and Refuge... Sunday, April 21, 2013

Happy Sunday morning to you! I have taken more time to sleep and rest, trying to recover from the fatigue. Since rest was what my body needed, rest is where my thoughts are this morning. Not only do our bodies need rest, but our souls need rest, which can only be found in God. He is our refuge, our solid rock and the only place where we find salvation and hope.

> Find rest, O my soul, in God alone; my hope comes from Him. He alone is my rock and my salvation; He is my fortress, I will not be shaken. My salvation and my honor depend on God; He is my mighty rock, my refuge. Trust in Him at all times, O people; pour out your hearts to Him, for God is our refuge. (Psalm 62:5-8)

In God is the only place our souls can find true rest. We have it here and now, on earth, as we accept the free gift of His salvation given through Jesus. And, we have it for an eternity in heaven.

This life can be very wearisome and feel much like living in a war zone. We are hit on all sides with many different struggles, trials, and difficulties. We may face sickness, divorce, financial problems, and interpersonal problems. But, when we focus our hearts on and place our trust in the

Lord, we find that He truly is our refuge in troubled times. He is the solid foundation upon which we can stand secure. He is our rock. I know that if my trust was not in Him at this time in my life, I would be shipwrecked and sinking and without the wonderful hope He has available.

We are encouraged to pour our hearts out to Him. He is listening. He loves us and wants to be our refuge. However, a refuge is only a place of security when it is used. Hmmm… in times of trouble, where do you turn first? Is it the Lord? Is your first thought to pray asking Him for His help, wisdom, and guidance? These are questions I ask myself, too.

Timing… Trusting…. Waiting… Monday, April 22, 2013

Hello! I gained extra sleep the last couple of days. What a blessing. My body desperately needed it. Long naps on both Saturday and Sunday refreshed me so much so that I am up earlier than I have to be this morning. I am even wide awake.

All in all, I am doing well. The sinuses are clearing, even though there is still a bit of nagging cough. The fatigue of the last few days should be less today. Yea! I suffered what felt like heartburn or acid reflux for a day or two after chemo, neither of which have ever plagued me before, but I have relief from it now. I am sure it was a side effect of the chemo and due to the fact that I ate less ice during the last treatment. Maybe just holding the ice in my mouth wasn't such a great idea. I could taste things fairly well for the last few days. Woo Hoo! I truly enjoy eating.

For those of you wondering, the "mangy dog" look is now gone. The only hairs I have left on my head are just a few loners, here and there. The patches were so pitiful looking. My head looks much better now than it did with the patches. Mom even decided that it looks well enough that I really don't have to cover it. Maybe a little tan to take away the white line that rings my face from last year's suntan would make it doable for the right occasion. Right now, however, the temperatures are too chilly to leave it uncovered. I never realized how much body heat the hair holds in.

The tumor has shrunk a lot. As I think about that, I remember asking my oncologist if it might be possible, since the tumor was shrinking, that the number of chemo treatments might be shortened. Not surprisingly, the answer was no. Chemo is no fun and makes me feel lousy. I hoped it could be shortened. This thought causes me to hmmm a little. The length of time the chemo takes to do its work is certainly not what I would choose it to be, nor is God's timing what I would always choose it to be. I continue to learn that God's timing is always perfect. He sees and knows what is ahead in our lives and what is needed for each moment to prepare us for the next. We don't.

> But I trust in You, O Lord; I say, "You are my God." My times are in your hands… Let your face shine on your servant, save me in your unfailing love. (Psalm 31:14-16)

My life and its span are in His hands. He created me and knows His plans for me. He knew when I took my first breath and He knows when I will take my last. His Word reminds us to wait upon Him and to remember that He is good (Psalm 27:13-14). As we wait, He encourages us to be strong and take heart. He also promises us that He will strengthen and uphold us. That is great news. We can never do it on our own. He gives us what we need as we trust Him. He reminds us not to be afraid, because He is with us (Isaiah 41:10). Oh, what great promises!

There are great promises for us as we wait in what seem like the darkest and most painful times in life. Whatever I am facing will not consume me, because He loves me (Lamentations 3:22-24). The Lord's compassion is there for us as we wait, always new and fresh and never failing. The promise is that whatever we are facing, even though there is pain for a time, rejoicing is on the other side. What great comfort that is.

Grateful for the help of others … Tuesday, April 23, 2013

Good Afternoon. It has been a tiresome day. The sinus issues and coughing kept me up much of the night. I decided to call in sick to work because I knew I needed rest. I am contemplating calling in for tomorrow, too. My fever has gone up and down since I got up. It has not hit the critical 101, but has come as high as 100.8. I will continue to monitor it. The headache has returned. I am certain it is related to the fever, sinuses, persistent coughing, and fatigue. The ability to taste has gone for the day. That is not unusual. It seems to come and go as I take the treatments. I am grateful I can taste on some days.

I made the decision to call in sick for work tomorrow. It is difficult for me to call in, but I know for my body's sake, it is wisdom. I surely do not want to slow the progress of the treatments and getting through with it all. As I think about how lousy I feel, I realize how grateful I am to have others around me to encourage, pray, and care for me. What a great blessing the Lord has given in those who have chosen to walk this road with me. I hmmm and think about how important it is to have others to walk with us (Ecclesiastes 4:9-12). As we do, we are strengthened.

God has given us each other for strength. Ultimately, He is our strength, but He graciously allows us to get in on the blessing of helping and encouraging others and working together. Isn't that just like God to give us the joy of being His hands and feet to others? The love and help from others warms my heart and greatly encourages me.

Obedience or Disobedience...Blessing or Consequence
Wednesday, April 24, 2013

I just got home from the pharmacy with more prescriptions. I now have a new antibiotic and an inhaler. I think it will help because the breathing treatment they gave me at the hospital last night helped. I had to take a trip to the emergency room. The fever necessitated it when it went over 101, I called the exchange and Dr. Gill called me back, letting me know that I must go. In the emergency room, they took chest x-rays, drew blood for testing, and gave me a breathing treatment. They wanted to be certain I did not have pneumonia. Praise the Lord! I don't. The ER doctor diagnosed it as bronchitis. I was also a bit dehydrated. They hooked me up to an IV to give me fluids while they did the other work. I did not drink as much yesterday because I slept most of the day.

My church prayer group sent out an email asking for prayer about the fever and trip to the emergency room. The Lord responded to the prayers of His people on my behalf. Thank you, Lord!

I feel some better today because I slept last night and coughed less. My abdominal muscles are sore from all the coughing and my ability to taste is still gone. A headache is a part of my symptoms, too. But, I have grown accustomed to these things and accept them as just a part of the way things are for now. I look forward to the day when things return to a healthy and more normal state. Until then, I will remain patient and trust the Lord to step me over each hurdle put before me. He is so faithful to do so. He will do that for you, too, if you trust and allow Him to. He continually reminds me that obedience, to all He asks, is the key to His peace and ability to rest in Him. Trust and obedience are where we find His peace. Hmmm… obedience is how we show God we love Him (I John 5:3a).

His commands and teachings are found in the Bible. In order to know them, you must spend time reading and studying. Do you love God? Are you being obedient? Whatever you put as a higher priority than God is what the Bible calls an idol. A simple definition of an idol is a false god. For you, it might be money, a hobby, another person, or any of a number of things. God must be first in your life in order for you to be obedient (Deuteronomy 5:7).

It is important to know that nothing will take the place of obedience. We often have to sacrifice things in different areas of our life as we walk with the Lord. But, be certain to know, sacrifice does not make up for a lack of obedience (I Samuel 15:22b). Obedience is first and foremost. Just reading and listening is not enough. Putting it into action is required (James 1:22).

The best part is, when we are obedient to God's Word, He promises to bless us. Just as with a parent/child relationship, with obedience comes blessing and disobedience carries consequences.

The most important part is that out of God's great love for us, He clearly provides us all we need to be obedient in His Word. He wants to bless us, so He gives us a road map to follow in order to receive His blessing. Are you seeking to follow the path He has set before you? Take some time with me to hmmm on these important truths.

Lies, Truth, and Sharing Wardrobes with a Rottweiler…
Thursday, April 25, 2013

Happy Sunny Afternoon. I hear the sounds of lawnmowers, weed eaters, hammering, and sawing coming from all over the neighborhood. It is another beautiful day that the Lord has made. I enjoyed most of it through the window because I have been inside most of the day. I am still recovering from upper respiratory issues. I followed doctor's orders and stayed home from work again today. Staying home was wisdom for giving my body more time to recover.

I have a large collection of bandanas from years past. My dogs always had bandana "clothes" to wear when I took them places or had company. I never imagined that I would be sharing a wardrobe with a Rottweiler, but sharing Ellie Mae's bandanas surely broadens the options I have for head coverings. At first, I thought the bandanas would be too small to cover my head, but after working with them, I found that if they are folded correctly, they work just fine. I think they are going to be better than some of the scarves this summer. In the heat, the cotton material will breathe and absorb sweat better. I am still chuckling to myself about sharing a wardrobe with a Rottweiler. Growing up, I always wanted a sister to share clothes with. Ellie Mae is not a sister, but I love her like family and we do get to share clothes.

I have been able to taste food today. I do not get the full flavor, but with a bit of imagination, I enjoy it anyway. I even stopped taking the water pill for swelling the last two days, and my ankles have remained my own and not those of a baby elephant. Yes, today has been a good day. I love hearing God's truth proclaimed and the deceptions of the devil exposed for the lies that they are. Hmmm... truth and lies. It is so very important that we speak truth. Satan is the father of all lies and is described in John 8:44.

Satan is a master deceiver and loves to distort and twist truth. When Jesus went into the wilderness to be tempted for forty days, Satan spoke to Jesus and even quoted Scripture. But as he did, he distorted the truth of God's Word and took the Scriptures out of context. The account of Jesus' temptation can be found in the beginning of the fourth chapters of both Matthew and Luke. We need to be familiar with it in order to combat the lies of the devil.

If you choose to deny the truth and believe the lies, you will have to suffer the consequences even to the point of destruction (Proverbs 19:5, 9b). The good news is, not only can we know the truth by studying God's Word, but we can ask for His help to continually speak the truth.

Singing... Praising... Joy... Friday, April 26, 2013

Praise the Lord for uninterrupted sleep. I am also praising Him because I do not have a headache at the moment. My body aches a bit, but that is another side effect I have grown accustomed to dealing with.

Today's only new side effect is a couple of mouth sores underneath my tongue. Chemo causes them. After a few days, they go away. The top of my tongue is also a little tender, but still very manageable. Given a little time, it will also subside. I still have shortness of breath, especially when I try to sing. I noticed that while at church. It might have been a blessing for those around me. I love to sing, but singing is not my strongest gifting. Hmmm... singing.

As people, we sing for lots of reasons. Most often, I sing because I have joy and because I want to worship the Lord. That is exactly what the Bible tells us to do. It does not matter if your voice is beautiful to anyone else. The Lord is the one to whom we are to sing. Those who have children will understand what a precious thing it is when your child sings to you. No matter what his or her little voice sounds like, it is precious in your ears. Our heartfelt singing of praise and worship is a precious sound in His ears.

God is absolutely worthy of our praise. We can praise Him for His faithfulness, His comfort, His wisdom, His peace, His provision, His power, His protection and the list goes on. "Great is the Lord and most worthy of praise; His greatness no one can fathom." (Psalm 145:3).

Each day, He gives me many reasons to praise Him. Joy and praise are closely linked together throughout the scriptures. Joy is always found and experienced in God's presence (Psalm 100:2). God inhabits the praises of His people. My encouragement to you is to hmmm on the greatness of God and thank Him, sing praise to Him for who He is and all He has done for you.

Love or Selfishness... Saturday, April 27, 2013

My first praise of the day is that I had the energy to make it through the workday. The second is that I tasted food all day today. A third is the minimal amount of nagging side effects. The stomach has been a bit more "fussy" feeling than usual, but beyond fatigue, that has been the worst side effect. The Lord continues to bless me with wonderful folks to encourage and be encouraged by. I even had one of my customers, whom I had not seen in a while to call the store just to check on me because the Lord had put me on her heart. She said she had been praying more than usual for me. Isn't that just like the Lord to prompt someone to pray especially hard for me on a week that included a trip to the emergency room?

I had a special moment with another customer, who I did not recognize as a regular. This lady's name is Tracie. I helped her with some problems at the self-checkout and she shared with me that life was especially hard for her right now. I had the chance to hug and pray over her. The hug and prayer brought tears down her cheeks. She said she knew that the Lord would never leave her nor forsake her, but life was so tough at this time that she felt like He had. She thanked me for praying for her and told me that she knew the Lord had sent me to her today. I have no idea what caused Tracie's heart such pain, but the Lord did.

We are all, daily, in need of love from others. I am very grateful for the love given to me by others and for the ability to give it as well. Hmmm... love and others.

> Love the Lord your God with all your heart and all your soul and with all your mind and with all your strength. The second is this; Love your neighbor as yourself. There is no commandment greater than these. (Mark 12:30-31)

I cannot help but think what a wonderful world this would be if we all would do just as these verses instruct. Unfortunately, all of us, at least at one point or another have allowed selfishness to get in the way of loving others. The Bible warns against selfishness and reminds us evil, wrath and anger will be the result (Romans 2:8).

Hmmm with me. With these truths in mind, search your hearts. Are you putting others before yourself, or are you putting your own wants and desires first? Seek to love others as you love yourself.

Hmmm... Sleep... Sunday, April 28, 2013

Good evening. I hope you all had a great Sunday. I went to first service at my church and then had the blessing of going to a neighboring church to listen to several testimonies of God's goodness and power. I was even blessed to give one myself. What a great morning it was. There is nothing like hanging out with my brothers and sisters in Christ.

I am still very tired today. My body aches, and my feet have regained the feeling of running across rough concrete without any shoes. I am also beginning to swell again. I took the water pill so I am sure that will mean numerous trips to the smallest room in the house tonight and less sleep. At least I do not have to be at work until later tomorrow morning, so I can sleep in a little longer. Hmmm... since I had sleep on the brain, I wondered what the Bible has to say about sleep. One of the first things I found is that the Bible reminds us that too much sleep and laziness will end you in poverty (Proverbs 6:9-11). The one who works will be granted sleep that is sweet.

> The sleep of a laborer is sweet, whether he eats little or much, but the abundance of a rich man permits him no sleep. (Ecclesiastes 5:12)

This verse also tells us that when we have an overabundance of things, they will be burdensome. The work needed to care for the things acquired, demands so much time and energy that it is easy to see that having excessive amounts of "things" was not worth the toll it takes to care for them.

We can sleep in peace because we know the Lord is watching over us and protecting us (Psalm 121:3-4). Not only is He watching over us, but His watchful eye never closes in slumber or sleep. We may need sleep, but He doesn't. That means His vigil protecting us is constant. He never takes a break to sleep, so we are never left vulnerable or without His protection. That is great news.

Work, Rest, and new head coverings... Monday, April 29, 2013

What a beautiful day! I love the smell of God's great outdoors wafting through the room. I slept longer and better last night. That went a long way toward easing the fatigue. My feet are still tender, but much better. The sores in my mouth are healing and I had a decent amount of taste when I ate today. The main frustration is that I still have a fair amount of coughing and drainage, but at least the fever is gone.

I found a great bargain today. As I walked by the Dollar Store next to my workplace, I looked in the window and saw a colorful display of scarves. I stepped in and found that they were only a $1 each. How cool is that? I also had one of my caring customers bring me a scarf and an interestingly made head cover. You pull it on like a sock cap and then tie a knot in the end that is on top of the head. I may have to play with tying the knot to get it to look just right. With today's additions, Ellie Mae may not have to share as much of her wardrobe with me. I wore one of her bandanas to work today. A few of the girls at work were having fun teasing me about it. I enjoyed the teasing. It makes work so much nicer when you can have fun with those you work with as well as the customers passing through. Hmmm... work.

God's Word tells us that we are to work. If we refuse to, then we should not eat (II Thessalonians 3:10b). We are to work as if we were working for the Lord. Whatever we do, we should be looking at it in that light because our bodies are made to be living sacrifices to the Lord.

> Whatever you do, work at it with all your heart, as working for the Lord, not for men, since you know that you will receive an inheritance from the Lord as a reward. It is the Lord Christ you are serving. (Colossians 3:23-24)

No matter how good or plentiful our works are, whether secular or religious in nature, they will never be enough to earn us a place in heaven. God's grace alone saves us and assures us a place in heaven as we put our faith in Him. Though our works are not what saves us (Ephesians 2:8-9), we are still required to work.

Our faith brings us into His salvation, and our faith requires action (James 2:17, 22). James goes even further to say that our faith is made complete by our works. Finally, God makes provision for us to rest from our work and commands us to do so. He sets one day aside for us to worship, rest, and be refreshed.

God set the example of a day of rest in the beginning when He created the heavens and the earth. He worked six days creating all of creation and then on the seventh, He rested (Genesis 2:2-3). God always gives us great examples to follow and instruction for how we should live our lives in the most effective manner. It is up to us to find out what His instruction is by reading His Word. As I write to you tonight, I see some places where I have fallen short of His ideal. I have asked for His forgiveness and set my heart and mind to strive for complete obedience. Where are you when it comes to God's instruction for your work? Are you wholly dedicated to His plan? That should always be our ultimate goal.

Sleepy… Tired… Tuesday, April 30, 2013

I had several customers encouraging me today. The way they love me warms my heart. I am always amazed by how the fact I am fighting cancer draws them out of their shells to have a conversation with me that they likely would not otherwise have. God uses those times to give me the opportunity to tell them about His goodness and grace. I am grateful.

I started swelling again today and just took a water pill to help reduce it. I did not take one last night, but realize now that I should have. That may be why my feet hurt and my ankles are stinging. The fatigue is greater than my ability to write this evening, so I am headed to bed. My head is already bobbing. I will look forward to our next time together. Sleep well, dear friends.

Battle… Authority… Wednesday, May 1, 2013

Happy beautiful day! I am always amazed at the never ending list of things that need to be done. If only my energy was the same. My energy was good for most of the workday, but the last couple of hours I began losing steam. I barely made it through the rest of the evening chores. My ankles were really swollen yesterday at work and even began to sting. I took a water pill again last night. Needless to say, I kept the trail hot, running across the hall to the smallest room in the house, all night long.

I had lots of customers and friends to love on and encourage and received the same in return from them. One, who just started chemo, came in giving me high fives of encouragement that we are going to beat the cancer. And, a couple of days ago, another came to me who just started hers. She was so glad that she was not the only lady to be losing her hair. It gave her great encouragement that she and I are going through the battle together.

This life truly is a battle, much more so than we realize. Yes, we all realize it is a battle to work, stay healthy, deal with difficult relationships and situations. But, most of us do not stop and think about the spiritual battle the world is in. This battle is for the heart and soul of mankind.

God loves mankind and wants to save each and every one. But, our enemy, Satan is out to steal and destroy every single soul that he can. It is up to each individual to make the most important decision in this battle. The spiritual battle that rages in and around us, reminds me of a verse.

> For our struggle is not against flesh and blood, but against the rulers, against the authorities, against the powers of this dark world and against the spiritual forces of evil in the heavenly realms. (Ephesians 6:12)

Our battle is not against other people as it sometimes seems, but against Satan and his band of demons. They are against us, because they are against God. Because the battle we are in is a spiritual one, we cannot fight it like we would fight an earthly war. The spiritual battle is very much in the mind. The verses in II Corinthians 10:3-5 show us that we are to "take captive every thought" making us obedient to Christ. It also tells us that we are to "demolish arguments and every pretension that sets itself up against the knowledge of Christ." He gives us authority to stand against Satan and his demons. Because Jesus has authority (Matthew 28:18), those who have accepted Him as their Savior and Lord also have authority.

That is great news for us. God even gave a great example when Jesus sent out workers into the towns ahead of Him. They returned filled with joy because the demons had to submit to them in the power of Jesus' name (Luke 10:17).

Chapter 5

Ellie Mae

Kimberly's Rottweiler

Since Ellie Mae is mentioned frequently in my writing, I wanted to share a little bit about my sweet girl with you. She is a rescued American Rottweiler, who normally weighs around 95 pounds. Like many people, she is sometimes a little less and sometimes a little more. When I brought her home, she was only six months old and had been pretty severely neglected. My sweet Ellie Mae was only 38 pounds of skin and bones. She was missing a portion of one ear and had a large scar on one side of her torso, but, oh what a lover she was. When I spent time with her at the shelter, I could not help but be crazy about her. It was love at first sight. I adopted her and made her my own.

Ellie Mae has the most loving disposition of all the dogs that I have ever owned. Never has she met another dog or human she did not offer love to. She has also been known to offer love to cats and horses. With her gentle and loving nature, a friend of mine convinced me she would be a great touch therapy dog. We went through the training and she and I became a certified touch therapy team. Our service consisted mainly of visits to a nursing home and the behavioral unit at a local hospital. Ellie Mae would always get excited when she knew we were going to make a visit. She never failed to share her happy wiggles and giant, wet kisses to those we visited. Ellie Mae loves to be petted. But, what she enjoys most is giving kisses.

She is a precious companion to me. The Lord uses her to kiss my face on the days I am down and to greet me every day with excited and happy wiggles, letting me know how thrilled she is to see me. She curls up next to me on the floor on the days I want to cuddle, and takes to the streets with me on the days I want to exercise. What a comfort and joy she is.

I often think how great it would be if people would learn to give the unconditional kind of love Ellie Mae gives. We would live in a much better world. As I think about it, unconditional love is exactly what the Lord gives to us. His *agape* love is unconditional, all day and every day. It is the exact love He is trying to teach us to allow Him to flow through us to others.

I am so grateful for the Lord's *agape* love for me and for giving me Ellie Mae as a great example. The Lord has given me a rare and precious gift in my sweet Ellie Mae. (For those of you wondering… Yes, Ellie Mae did get her name from the television show, "The Beverly Hillbillies.")

Chemotherapy II

Second Round of Chemo Treatments
12 Weekly Treatments

Chapter 6

Chemo is Working

May 2, 2013 – May 31, 2013

Submission… Authority… Chemo… Thursday, May 2, 2013

Hello! It's me again. It's been gorgeous day. The yard is now carpeted with a solid green turf. And, as I breathed deeply the aromas of the neighborhood, wonderful fragrances of fresh cut grass and barbeque filled my nostrils.

Yesterday, I made it through all eight hours of work with flying colors. Today is the National Day of Prayer, when Christians all across the nation pray for our country and its leaders. I know of no time in this nation's history when we need prayer more than we do now. God's people are the ones who can make a difference if they will commit themselves to the Lord and His instruction.

> If My people, who are called by My name, will humble themselves and pray and seek My face and turn from their wicked ways, then I will hear from heaven and will forgive their sin and will heal their land. (II Chronicles 7:14)

Today, the chemo side effects are mild. The worst things are still fatigue and a continual cough with draining sinuses. Though progress is slow, the cough no longer keeps me awake at night.

Today, I start my second set of chemotherapy treatments. These are scheduled for every Thursday for the next twelve weeks. I am glad to be through the first set and starting on the next. It means I am closer to the end. At this point, I have fewer negative feelings about this round. First, I do not have to eat ice during these treatments. I really hated that part.

Second, this round uses a drug which does not have as many side effects as the last two drugs I was given. Yea, again!

As Christians, we have the authority of Christ to defeat Satan and his demons. But, we are only able to exercise Jesus' authority when we are submitted to Him (James 4:7). If you are not first submitted to God's authority, you cannot expect the devil to flee from you. I was reminded that at the heart of every sin is rebellion. As I pondered that truth, I realized it had to be true. If we are submitted to God, then we are being obedient. When we are not standing with Christ, we are against Him. The other authority will end up being Satan. We cannot serve two opposing authorities or two masters (Matthew 6:24a).

Search your heart. Are you truly submitted to God as your authority? If you are rebelling, you cannot expect to walk in the authority Christ gives His followers, allowing you to defeat the devil and his demons. I want the victory. What about you?

Wonderful Praises! *Friday, May 3, 2013*

Good Morning! I have lots of good news and praises to share. Yesterday was the first day of the second round of chemo treatments. I started the new drug and, so far, I feel so much better than with the last two drugs I was given. I do not have to continue taking the steroid which was necessary with the previous chemo drugs. That is great. Maybe I won't be as hungry as a horse every day.

Another wonderful praise and the best for the day, is that when Dr. Gill felt the spot where the tumor was, she said that if this was my first appointment with her, she would not be concerned with anything that she felt. I knew I did not feel it anymore, but it is always great to have an expert's confirmation. Praise the Lord for answering prayer.

Yesterday's treatment did not cause me to feel nearly as bad as the previous ones, plus I did not have to endure the agony of eating ice. I know it sounds silly, but eating ice was one of the worst parts for me. Not only did it make my teeth hurt, but as the ice hit my stomach I would feel nausea. It also chilled my body to the point of shaking. Presently, I cannot even think of ice without my stomach turning. I am sure that will go away with time, but for now, "Yuk" is how I feel when I think of ice.

Father continues to bless me with encouraging folks all through my treatment days. Melinda drew my blood again. She has a genuine smile and a heart that reaches out, letting me know she really cares. The same goes for Dr. Gill. It is wonderful to have a doctor who truly cares and makes me feel comfortable and at ease. The caring treatment continued with the nurses in the unit where the chemo is administered. Jessica came to give me a hug and check to see how I was feeling. She teasingly gave Julie, my nurse for the day, a playful admonition to take good care of me.

This chemo drug is mixed with a component which can cause allergic reactions. Because of that I was given a mega dose of Benadryl before the treatment started. Before Julie was halfway through administering it, I began to feel my head getting fuzzy and my fingers becoming harder to control. My words began to slur and it took me longer to react to the things around me. By the time my body received it all, I felt like I was fighting to come out from under anesthesia. Mom knew I was struggling and told me to try to sleep. I quickly fell asleep and slept most of the way through the treatment. Since the Benadryl hit me so hard and I did not seem to have any allergic reaction, Dr. Gill told me that she would decrease the Benadryl dose for the next treatment.

I continue to keep my eyelashes and eyebrows, which is a wonderful answer to prayer. Dr. Gill advised that numbness often occurs with this particular chemo drug. I can only imagine how difficult it might be for me to handle money at work if my fingers are numb.

Often, when we come to God in prayer, we come seeking His hand. We seek His hand of provision, His hand of protection, and His helping hand. This is not to say that we do not have need of those things and more. But more importantly we need to come seeking His face first. When we seek His face we are seeking Him for who He is, not just what He can give us (II Chronicles 7:14).

> Hear my voice when I call, O Lord; be merciful to me and answer me. My heart says of you "Seek His face!" Your face, Lord will I seek. (Psalm 27:7-8)

God is not a genie from a magic lamp. He is our loving Father, who desires a deep and intimate relationship with us. He is so worthy of our praise, honor, and love with or without all that comes from His hand. Seek His face today and enjoy His presence.

Feeling Good... Prepared Place... Saturday, May 4, 2013

Hello, again. I felt really good yesterday, considering it was the first day after chemo. What a blessing. I am hoping it stays this way all through this cycle of treatments.

> Do not let your hearts be troubled. Trust in God. Trust also in Me. In My Father's house are many rooms; if it were not so, I would have told you. I am going there to prepare a place for you. And if I go and prepare a place for you, I will come back and take you to be with me that you also may be where I am. (John 14:1-3)

Shortly before Jesus was to be crucified He comforted His disciples with this promise and it is a promise for all God's children. When we accept Jesus as Lord by placing our trust in Him, we are adopted into the family of God and given a place in heaven. God is preparing a special place for each and every one of us (I Corinthians 2:9b). Isn't that exciting?

God loves you and me so much that He has prepared a place for us so fabulous that our mind cannot even conceive how great it is. Think of the best place you could ever live... the best house, the best weather, the best scenery, the best amenities of every kind... even as you picture it in your mind, know that the place God has prepared for you will cause even your best imaginations to pale in comparison to His heavenly home for you.

What a wonderful thought. Then, to top it off, there will be no more tears, death, mourning, crying, or pain ever again. When I think of what He has prepared for me, it takes the fear out of leaving this world that has so much pain and sorrow.

Though my mind cannot wrap itself around it all, He has placed within my spirit the wonderful knowledge that He has it all perfectly planned just for me and for you, too.

Hmmm... Frustration, Strength, Maturity...Sunday, May 5, 2013

Good morning, friends and loved ones. The different chemo drug has not caused me to feel nearly as lousy as the previous ones. I thank the Lord for that blessing. I have a headache and lack energy; but the energy is more than with the previous treatments.

Recently, I have found myself wishing for more spiritual maturity than I currently possess. I have been feeling a bit frustrated with myself because I have not been maturing as rapidly as I would like. The Lord gave me great comfort as I read His Scriptures and reminded me that He is the one to bring me to spiritual maturity.

It is not a work that I can do on my own and I can be confident of His promise to complete the work in me that He started (Philippians 1:6). I cannot live up to anything that I have not yet learned, but I am expected to put into practice what He has already taught me (Philippians 3:16).

God knows we cannot live the Christian life without His help. That is why He sent Holy Spirit to help us when we received Jesus as our Savior (John 14:26). Even the disciples, who spent much time with Jesus, could not do all that they were instructed to do without help.

After His death and resurrection, Jesus told them to wait, not leaving Jerusalem, until they were given Holy Spirit (Acts 1:4, 8). With the promise of Holy Spirit, came the promise of power.

Holy Spirit's power enables us to live the Christian life and to be witnesses for Jesus. We can never do it on our own. When we try, we are destined to failure. But, when we trust Holy Spirit and rely on His ability, we have victory.

Special Blessings, Love, Rejoicing, Singing...Monday, May 6, 2013

Happy, beautiful morning! When I took Ellie Mae out for her morning sniff-over the yard, the temperature had risen and the birds were singing. I was able to attend both morning and evening services at church. The love of my church family, as well as their encouragement and generosity blew me away. The ladies showered me with scarves and also a generous gift. The Lord also sent me a special volunteer to help by mowing the grass at the home my husband and I lived in. I am trying to sell it. What a burden that lifts from me.

As I think about all the special blessings and how Father continues to provide for all my needs, I cannot help but hmmm on His love for me.

"Because he loves me," says the Lord, "I will rescue him; I will protect him, for he acknowledges My name. He will call upon Me, and I will answer him; I will be with him in trouble, I will deliver and honor him." (Psalm 91:14-15)

As I sit here and hmmm that thought, my heart can't help but be warmed and filled with joy. The Lord loves me and you so much so that He will protect us and deliver us from trouble and even honor us. My heart and mind are filled with appreciation of His love for me.

My Needs... His Promise and Provision... Wednesday, May 8, 2013

Yesterday, we were given beautiful sunshine. It was so nice that Mom, Ellie Mae and I went for a walk after dinner. My only disappointment was that I did not have the energy or stamina that I had before. The hills were much harder to climb and I did not have the energy to do the whole subdivision as I did before the chemo treatments. Some days when I move too fast for too long, I have to stop for a break, or I get a little light headed and out of breath. But, even though I cannot do all that I used to do, I praise the Lord because I can still do all that I need to. Hmmm... my needs.

The Lord reminds me that there is a difference between what I want and what I need. He will always give me what I need. It is His promise. I have repeatedly seen Him give me, through others, what I need in this season. He always provides. Hmmm... the Lord's Provisions. Not only does He promise to satisfy our needs, He also reminds us that He knows what we need before we even ask Him (Matthew 6:8b).

We are instructed to pray about everything. When we trust Him, we will not be anxious or fearful about anything. In God's economy, when He speaks something, it is considered done, even though the actual fulfillment of what He has promised is not yet seen.

What do you need today? Is it a need or just a want? If it is truly a need and you are God's child, He has promised to meet it.

Safe in His Hand... Resting in His Shadow... Thursday, May 9, 2013

I am starting early today because I must be at work for the morning and then head to the hospital for today's chemo treatment. I am counting down. There are eleven more before I am finished. I am praying the Benadryl does not knock me out today like it did last week. After chemo, I plan to sit in on counseling sessions with Dr. Porter and won't be very helpful or learning anything if I am sound asleep or fighting to stay awake.

I made it through all of the things that I needed to do yesterday. I had a headache and my feet hurt beginning very early in the day. I had no relief until I was able to get off of them. The ache in my feet has plagued me for quite a few days now. "My dogs are barking" as they say. I was also fatigued which has become normal for this phase of life with cancer. It is good that I can push through much of it. There are times, however, that the Lord reminds me that it is time to rest. I love naps. They make it easier to "keep on keeping on." Hmmm... rest.

> He who dwells in the shelter of the Most High will rest in the shadow of the Almighty. I will say of the Lord, "He is my refuge and my fortress, my God in whom I trust." (Psalm 91:1)

I visualize myself in the battle of life. I see God going before me, clearing the enemy from my path. In my mind's eye, I see myself stepping directly in His footprints as I walk in His shadow. I am able to rest as the enemy and battle rage all around me because I am sheltered by the Lord. What a great comfort that is.

Good News! Chemo... Laughter and Joy...Friday, May 10, 2013

Hello, friends and family. Yesterday began with four hours at work and lots of caring customers and coworkers. Then, "Hoke" picked up "Miss Daisy," taking her and her Mom to the hospital. My cheerleaders were all with me. Words cannot fully describe how deeply I am blessed by having them there as I take the treatments.

My blood counts were in great shape. As Dr. Gill examined the tumor area, she repeated the fact that she could not feel the tumor anymore. Praise the Lord. She also informed me that the problem I am having with my feet is called neuropathy. The chemo affects my nerves, which affects my feet. I no longer have feeling in my big toes. They are numb. As Dr. Gill examined my feet, she also examined the swelling in my ankles and feet. My right one had quite a bit more swelling than the left. To be certain that it was not a blood clot, she sent me down for tests. The technician tested both legs. No blood clots in either leg.

After my visit with Dr. Gill, my cheerleaders and I headed for the treatment area. When I arrived, I had a wonderful surprise. Jessica was my nurse for the day. I also got a chance to visit with Heather and Julie, who have been my nurses for other treatments. Before we started the treatment, Dr. Porter prayed with us and Jessica and Heather joined us for the prayer time. This time, Dr. Gill cut the dose of Benadryl in half, so I was not nearly as sleepy. When Jessica first injected the Benadryl, I could feel the body reacting to it. But, in a short time, I was able to shake it off and enjoy the fun and fellowship for the rest of the time.

I learned a new term yesterday. I could not help but laugh about it. Jessica told me that I would be ready to go just as soon as she "decanulated" me. That word makes it sound quite serious. I first thought, "Wow! What does that mean they have to do to me?" Come to find out, all it means is to have the needle removed from my port. So, I get decanulated weekly now. How do you like that? Maybe you had to be there, but it tickled my funny bone. It doesn't take much. I love to laugh. It releases something in me that bubbles up from deep inside and makes me happy.

Hmmm... laughter... joy. As I think about the wonderful gift God has given us in laughter and how grateful I am that He gave us a sense of humor. Having a sense of humor and the ability to laugh are just two of the ways we are made in God's image. Not only do we laugh, but the Lord himself laughs. "The One enthroned in heaven laughs..." (Psalm 2:4a).

My favorite verse regarding laughter is in Job. Job faced an immense amount of disaster and hardship in his life. One of his friends named Bildad came to comfort him in his time of mourning, and spoke words, which were more prophetic than either of them knew at the time. God was soon to bring Job up from disaster and restore more to him than he had lost at the hands of Satan. "He (*God*) will yet fill your mouth with laughter and your lips with shouts of joy."(Job 8:21).

God fills my mouth with laughter and gives me great joy even as I walk through this turbulent time. I am grateful as I think of all that has happened and the faithfulness of the Lord through the storms. Not only has He calmed me, but He walked with me and gave me others who encouraged me. He has given me so much joy that I can laugh and be happy. His presence is the source of true joy. I have wept many tears in past months, but He has brought me joy and laughter (Luke 6:21b, Psalm 30:5b). I thank Him and praise Him for those great gifts in my life.

Freedom... Sin and Death... Eternal Life...Saturday, May 11, 2013

Good morning! I felt good yesterday. I was able to stay off my feet, so they didn't bother me at all. My hands did not tingle. The headache was minimal, and I had the energy to do all that I needed. Praise! Praise! Praise! My taste buds are still working well. I am beginning to wonder if this round of chemo treatments will affect them since I have experienced the ability to taste for many days now. Either way, I will enjoy tasting while I can. I no longer take it for granted. I was blessed to spend the day with Dr. Porter and those who came for counseling. As you know, that is one of my favorite things to do. I love to watch the Lord work setting people free from strongholds. When the Lord sets you free, you are free indeed. Hmmm... free... freedom.

> For the wages of sin is death; but the gift of God is eternal life in Christ Jesus our Lord. (Romans 6:23)

Jesus paid the penalty of death for us. His death and His blood give us freedom (Revelation 1:5b). This is the ultimate freedom. We are free from the demand of eternal death which our sin placed on us. What a gift we have been given. Have you accepted the freedom Jesus offers you?

Another Buzz Cut, Freedom, Strongholds... Sunday, May 12, 2013

Hello all! I will start by sharing with you that my Mom got another buzz cut. It is so thoughtful of her to do that for me. My Mom is the best. Her love and encouragement mean more to me than she knows. I even have tears as I think about it now. I am so glad to have her with me daily as I walk this road. I may be 44 years old, but it is still a wonderful blessing to have the love, comfort and encouragement of my Mom.

I was blessed to be able to take a short nap in the sun when I got home from work. I worked in the flower shop to help out for Mother's Day. It was more physical than I have been doing and my body felt it. I was beginning to get a bit shaky and light headed when I finished. The faster pace of moving, lifting, and bending up and down seemed to be causing the problems. The praise is that I was still able to do all I needed to get the job done.

I look forward to freedom from the side effects when all the treatments are done and the cancer is determined to be gone. Hmmm... freedom. Today I will focus on freedom from strongholds.

Some of you may have heard of "besetting sins." These sins are ones that a Christian seems compelled to continue committing. They are also known as strongholds. Satan uses strongholds to manipulate and control Christians. The good news is that Christians' spiritual weapons can demolish the strongholds, setting them free (II Corinthians 10:3-5).

Satan has no hold on Jesus and should have no control over Christians. Disobedience and unconfessed sin gives Satan and his demonic forces a place from which to manipulate until the sin is confessed and abandoned. Although confessed sins have been forgiven when a Christian accepts and receives Christ as their Savior, there is also the possibility that demonic strongholds came to the Christian from their ancestors at the moment of conception. These strongholds are known as family curses (Genesis 20:5-6).

Jesus sets us free from the penalty of our sins when we accept Him as Savior and Lord. So, in no way am I suggesting that a Christian can be demon possessed. When Christians are accepted into God's family, they are sealed by His Spirit and guaranteed their place in heaven (II Corinthians 1:21-22).

> If we confess our sins, He is faithful and just and will forgive us our sins and purify us from all unrighteousness. (I John 1:9)

It is imperative that a Christian first be submitted to God. Then he or she can resist the devil. After these two steps are taken, the Christian can then draw near to God and He will draw near to them (James 4:7-8).

Hmmm... who are you submitting to control your life? A loving Heavenly Father who desires to bless you, or evil Satan who desires to steal, kill, and destroy you? The good news is that you have the ability to choose. The choice is yours, and so are the consequences.

Good Seeds, Bad Seeds and a Harvest...Monday, May 13, 2013

Good Morning! It is tough getting out of bed some mornings to spend the time with you and God's Word, but it is always worth the effort. Even if my body is not energized, at least my soul and spirit can be.

The only side effects to bother me yesterday were fatigue and an unhappy stomach. Since starting chemo, my stomach is never completely happy. On Sunday, I spent the morning with my church family. They always provide great encouragement. Time spent in worship always gives my spiritual batteries a recharge. As I read this morning, the following verse stood out to me and I took some time to contemplate.

> Do not be deceived: God cannot be mocked. A man reaps what he sows. The one who sows to please his sinful nature, from that nature will reap destruction; the one who sows to please the Spirit (Holy Spirit) will reap eternal life. (Galatians 6:7)

Just as a farmer, reaps a crop harvest from the seed he has sown, we will reap a harvest from the seeds we sow through our decisions. All we give, all we say, all we think, and all we do will reap for us a harvest of consequences, either good or bad. Not only do we receive good or bad depending upon the choices we make, but we will receive with greater liberality when we sow liberally. On the other hand if we sow minimally, we reap minimally.

> Give and it will be given to you. A good measure, pressed down, shaken together and running over, it will be poured into your lap. For with the measure you use, it will be measured to you. (Luke 6:38)

What kind of seeds are you sowing? The only way to change the consequences is to change your actions

Confession... Mercy... Forgiveness...Tuesday, May 14, 2013

Good evening! I am grateful for the warm weather. It gave me a chance to play with Ellie Mae and her football this afternoon and to let some of the sun's rays hit my head. I would like to tan my head just a bit, so that the difference in color between my face and head blend. A little tan on the face would be good, too. Then, maybe "Miss Maybelline" and "Miss Cover Girl" won't have to work so hard.

Today was tough. Fatigue nagged at me as I tried to complete the workday. The last three hours were difficult, but God gave me strength to make it through.

Father continues to bless me with the kindnesses of others. I cannot begin to thank them enough for all the prayers, gifts, cards, hugs, encouragement, and special things done for me. Many have blessed me and lifted me, making this season of life much easier.

As I studied this morning, I was reminded of the importance of confessing sin. Confessing sin is not just an option for a Christian, it is a necessity. We must recognize the sins we have committed. If we ask, the Lord will reveal them to us (Job 13:23). No matter how hard we try, sin cannot be truly hidden from God anyway (Proverbs 28:13). If we attempt to cover our sin, we forfeit God's mercy, forgiveness, and prosperity.

Sin brings stress, heaviness, and torment when we refuse to confess (Psalm 38:4). We have all sinned, but as we confess them to the Lord, he removes the burden, forgiving and purifying us (I John 1:8-9). Search your heart. He longs to lift the burden, guilt, and shame from you because He loves you. Will you allow Him to?

Confession.... Others... Healing....Wednesday, May 15, 2013

Good Evening! It is beautiful again. I was even able to slip in a nap in the sun after I got home from work today. I felt better today. The fatigue was not as bad. I have taken Dr. Gill's recommendation to try the generic of Prilosec to see if it will relieve the unhappy stomach. The instructions on the box say that it takes one to four days for full effect, so, I will patiently wait and see if it will net the desired results. This morning, my feet started to burn like I was standing on hot asphalt. I prayed and asked the Lord to take the sensation away and He quickly answered that prayer. The pain of the neuropathy in my feet only lasted about an hour and a half today. Painful feet are no fun when you have to be on them for eight hours.

God meets our needs with Himself, but He often allows us to get in on the blessing of meeting the needs of others. As we live in community with others, there is great blessing. There is also the chance that we will hurt others with our sin. Not only is it imperative for us to confess our sins to

God, but it is also essential that we confess our sins one to another and be reconciled to each other.

In Matthew 5:23-24, it even goes so far as to tell us that before we are to present our gifts and offerings to the Lord, we are to be reconciled to those who have something against us first. There is something special about confessing our sins one to another. Not only does it help to reconcile relationships, but it brings healing to our hearts as we pray for each other (James 5:16).

Isn't that just like our God? He will bless us with healing as we are obedient, confessing our sins to each other and reaching out to help others by praying for them. Out of God's great compassion and the sacrifice Jesus made for us, when we accept Jesus as Lord and Savior, our sins will be forgiven. Not only does He remove them, but they are taken as far from us as "the east is from the west" (Psalm 103:12). Hmmm... that distance is unfathomable. What love our Lord has for us.

Naps... Revival... Joy ....Thursday, May 16, 2013

Good morning, dear friends and family! It is dark and early as I sit before the computer screen. Even though I must rise early, it is my favorite time of the day.

The revival of our desire to seek, know, and grow in the Lord was one of the things my pastor shared in Bible study last night, and it struck a chord in my heart. As Christians, there are times in our walk with the Lord when we have chosen to draw nearer to Him. At other times we drift, losing our passion and fire, as well as our desire for Him to do a deeper work in us to bring spiritual growth.

When we have stagnated in our walk with Christ, we need the Lord to revive us by leading us out of that dry and stale place, bringing us back to intimacy with Him where we have His joy, complete joy (John 15:11b).

The Lord is the only one who can bring His joy and revival to our hearts. Complacency often precedes destruction (Proverbs 1:32b) and will destroy the growth and joy our relationship with Him provides, as well as the impact for Christ our life can have on others. That is a high price to pay for spiritual laziness.

Hmmm... do you have the abundant, full, and impactful life Jesus died to give you? Search your heart. Are you truly passionate for the Lord or are you just going through the motions of the Christian life without the joy, peace, and strength Jesus gives?

Chemo, Faithfulness, Stones of Remembrance Friday, May 17, 2013

Happy Morning to you all! I am pleased that I do not have to work today. Yea! Extra rest will help knock the edge off of the fatigue. I will start our time together with an update and praises from yesterday. It is a great blessing to have my parents with me. The morning started with blood tests. All of my blood counts were good. Praise the Lord! After having blood drawn, I went to the oncology department to see Dr. Gill. While waiting, I got a chance to visit with Mary Ellen, who is in charge of the cancer resource center. What a precious lady. She helps and encourages folks as they begin their cancer journeys.

Seeing Dr. Gill is always a favorite part of my trip to the hospital. As she examined me, she confirmed again that she could feel nothing abnormal in the tumor area. Dr. Gill reduced the steroids, which tend to grind my body's plumbing (digestive tract) to a halt.

When Dr. Gill and I talked, I asked her what she thought treatment would look like after chemo. She said there were two most likely scenarios. One would be a mastectomy, but she doubted it would be that one. The other she believed to more likely, would be a lumpectomy with six and half weeks of radiation five days a week. That does not sound great either, but she said radiation was a cake walk compared to chemo. She also said that radiation treatments could be set up for a facility closer to home. With treatments being Monday through Friday, a shorter drive for treatments would be a blessing. As I hmmm these thoughts, I realize... what are six and half weeks more compared to a mastectomy?

After hugging Dr. Gill, I headed back for treatment. I found Jessica and Heather, two of my favorite nurses, there. We had a little fun taking pictures together today. Gen, my favorite volunteer, also joined us.

I only have nine more chemo treatments. But, I have a touch of sadness as I think about not seeing the folks I have come to love at St. Luke's hospital. I plan to make a scrap book of my journey in order to help remember God's faithfulness through the whole process as well as all the wonderful people. Hmmm... remembering God's faithfulness.

I remember how God told the Israelites to set up stones of remembrance so that they and the following generations would remember His faithfulness when He dried up the Red Sea as they left Egypt, and then the Jordan River, when He brought them into the Promised Land.

The whole story of the Israelites crossing over the Jordan can be found in Joshua 3-4. It is a great testimony of God's love, power, and faithfulness. God wants us to do the same type of thing to set up remembrances of His past faithfulness to us. It may just be a journal or something more physical. Take a moment to think. When have you seen God's mighty hand at work on your behalf? Have you thanked Him for it? Do you make a special effort to remember how He exercised His power and faithfulness and blessings?

He wants us to remember. He knows that as we go through rough and stormy seasons of life, we will be able to look back at those "stones of remembrance" from our own lives and draw strength and courage from them. God is telling us, "I am faithful; remember that and take heart. I will work on your behalf. I love you." I find special strength and encouragement when I look back at "stones of remembrance" in my own life. Make a list of the times when the Lord's faithfulness meant the most to you, and keep it close at hand (Psalm 77:11). The next storm in your life is likely not far off. You will find strength in your remembrance of His faithfulness.

Hair, Protection, Obedience, and Security....
Saturday, May 18, 2013

Hello! I slept in two days in a row. My work shift today is a late one, so the sleep this morning was great. Yesterday started with all ten toes being numb, but this morning only the big ones are totally numb. The numbness is from neuropathy caused by the chemo. Numbness is much easier to handle than the bottoms of my feet feeling like they are on fire. I felt really good all day. I even felt spry enough to have a rousing game of soccer with A.J., my great nephew, who just graduated from preschool yesterday. It was fun. I could tell I pooped-out a lot easier than usual, but it was still nice to feel up to playing.

Mom and Dad built a special framework that attaches to the back of my dresser. It is specially made to hold all kinds of scarves and hats, making it easier to keep them organized and unwrinkled. It is really wonderful. I think Mom masterminded it and did the sewing involved, while Dad did the carpentry. I love it! It has strips of cloth hanging from the top where I can clothespin the scarves all the way down the length of each strip of cloth. And, my baseball hats sit perfectly behind the top board.

I gained an appreciation for what all of you guys with little or no hair on top feel when you knock your head into something. Yesterday, I dropped a spoon in the floor while I was drying and putting away dishes. As I stood up from retrieving it, I skinned my head on the corner of the cabinet door. Ouch! I am beginning to understand how much protection hair gives a scalp.

Hmmm... protection, God's Word is full of protection promises. His protective eye is always watching over us (Psalm 121:8). I find great comfort in that truth. As I think about God's protection, Jesus prayed for the Father to protect His disciples (John 17:11b-12a) and those who will believe in Him.

Fatigue... Suffering... Benefits... Glory.....Sunday, May 19, 2013

Good afternoon! It seems odd to sit down at this time of day to spend time with you, but my body would not move very fast this morning. Yesterday was Saturday in the grocery store and Super Triple Coupon Week as well. That means, it was really busy and more than the average amount of headaches to deal with. But, the praises are, I made it all the way through my work shift and then to church this morning. When I got to church, I had lots more energy than when I left the house. It always seems to work that way. Being in the Lord's house and with His people always gives me a giant boost.

The most natural thing for us to think is that suffering is bad and we want to immediately stop it. That is not the view that the Bible gives us of suffering. As I hmmm, the first and most obvious thing is the suffering of Jesus Christ leading up to His crucifixion and death on the cross. It was God's will and plan for Jesus to suffer on our behalf, granting us the greatest gifts imaginable, forgiveness for sin and eternal life (John 3:16-17). Sin causes suffering in the world.

> In bringing many sons to glory, it was fitting that God, for whom and through whom everything exists, should make the author of their salvation (*Jesus*) perfect through suffering. (Hebrews 2:10)

Not only did Jesus' suffering pay the price for our sin, but He gave us an example to follow. We are to entrust ourselves to the Lord, without retaliating against those who wrong us, enduring suffering for doing what is good (1 Peter 2:20-24).

Suffering for Christ has benefits great enough to rejoice in: Perseverance, Character, Hope, Maturity, and Completeness. (Romans 5:3). Hmmm a little bit with me. Are you suffering for your faith in your everyday life? How are you handling it? With joy, honored that you are considered worthy to suffer for Him, or with grumbling and complaints? Honestly, none of us want to suffer. But, aren't the benefits worth the temporary pain?

Hmmm... Higher thoughts and ways.... Monday, May 20, 2013

Good Morning! I slept through my alarm this morning and have less time to hmmm. I think my body's unwillingness to wake up is chemo fatigue. As a matter of fact, the temptation is to shut the computer off and crawl back in bed, but I have to work today. Maybe I can sneak a nap in this afternoon.

During church time, the fatigue did not bother me at all, with the exception of climbing two flights of stairs. I know that does not seem like much, but by the time I got to the top, I was out of breath. Not only do I not have the stamina I had before, but I do not have the muscle strength either. It feels frustrating, but I continue to remind myself that these particular struggles are for a season. I must continue with patience and perseverance. God has given me an extreme amount of grace during this time. Even though I am often tired and weaker than I would like, I have been able to do what was needed. The Lord promises to supply all my needs and He has even supplied an abundance of my wants as well.

As I look back over this season of life, I see God's sovereign hand of mercy guiding me and protecting me in ways that I could not always understand at the moment. Things which appeared as if they could not possibly have any redeeming value at the time ended up bringing blessings. We must remember that the way we see and do things is not the way that God sees and does them (Isaiah 55:8-9).

Obviously, I would not have chosen all the things that have happened to me in the last ten months, but I am far enough into them that I can see how God is using them for my good. I also see how He prepared me to face the storms that came in rapid succession. As crazy as it might sound to some, especially those who do not know the Lord, I would not give back all the things the Lord worked in me during this time, for not having to endure the painful circumstances. I realize, in many ways, I am happier than I have been in a long time, despite all of the challenges I have and am still facing.

Fatigue, Anger, Resentment, Unforgiveness...
Monday Evening, May 20, 2013

Hello all. Today was difficult because of fatigue. I ended up going home from work early. I could have toughed it through, but my body told me it was wise to go home. When I got home, I took a two hour nap. It was just what I needed. I spent the rest of the day working on paperwork for the divorce attorney and was positively not a highlight to my day, but it had to be done. Satan was trying to convince me to allow bitterness, resentment, anger, and unforgiveness in my heart toward my husband. He also knew I was physically tired and dealing with thoughts of the divorce stirred up painful emotions. It would be easy to be angry and bitter toward my husband because of the pain and difficulties, but God has been good to give me the ability to resist Satan when he tries to insert these ugly things in my heart. Hmmm... Anger, Bitterness, Resentment, Unforgiveness...

God's Word tells us that bitterness, resentment and anger should be eliminated from our lives. If we are to serve the Lord, we are also to live a life of kindness and forgiveness (II Timothy 2:24).

I have been forgiven much by the Lord and must be just as willing to forgive others (Ephesians 4:31). If I give bitterness room to grow, it would not only cause me harm, but it would also negatively affect the others my life touches (Hebrews 12:15). Bitterness and anger give Satan a foothold in our lives. It is inevitable that we are going to experience the emotion of anger, but when we harbor it by allowing it to become bitterness, we step off into sin.

> In your anger do not sin: Do not let the sun go down while you are still angry, and do not give the devil a foothold. (Ephesians 4:26-27)

The warning to not allow the sun go down on our anger is a reminder for us to deal with our anger quickly by rejecting it from our hearts and minds.

Proverbs 29:11 warns us that we are fools if we lose our temper, but wise when we use self-control.

We are warned to be slow to anger (James 1:19-20), because anger thwarts our ability to live righteous lives that will be pleasing to the Lord. How many lives are affected by your decision to allow the rottenness of anger and bitterness to fester in your life? Allowing Satan a small corner of your heart and mind, will soon allow him to take more control than you want to give him. Are you harboring anger and bitterness? Is there anyone you have not forgiven?

Weak yet Strong...Wednesday, May 22, 2013

Happy early morning to you! It is a quiet time with the rest of the house is asleep, except for Ellie Mae and me. Yesterday, I made it through the whole workday. My energy began to run low and the last couple of hours were tough. My muscles are aching. They have been doing so for several days now. It feels like the ache of overuse. Dodi, a friend of mine gave me the thoughtful gift of a massage. I no longer have the physical strength I once had. That is frustrating, but, I am still able to do all that I need to do, so that is a praise. In time, strength and energy will return. Hmmm... weakness... strength.

These scriptures are a great encouragement to me any time I feel weak and am facing difficulties and painful times.

> But He said to me, "My grace is sufficient for you; My power is made perfect in weakness." Therefore I will boast all the more gladly about my weaknesses, so that Christ's power may rest on me. That is why, for Christ's sake, I delight in weaknesses, in insults, in hardships, in persecutions, in difficulties. For when I am weak then I am strong. (II Corinthians 12:9-10)

First, we have God's promise that no matter what we are facing, His grace will be sufficient for it. When He tells us His grace is sufficient, that means *always*, not sometimes, not in specific situations, but *always*. God's power is shown perfectly and completely when I am weak. My weakness is actually an asset and a delight at this point. I and the world around me can see that it is positively God's awesome power allowing me to walk through whatever challenge has come my way. Praise the Lord! "When I am weak then I am strong" in His perfect and all powerful strength. I am made strong through God's Holy Spirit (Romans 8:26b). That is enough to make me want to shout. "I can do everything through Him who gives me strength." (Philippians 4:13).

When challenges and trials come our way, His strength and grace are there to carry us through. What a great comfort these truths are. Hmmm… what is God asking you to do today? Are you trying to do it in your strength or are you allowing Him to do it through you? Trust Him today.

Wholehearted Devotion and Promises… Thursday, May 23, 2013

As I start the day, I look forward to whatever it holds. I work and then go to the hospital for chemo. Even with all the negative physical effects, the treatments, though not fun, have not been as bad as I thought they might be. I find that to be especially true this second round of treatments. The Lord reminds me it is only because I have kept my focus on Him and not the negative aspects that I can smile and enjoy this period of time. The Lord gives us many promises to hold onto in troubled seasons. Hmmm… devotion… wholehearted. He instructs us to seek Him with all that we are, to devote both our hearts and souls to Him (I Chronicles 22:19a).

When I looked up the word *devote* in Webster's dictionary, the definitions are to give all or a large part of one's time or resources and to apply habitually. Hmmm… we must habitually set our hearts and souls apart to seek the Lord in a wholehearted manner.

The Lord knows our hearts. He knows whether we are truly devoted or just giving Him lip service (I Chronicles 28:9b-10). He knows our minds, and every thought and motivation. He recently convicted me that, though I loved Him and was serving Him, I was not doing it with wholeheartedness because I had allowed an area of disobedience. Being wholehearted is more important than we realize (I Kings 8:23-24). Search your heart. What area are you holding back? What are you giving your time, thoughts, or energy to that is not pleasing to Him? I want what He has promised, don't you?

A Fun Chemo Day, What is Behind and Ahead, Fri, May 24, 2013

What a beautiful morning. Ellie Mae and I just came in from her morning sniff over of the yard. The sunshine is bright. The grass is shimmering, covered with sparkling diamonds of morning dew.

At work, one customer gave me a purse that had been her sister's, who died of breast cancer. The purse had black fringe around the top resembling hair and a button that read, *"I Am Having a NO Hair Day!"* It was a very emotional moment for my customer, who had big tears in her eyes as she shared her sister's story. It was a blessing to have enough time to hug and love on her before my next customer. Cancer affects so many lives. Until I was diagnosed with it, I did not realize just how many people are hurting and suffering. Many of my customers are or know those who are afflicted with it. My heart breaks for them as I visit with them, seeing their deep pain.

After work, I "hot footed" it to the hospital. After having my blood drawn, I had my oncologist's appointment. My blood counts were fine. The doctor jogged with me around the oncology department to check my heart and lungs, making sure they were not being too adversely affected. The jog was fun. I laughed the whole way around the office lobby as Colby, another of my fabulous nurses, teased and cheered me on. On most treatment days, Colby is the one to weigh me and to check my temperature and blood pressure. What fun she is! She keeps an eye on my weight, reminding me when I am the same or just a touch under the last visit. "One cheeseburger can change that." If I am over, she asks me if I have been eating cheeseburgers. The results of the jog determined I was fine. I thank the Lord for giving me reassurance through the doctor.

After the appointment with the oncologist, I headed back for chemo. Dad, Mom, and Dr. Porter accompanied me today. I love having them all with me; they are a great encouragement. Many of my favorite folks were on duty in the chemo area. Their smiles, hugs, sweet words and encouragement always make my day. We had lots of fun this week, taking pictures.

Dr. Porter brought a bowl with big bags of candy for those working in the unit. It was full when he brought it and they "hit it" so much that there was only a layer covering the bottom of the bowl by the time we left. The folks working that area of St. Luke's are considerate and helpful to us. As we enjoyed our time talking and laughing, another of the nurses came by and visited for a while. She said, "Your spot is always where the party is." Laughter and fun always seem to draw folks in. Really, I believe it is the joy of the Lord that is so hard to resist.

After yesterday's treatment, I am down to just eight more! Yea! I am glad to have those behind me and looking forward to knocking out the ones ahead of me. Hmmm... behind... ahead.

> Not that I have already obtained all this, or have I already been make perfect, but I press on to take hold of that for which Christ Jesus took hold of me. Brothers, I do not consider myself yet to have taken hold of it. But one thing I do: Forgetting what is behind and straining toward what is ahead, I press on toward the goal to win the prize for which God has called me heavenward in Christ Jesus. (Philippians 3:12-14)

First, none of us have already attained the perfection of being conformed to the image of Jesus. This life is a learning and growing process. When we first come to the Lord and surrender our heart and life to Him, the conforming and transforming process begins. As we allow Holy Spirit to lead and guide us, the Lord knocks off our rough sinful edges, growing in us the fruit of His Spirit (Galatians 5:22).

How do we do that? We "forget what is behind," which means we put our sinful past behind us, considering it finished and no longer a part of our life. Then we "strain toward what is ahead." What is ahead? It is heaven, eternal glory and an eternity with the Lord. What a great prize. As we push forward, allowing the transformation process in our life, we are storing up treasures for ourselves in heaven. God blesses and rewards our obedience (Matthew 6:19-20).

As Christians, our true citizenship is in heaven, where we will have a glorious body like the one that Jesus has (Philippians 3:20-21). It will no longer be subject to weakness, decay, and death because of sin. I look forward to that day, especially as I feel all the aches and pains of this earthly body.

Blessed By Friends... His Friend...Saturday, May 25, 2013

Hello, friends and family! Last night, I saw a gorgeous moon, bright and full, with a soft shimmering haze encircling it. It was perfectly nestled in the dark sky just above the horizon with a smattering of stars splashed in the expanse around it. I love Father's handiwork in nature. Nothing is more beautiful.

    Yesterday was a day off from work. I needed it to catch up on paperwork. I finished it. Praise the Lord! I had a massage which was a blessing. I had aching muscles that appreciated the attention. This morning, many of them no longer ache. A friend gave me the gift of the massage. Many friends have given me gifts in this season. I have a friend that blesses me with manicures. And, still others bless me with gift cards, scarves, hats, and many other things. What a treasure my friends have been to me in this season! I cannot thank the Lord enough for all of their encouragement, love, prayers, cards, emails and thoughtful gifts. Hmmm... friends. We all have human friends. But do you realize if you are obedient to Jesus Christ, you are His friend?

> Greater love has no one than this that he lay down his life for his friends. You are My friends, if you do what I command. (John 15:13-14)

Our side of the friendship equation with Jesus is obedience to show we love Him. On His side, Jesus laid His life down for us. When you look at the price we pay to have a friendship with Him compared to the price He paid, our side is a small sacrifice. The great love Jesus has for us is beyond comprehension and is eternal.

    Are you enjoying the intimate friendship Jesus died to give you? Do you spend time in prayer talking with Him as you would a close friend? Are you daily reading His Word to know Him better?

Sunshine, Confidence, Faith, Testimony....Sunday, May 26, 2013

Good afternoon! I was up early for church and after lunch took a walk with Ellie Mae and Mom. The sun was shining beautifully and I wanted to get a little exercise and to get a little suntan on this white head of mine. I can see the defining line between my face and scalp starting to fade. As the temperatures rise, I realize the head coverings are hot. Last night at work, I was sweating and thinking it would be nice to take the scarf off to cool down. I decided against it because seeing my bald head would make some of the customers uncomfortable.

With each passing day, I am more and more comfortable with the place in life I find myself, even without hair. God is so good to have prepared me and then continued the process of working comfort, strength, peace, boldness, and confidence in me. The fear He removed and the courage and confidence He continues to give amazes me. Otherwise, I would be unable to open my life to you, testifying boldly about His grace, faithfulness, and love.

Hmmm... testify. In Webster's dictionary, definitions of *testimony* are: witness, evidence, and profession. If we testify, we are witnesses professing and giving evidence to what we believe and know. Each Christian has a unique testimony concerning what the Lord has done for them, and who Jesus is. Jesus told His disciples Holy Spirit would testify about Him and that they must testify about Him (John 15:26-27). Fear, cowardice or timidity can hinder us from giving testimony.

Satan gives a spirit of fear or timidity, while God gives a spirit of power, love and self-discipline. Satan tries to discourage us with fear, but God gives us power and confidence (I John 4:14). We live in a world that is lost and dying without the salvation Jesus offers. If we, as Christians, don't tell them the good news, who will?

In Romans 10:14, the word *preaching* means to herald or proclaim. Hmmm... if you say you believe, are you speaking and testifying as He commands? If not, why? If you do not tell those in your sphere of influence, who will? I want to hear Him tell me, "Well done, good and faithful servant." What about you?

Fatigue... Adversity... Benefits... Monday, May 27, 2013

Hello! When the alarm went off, I did not have the energy to get up, so I slept in a little longer, then went to work. Soon after arriving, the energy quickly depleted, so I left after only working four hours and headed home for a nap. Even after the nap, I don't feel like I have much "spit and vinegar" (full of energy, having a little spunk or "get up and go" attitude). I have a headache and might be developing a sinus infection. I suspect I will have to double up on the water pill because of extra swelling in my ankles and feet. Dr. Gill told me that the job I have does not help the swelling, since I am on my feet all eight hours. The praise is, I have worked almost all of my shifts all the way through on a regular basis. I think, I have only missed four days of work since chemo started. However, on the days I have chemo treatments, I am only scheduled to work four hours because I go to the hospital straight from work.

I've done very little all afternoon besides nap. Today's fatigue is worse than it has been for a while. As I was reading my Bible today, I was reminded of something one of the ladies in my Sunday school class said to me. She said that she sometimes gets angry because of the troubles I have to go through. I have had others express that thought to me as well. It shows their love and care for me, and I am grateful. Others have wondered aloud, "Why you?" Typically, my response is, "Why not me?" Why should I be exempt from trouble? Hmmm… trouble. Jesus promised us trouble would come (John 16:33).

Trouble has come for me and in abundance in this season of life. But, He gives me the reassurance that He has overcome. Because I am His child, I am in Him. Therefore, I also can overcome. As I remain in Him, He will remain in me, and I will thrive and bear fruit (John 15:4-5). That is great news!

Adversity is the only thing that will show us experientially just how faithful the Lord is. In the good seasons of life, we do not have to rely on Him as we do in the difficult ones. Times of adversity are where we develop perseverance, character and hope (Romans 5:3-4). Those are all things I want Him to work in me. Therefore, I am able to rejoice in this season, even though it carries with it much pain and difficulty. That brings me to the verses that prompted my hmmms for today.

> Though the fig tree does not bud and there are no grapes on the vines, though the olive crop fails and the fields produce no food, though there are no sheep in the pen and no cattle in the stalls, yet I will rejoice in the Lord; I will be joyful in God my Savior. The Sovereign Lord is my strength; He makes my feet like the feet of a deer; He enables me to go on the heights. (Habakkuk 3:17-19)

Regardless of circumstances, we are to trust in the Lord. Even when God allows suffering and loss. No matter what we lose or are challenged with, as Christians, we have the eternal hope and promise that the pain of this life is fleeting. Once we reach heaven, there will be no more pain, no more tears, no more suffering (Revelation 21:4).

My pastor spoke on eternity Sunday. We are to live with the awareness that we are eternal beings headed toward eternity from the time we are born. Look at everything from God's perspective, to grow you, develop a deeper trust and faith in you, to draw you into a more intimate relationship, and to teach you. Adversity is never fun, but the benefits gained by trusting the Lord through it are phenomenal.

Ellie Mae: Patience, Waiting, and Blessing...
Tuesday, May 28, 2013

Good evening, friends and family. The first praise of the day is that I made it through all eight hours of work. Because of the continued fatigue, I had to push myself. Other side effects included a mild headache and increased numbness in my feet. Today, not only were all of my toes numb, but the areas all the way back to the balls of my feet were numb.

After arriving home, fatigue overtook me and I headed to bed. After the nap, I took Ellie Mae out for her sniff over of the yard. While we were out, she ran into the garage and got her football to let me know she wanted to play. I felt bad that she had been cooped up all evening while I took a nap and had not been able to play, so we played till she got tired. She is so patient with me when I want to take a nap or spend time studying or on the computer. She quietly waits till I am ready to take her out. Hmmm... wait.

As I think about Ellie Mae waiting on me, I realize that she calmly and patiently waits on me because she trusts me. She knows I will feed her, take her out into the yard, and provide for all her needs in due time. She is a great example of how I should wait on the Lord. Ellie Mae does not get excited and antsy while she waits; she lies on her bed and quietly rests. She has no doubt that I will take care of her. We are to be still and wait patiently for the Lord (Psalm 37:7), just as Ellie Mae does with me.

Hmmm... I wonder. Do we have the same confident assurance that He will take care of us and provide for all our needs? Do we get impatient while we wait, or wait in calm assurance and trust? He knows what is best for us and will work things out in His timing. He is never early or late. He is always right on time to give His grace and compassion.

We will be blessed because we wait for Him (Isaiah 30:18). I want His blessing. How about you? Remember, the Lord always rewards faith, trust, and obedience.

Ellie Mae's Desires, Desires of our Hearts...Wed, May 29, 2013

Hello! I want to start the update today with praise. I had more energy today. I surely do not enjoy feeling fatigued, but the Lord gives me His grace. It was, is, and always will be sufficient. I am beginning to feel better just in time for another chemo treatment tomorrow.

Pam, a good friend of mine, who I have known for over thirty years is coming to town. I want to feel good for her visit. Pam is the only friend I kept up with from high school. She and I were friends as far back as grade school. If I remember right, we even played T-ball together when we were just little bitty squirts. To be able to see her is a fantastic praise.

The Lord is always good to give me many reasons to praise Him. I encountered more caring customers today. Their and my coworkers concern for me always blesses me. The weather has been fabulous, even if it was hot. Ellie Mae is not a lover of the heat and gets hot easily. Right now, she is lying on her bed across the room from me in front of the fan. She doesn't sound spoiled at all, does she? I told you she knows that I will take good care of her. Not only do I take care of her needs, but many of the things I know she desires. A great example is the fan I put on the floor to cool her. She loves that. Hmmm... needs...desires.

The Lord knows and promises to meet His children's needs. Not only does He meet their needs, but He will also give them their desires, within the guidelines He sets forth. What are some of those guidelines? The first is that we *delight* ourselves in Him (Psalm 37:4).

A definition in Webster's dictionary for *delight* is to take great pleasure in. When we are finding our pleasure in the Lord, we will be pleased with what pleases Him. A second guideline is *righteousness*. In other words, we are to be upright, blameless and innocent. However, it is only through and in Christ Jesus that we can be righteous. It is His righteousness that covers us (Proverbs 10:24b).

A third guideline is *reverencing (fearing)* the Lord. I like Webster's definition of reverence. It is, "awe combined with respect." God is absolutely awesome, worthy and deserving our respect (Psalm 145:19).

A fourth guideline is that we must be *seeking* Him (Psalm 34:10). He satisfies our desires with good things. We won't lack for any of them when we wholeheartedly seek to please the Lord. God promises us that when we ask anything in accordance with His will, we will have it. That is great news!

> This is the confidence that we have approaching God: that if we ask anything according to His will, He hears us. And if we know that He hears us, whatever we ask, we know that we have what we asked of Him. (I John 5:14-15)

We all have desires in our hearts. Are your desires, God's desires? Do you delight yourself in Him? Are you seeking Him? In order to expect the Lord to give us the desires of our hearts, we must follow His guidelines.

Good News, Compassion, Dust, and Sympathy...Thursday, May 30, 2013

What a great day! It was fabulous from the time I got off the floor to rise for the morning. I know. You are wondering... "What was she doing on the floor?" I put my feet up on the bed, higher than my heart, in order to help the swelling in my feet and ankles go down. The swelling is causing the spider veins I already had to worsen and my legs are showing more discoloration. I have varicose veins, compliments of heredity and a job that had me on my feet for the last 27 years.

"Hoke" drove "Miss Daisy" and her Mom to the hospital again. First, I had blood drawn in order to be certain my counts were good and my organs were all still functioning properly. Praise the Lord! All were good. Today, Dr. Gill told me that I was doing better than any of her other cancer patients. She acknowledged that God has given me a lot of grace and a great support system. Those things are the things she attributes to my ability to do so well. She is absolutely right.

God's grace is sufficient. More than sufficient! She said she hasn't seen any of her other cancer patients continue to work as I do and be able to do all the other things God has allowed me to do as well. It is only through His strength and provision that I have that ability. I thank Him and praise Him for it. I believe He has given it as an answer to the prayers by all the prayer warriors, lifting me before Father's throne.

I learned another interesting tidbit today. I asked Dr. Gill about the change in my body's feminine cycles and experiencing sudden outbreaks of sweat when I was comfortable just a few seconds prior. She told me that the chemo had thrown me into menopause.

That explains the sudden hot flashes and change in cycles. She said when the chemo is finished I will most likely come back out of it. (Okay! Ladies from my Sunday school class, I got it! I understand what you all have been talking about now. I see how you can be perfectly fine one minute and then roasting the next.) I also notice, as much as I hated having a fan on when I was sleeping before the chemo treatments, I often turn the ceiling fan on over my bed. And, I flip the covers off and on several times in the night. It all makes sense now.

Today, as my chemo IV dripped, I got up and wandered through the unit, rolling my IV pole with me. I visited with some of the staff and two ladies I met at the lab area earlier. It was a divine appointment. Earlier, one admired the phone case I purchased last week. It was black leather with tooling and a lot of "bling" on it. The Lord prompted me to give it to her, so I did. Both ladies hugged me, and one got big tears in her eyes and kissed me. She thanked me and I told her to thank the Lord since it was from Him. Anything I have is only because He gave me the ability to have it, so ultimately, it is from Him. These two ladies were in the transfusion unit getting treatments at the same time as me. It was a precious time of conversation and fellowship.

Today, one of my friends bemoaned something the Lord convicted her of as He spoke to her heart, and she reiterated her desire to please Him.

> As a father has compassion on his children, so the Lord has compassion on those who fear Him; for He knows how we are formed, He remembers that we are dust. (Psalm 103:13-14)

This life is difficult. We have challenges every day. We have an enemy who is constantly trying to divert our attention away from the Lord, tempting us to sin. Our flesh is weak, filled with selfish and wayward tendencies. Even though we are on our way to maturity, we are not yet perfect. God knows why we do what we do, and why we think what we think. Despite our imperfections and tendencies toward sin, He loves us and has compassion on us. God knows obedience is difficult for us, and when we fail, He continues to love us.

We are dust, dear friends. He does not expect us to be perfect immediately. When He breathed His breath of eternal life into us as we gave our hearts and lives to Jesus, He gave us Holy Spirit and started the process of molding and making us into the wonderful image of His Son, our precious Savior. Jesus understands and sympathizes with the anguish and suffering we experience.

Inner truth…Friday, May 31, 2013

Good evening, dear friends. It is late as I sit down to the computer. I sat down some time ago but had to get up and go to the basement because of tornado warnings. We were blessed. There was no damage and all we had was rain. I accomplished quite a few things in the morning and then Pam came and took me to lunch. We decided that instead of it being two years since we had seen each other, it really had been three and a half. It was great to just sit and catch up with each other's lives.

I am exhausted and my scratchy throat increased this afternoon. So, I think I will leave you with a thought for the day and head to bed for rest.

"Surely You desire truth in the inner parts; You teach me wisdom in the inmost place." (Psalm 51:6). This verse reminds me that I am not only to always speak the truth, but I am also to acknowledge the truth within my own heart, mind and soul. We often refuse to face truth because we do not want to see nor act upon it. It seems easier to deny truth than to face it.

Look deep within. Ask the Lord to show you any lies or dishonesty within. Whatever He reveals, ask His forgiveness, then act on the truth and discard the lie. He is faithful to forgive and to give His love and peace.

Chapter 7

Fatigue is a Daily Companion

June 1, 2013 – June 30, 2013

Seize the Day...Saturday, June 1, 2013

Good morning. I have a late work shift and am starting the day tired and exhausted. Fatigue is a daily companion. The double dose of the water pill kept me up, warming the trail from the bedroom to the smallest room in the house. Even after two days of double doses, I still have quite a bit of swelling in my ankles and feet. The hot flashes are not helping me sleep either. I will go to sleep, comfortably under a few covers, only to wake up sweating and throwing the covers off. Then, the next thing I know, I am reaching back down to pull the covers back up. As I think about the hot flashes, I chuckle to myself, remembering the ladies in my Sunday school class talking about them. Well, if nothing else, I suppose I will know what to expect when menopause starts officially and permanently a few years down the road. Because of the ladies and their stories about hot flashes, I can laugh as I experience them. Praise the Lord for the humor He gives me through others.

    We often like to say that we will do this or that tomorrow or that a certain thing will happen. We can speculate about tomorrow, but we have no way of truly knowing what tomorrow will bring (Proverbs 27:1). How many times have we started a day, assuming that it will be like any other day, and then been surprised or blindsided by something?

> Why, you do not even know what will happen tomorrow. What is your life? You are a mist that appears for a little while then

vanishes. Instead you ought to say, "If it is the Lord's will, we will live and do this or that." (James 4:14-15)

Our life on earth is short and quickly vanishing, but it is in the Lord's hands. We should live each moment of this life as if it will be our last. We should tell those we love, that we love them and then show them. We are also to tell the world around us of God's great love for them and the salvation He offers through Jesus.

We may not have tomorrow and those in our sphere of influence may not have tomorrow. Hmmm… what is it that the Lord is asking you to do? Who do you need to tell or show that you love them? Is there someone in your life that you need to confess a wrong to and ask forgiveness? Do you need to make amends for a wrong you have committed against someone? The Lord gives us adequate time to do all He calls us to do. It often does not seem like it, but if we do what He asks, as soon as He asks, we will have sufficient time for each and every task.

Tomorrow may never come for you or me. Let us live today and every day with that truth in the forefront of our mind. A chorus in a song a friend shared with me says it wonderfully.

> So while there is time to live, to laugh, to love, to run, to build, to pray… Before it's too late, seize the day! So I ponder the truth I almost missed, that perhaps for such a time as this, a Sovereign God has put me where I am.
>
> (*Carpe Diem*, song by Ron Johnson and by Christian musician, Dan Smith on his Not Ashamed album, 1996.)

God placed you and me here for such a time as this. It is up to us. Will we seize the day?

Outward Appearances and the Heart…Sunday, June 2, 2013

Good afternoon. As I start our time together, I am still stretching from a long nap and my mind is still fuzzy from sleep. The fatigue has been stronger the last couple of days and a headache has accompanied it. When I sit down and get still, my body wants to check out and go to sleep.

I made it all the way through the work shift last night. Business was slower than usual for a Saturday night. Therefore, I did not have to talk as much which saved my voice. Then, I was able to get up and go to church this morning with sufficient energy.

As I think about the way that the world looks at people and their appearance, for example, a body that is too fat or skinny, a nose that is too big or small, a face that is not pretty or handsome, hair that is too gray or too sparse, eyes that are too big, lips that are too small, and the list goes on. I am glad that God does not look at me the same way the world does. God does not look at our physical appearance but our inner character and condition of our heart. "The Lord does not look at the things man looks at. Man looks at the outward appearance, but the Lord looks at the heart." (I Samuel 16:7b).

The Lord sees who we really are deep inside, not who we appear to be on the outside. We can put on makeup, fancy clothes, jewelry, and do all kinds of things to improve our outward appearance, as well as pretend that we have character qualities that we do not truly possess. However, what we do to enhance the outer appearance does not change who we are on the inside. There is nothing in our hearts that can be hidden from the Lord. Don't deceive yourself into thinking you can hide the condition of your heart from God, even if you think you have successfully hidden it from the people around you.

Hmmm… is there something in your heart you know should not be there? Are you deceiving yourself, thinking that no one will ever know? God has already seen it. The only way to be free of it is to confess it to the Lord and ask Him to remove it. He will be faithful to do it. The condition of your heart has eternal consequences.

Sovereignty, Seasons, and Trust…Monday, June 3, 2013

Hello. My throat is no longer sore, just hoarse. I have less fatigue today than the past couple of days. That is a big praise. Fatigue is the most difficult side effect.

After a short rest when I got home, my niece, Abby and I took a walk around the neighborhood. Walking with her caused me to push myself to keep up. Last year at this time, I was walking and jogging six to ten miles three to five times a week. I miss my ability to do that. It gives me great pleasure to walk in God's great outdoors. But, I must remember, this is just a season. The seasons will change and I will be able to do more again.

At my last appointment with Dr. Gill, I asked her how long it takes after chemo is finished to get back the energy I had before. She said it takes about a year. I hope and pray that it does not take quite that long.

Hmmm... seasons. As I think about seasons of life, I am reminded of the scripture in Ecclesiastes 3:1-8 that tells us that God, in His sovereignty, set forth a time for everything and every season. The times and seasons of our lives are in God's hands. "But I trust in You, O Lord; I say, You are my God. My times are in Your hands..." (Psalm 31:14-15a). His great promise and desire is to do good to us.

God is sovereign, our lives are in His hands, and He plans to prosper us, giving us a future and a hope. Are those not enough reasons to trust Him? My encouragement to you is to enjoy the pleasurable seasons of life, thanking God for them. Then, look to Him in the difficult ones and trust Him to carry you through.

Light and Direction...Tuesday, June 4, 2013

Good evening! It was another workday for me. I am still dealing with fatigue. I took a two hour nap when I got home from work. The neuropathy is still tolerable. There are short spans of time when my feet and ankles look almost normal, but more often than not, they are swollen. I am continuing to take the double doses of medicine to help. I am also being more intentional about not adding extra salt to my food and trying to put my feet and legs up when I have the opportunity.

The generic for Prilosec, Omeprazole, that Dr. Gill recommended, has kept my stomach discomfort to a minimum. I am normally reluctant to take any kind of medication, but some are a necessity. The first time Dr. Gill recommended the Prilosec, I hesitated to take it because of my normal reluctance to take medication. If I had followed her recommendation when she first gave it, I could have saved myself several days of discomfort. It is always wise to follow the direction and instruction of one who knows what is best. When we do, we are saved from the consequences. Hmmm... instruction... consequences.

As I think about consequences of our ignorance and the blessing of following instruction, I think of God's Word. It is the ultimate instruction for our lives and will save us from many awful consequences when we obey its direction. It shows us the way to live (Psalm 119:105) and gives us direction, and just like a lamp on a dark night, shows us the dangerous spots so we can avoid them. Not only will we not stumble, but we will have peace as we walk in the light of His Word (Psalm 119:163).

God tells us what sin is and how to avoid it. He knows when we sin; we will have to deal with the consequences. By hiding His Word in our hearts, making it a part of our belief system, choosing to reject sin, we will avoid the consequences of sin (Psalm 119:11).

His instruction to us is not only true for yesterday, but for today and tomorrow. They are eternal. Best of all, when we obey His Word and seek Him, we will be blessed. Seek the Lord and His instruction for your life, dear friends.

Lifted... Thursday, June 6, 2013

Good morning. I am joining you today rather than last night because I ran out of energy and could not keep my eyes open. After work, I took care of Ellie Mae and a few other things and went to church for Bible study and then sat in on a counseling session. The day was long, but I had energy to make it through. And as you know, my time with my church family always puts wind in my sails and lifts me.

Hmmm... lifts. As I think about the way the Lord uses others to lift me, I think of how He used the loving words of my Dad to lift me when I was feeling low just a couple of days ago and how he sent a sweet customer to give me a vase with a single pink rose and baby's breath yesterday. Not only does the Lord use my church family, blood family, friends, and customers to lift me, but He gives you and me the ultimate lift. First, He lifts us from the muck and filth of our sin and places our feet firmly in Him that we might stand secure in our salvation (Psalm 40:2).

The Lord knows the mess we get ourselves into with sin. He alone can lift us from it. He is faithful to every promise He gives. As we acknowledge Him, bowing before Him with a humble heart, He will lift us (Psalm 145:13-14). If we do not come from a place of humility, the Lord will not give us the lift He desires, and that we desperately need. We often want to be lifted from painful situations before the Lord has completed the work He desires to do in us. We must wait upon Him, trusting and knowing that in His perfect timing, He will lift us up.

> Humble yourselves, therefore, under God's mighty hand, that He may lift you up in due time. Cast all your anxiety on Him because He cares for you. (I Peter 5:6-7)

When we are humble before the Lord, not arrogant and prideful and trust Him to take care of us, He will lift us up in His perfect timing. We can rest in that fact, dear friends. His promises are always true. Do you need the Lord's lift in your life? Are you humble before Him? Look into your heart. Be honest with yourself and God. Trust Him and humble yourself. He will lift you up.

Swollen feet, Chemo, Disappointment, Trust...Friday, June 7, 2013

Hello friends and family. As we start our time together, I am thinking back over things I have shared with you. How we should trust the Lord... How His timing is perfect... How we must wait upon Him... How we say that we will do this or that in a day and really don't know what the day will hold. Well, my day did not go as I had planned yesterday.

As you know, my chemo treatments are scheduled on Thursdays. As usual, the first stop is always the lab where blood is drawn to check the blood counts and organ function. Then I have an appointment with Dr. Gill and finally, chemo. Well, yesterday things did not go as planned. When I had my appointment time with Dr. Gill, I found out that my white blood cell count was too low for chemo. I needed a 1.2 count and I had a 1.1. Dr. Gill's concern was that if I had chemo yesterday, I could end up with a bad infection and a three or four day stay in the hospital. Needless to say I do not want that. However, I would be a liar if I said that I was not disappointed. She assured me that having to wait to give chemo is a normal occurrence and they expect it to happen. The way she described it is, I (my immune system) am like a boxer getting hit with hard punches (chemo), getting knocked to the mat. Each time I get knocked down it gets harder for me (the body) to get back up. This time the body was slower getting back up. When I asked, she said the antibiotics I just finished for the sinus infection could have had an impact as well. I also asked if the lower count could have had an impact on the more severe fatigue I experienced. She said that was possible, too. I want to finish the treatments as soon as possible and get to the other side of this season of life. Hmmm... disappointment.

As you know, swelling in my feet and ankles has been an ongoing problem for me with the chemo treatments. Miss Linnie, Dr. Porter's wife, and others had mentioned the support stockings that are worn for varicose veins and used after surgery to help with circulation. I asked Dr. Gill about them and she agreed that they could definitely be of help. She wrote a prescription for me. Since I did not have chemo yesterday, I had extra time to go to the medical supply store to try to get some. They measured me but, they did not have my size in stock, so it should be seven to ten days for the order to come in.

Dr. Gill also had me to triple the amount of the water pill I am taking. I also have to increase the potassium supplement they are giving by four times. Praise the Lord! The ankles look much better this morning. It is my prayer that the increased dosage and support stockings will be all that is needed to provide adequate circulation to my feet and ankles. The ongoing difficulty with the swelling in my feet and ankles has also prompted me to put a foam wedge at the bottom of my bed while I am sleeping at night, raising my feet higher than my heart. It is disappointing to have to continue to fight the swelling. Hmmm… disappointing.

The Lord knows all that is in my heart and mind and knows what I think and feel before I ever think or feel it. He knew how disappointed I would feel when I found out that I would not be able to take chemo today. Thinking about it, I can see why He had me share with you that He would lift us up in His timing and not ours. He knew I would need to focus on that truth as I felt today's disappointment.

The Lord gives us His hope in our difficult times. His hope will not disappoint us because it is given to us through His Holy Spirit (Romans 5:5). Holy Spirit reminds me of His promises and truth when I am feeling down and disappointed. As I prayed, Holy Spirit gave peace to my heart and reassured me that He had it all under control and firmly in His hands. If we do not keep that truth firmly in focus, the devil will derail us from the Lord's plan for our lives. When we hit times of disappointment, it is important for us to cry out to God, placing our trust in Him (Psalm 22:3).

God's plan for our lives is perfect. When we follow Him and trust Him, we will not be disappointed. I cannot trust my own understanding of my situations. I must acknowledge the Lord and allow Him to direct my life.

> Trust in the Lord with all your heart and lean not on your own understanding; in all your ways acknowledge Him and He will make your paths straight. (Proverbs 3:5-6)

The Lord will direct the path of my life for my good, if I trust Him, agreeing His way is always best, even when it does not look like it to my human eyes.

Hmmm... what disappointments are you facing today? Have you looked to the Lord to help you see His perspective? Where is your focus, on your feelings or the Lord and His eternal purpose to use the difficult situation to grow you? Disappointment is not easy. I faced a great number of disappointments in the last several months that would have been devastating if it had not been for the Lord's sustaining hand. He is faithful, dear friends. He will not disappoint you if you will trust Him.

Complaints or Gratitude...Saturday, June 8, 2013

Hello, dear friends. As I contemplated the feelings of disappointment from Thursday I see how Satan tried to tempt me to complain because things had not gone as I wanted. Hmmm... complain. Whatever our circumstances, God calls us to live without complaining.

> Do everything without complaining or arguing, so that you may become blameless and pure children of God without fault in a crooked and depraved generation in which you shine like stars in the universe... (Philippians 2:14-15)

As Christians, we are called to a higher standard than the world adheres to. God calls us to a life of gratitude, not of grumbling. We are to do all we do with thanksgiving to the Lord (Colossians 3:17).

No matter what we do or say, it should always have the following questions in mind. Is this what Jesus would do? Is this what Jesus would say? Jesus is the model we are to pattern our lives after. Jesus is not a complainer. He accepted all that came His way, trusting God, the Father to take care of Him. He even went to the cross, suffering insults, ridicule, beatings, scourging, and finally the crucifixion never uttering a complaint.

Look at your life. Do you find complaints or gratitude? It is easy to complain when things are not as you would like them to be. Life is not always fair, and when those around us, especially those we love, hurt us or disrespect us, we immediately want to complain. Living your life with Jesus as your model causes you to stand out as different from the world. He lived His life blamelessly and pure. That is to be our standard. Only with Holy Spirit's help can we follow Jesus' example. When you find complaints and ingratitude in your heart and life, ask the Lord to remove them and give you a heart of gratitude.

Rain... Difficulties... Grace... Faith... Sunday, June 9, 2013

Happy afternoon! I am on the deck, listening to gentle rain softly tapping, soft and soothing. I enjoy the sound of the pitter patter of raindrops on a roof. I like the smell of rain, too, and can often tell it is coming just by the smell in the air. Hmmm... rain... He sends the rain.

As a Christian, it is often hard to understand why the Lord would allow bad things to happen to those who we consider to be good people. It is also an excuse that non-Christians use to justify their disbelief in God or their belief that the Lord is not a good God. It is also difficult to understand why God allows evil people to seemingly prosper in this world. I will not begin to try to fully explain why God allows the things He does, but I will share with you some of my experience and what I know to be true.

I have learned to trust that the Lord has a purpose for what He allows in my life. I do not always see the reasons why, but know He has them. Even though He has allowed me more suffering in the last several months than I thought possible for me to withstand, He is completely faithful, giving me His comfort and His strength to face it. He continually uses these challenging days, to draw me closer to Him and teach me how to trust Him more wholeheartedly. He has drawn me deeper into His Word and truth and repeatedly given me the opportunity to share His goodness and faithfulness with others. I would not trade all He has done in me for the ability to not to walk the road He has allowed me to travel these last eleven months. Bankruptcy, divorce, losing my home and cancer are horrible things to face, but the pain they brought is nothing compared to the joy of the intimacy I have experienced with the Lord.

When God allows seasons of pain, tragedy, or heartache, He is faithful to give us the grace to walk through them. No matter what we face, His grace is sufficient and will carry us through if we will trust Him. His power is infinitely stronger than our own. Our strength will never take us through life's challenges with victory. Because we trust Jesus as Savior, we can boldly approach God in our time of need with confidence and assurance that He will give us the grace we need for every situation of life. (Read more in Romans 5:1-2; Hebrews 4:16.)

Even though we may not understand why we face the difficulties we do, we can rest assured that the Lord will provide all we need to face trials and troubles and use them for our good. Just as children do not always understand why parents do the things they do, we, as God's children, do not always understand why God allows the things that He does. As children must trust their parents to have their best at heart, so must we trust our Heavenly Father.

Are you in a difficult and painful time of life? Seek the Lord and His grace. Ask, trust and believe Him for it. His grace for our salvation comes through faith, belief and trust. His grace for difficult times comes the same way.

Difficulties... Grateful Hearts... Joy... Tuesday, June 11, 2013

Good morning, friends and family. The morning was a struggle with fatigue but I began to feel a little better as the day progressed. I still had swelling, tenderness, and stinging. If that is the worst of it, it is nothing. I learned one of the keys to facing the difficulties of life is having a grateful heart and thanking the Lord for the many blessings He has given me. When my eyes are focused on Him and my blessings and not on my struggles, I have more joy, peace and strength to face each and every day. Hmmm... grateful... thankful.

Satan is always looking for ways to convince us to have a "pity party" over circumstances in our lives. But, as we refuse the devil's lies and focus our hearts and minds on the Lord and His goodness and thank Him, no matter our present circumstance, God's joy and peace will be in us. The Lord does not want us to ignore the difficulties we have in life, but to talk with Him about them. "Cast all your anxiety on Him because He cares for you." (I Peter 5:7).

God loves us. He is the only one who can handle all our struggles, giving us peace and joy in the midst of them. As usual, my hmmms bring questions to mind. Are your words and actions consistent with the teachings of Jesus? Where is your heart and mind focused? Is it on your difficult circumstances or on the Lord and His blessings? In difficult times, at the very least, you can thank Him for the good He promises to work in you as a result of the difficulty (Colossians 3:17). Trust Him, dear friends and family. Thank Him for His sacrifice for you. Thank Him for the peace, love and joy He has made available to you through His Holy Spirit.

Guarding the Heart...Wednesday, June 12, 2013

Hello. I have great news to start the day. I checked on the condition of my ankles and feet. My ankles were my own again and not those of a baby elephant. Praise the Lord! He answered prayers for me. Even after eight hours of work, they were not as swollen as they have been in days past. It gets better yet. After a short rest after work, I took a walk and was able to walk the whole subdivision twice...hills and all! This was more than I could do last week and it felt great.

The workday was a good one. I had more energy than I have had in quite a while. As each day passes, I see the Lord's hand strategically placing different people in my day. So many touch my heart with their kind words and concern. The Lord put a great love in my heart for people. I think it is why I enjoy my job. My contact with people brings great joy to my heart. Hmmm... my heart.

> Above all else, guard your heart, for it is the wellspring of life. Put away perversity from your mouth; keep corrupt talk from your lips. Let your eyes look straight ahead, fix your gaze directly before you. Make level paths for your feet and take only ways that are firm. Do not swerve to the right or to the left; keep your foot from evil. (Proverbs 4:23-27)

The main point is to remind us how important it is for us to guard our hearts from evil. We must guard what we say, where we focus our eyes, where we go, and what we do. Each word we say, thought we think, action we take, and decision we make will not only chart the course for our life but either defile or build up our hearts.

We are to store up good things in our hearts. They are the "wellspring of life." Our emotional, spiritual, physical, and psychological well-being and health are dependent on the heart and what is contained there.

Search your heart. What do you find there? What words flow from your mouth? Are they words of life? Do you build others and yourself up or tear them down? Guard your hearts, dear friends. Ask the Lord for His help.

Chemo... Courage... His Command....Thursday, June 13, 2013

Hey there! I will start with praise today. The swelling in my feet has, again, come down over night. My feet hurt the last couple hours of work. The left one is especially painful. I have yet to receive the compression socks and eagerly await their arrival.

The next praise is, after working this morning, I am on vacation. My brother and his family are coming in from Denver to spend some time with us. I am really looking forward to it. I do not get to see them very often.

Today is another chemo day. My blood counts should be good today, especially since they were so close last week. I suppose my body needed a break. It was good to have the break, even though I would rather not miss a treatment. There are many things in life I cannot control and could cause me to worry, but God reminds me to take heart and be courageous. I need not worry. Hmmm... courageous. God instructs us to "be strong and courageous."

> Have I not commanded you? Be strong and courageous. Do not be terrified; do not be discouraged, for the Lord your God will be with you wherever you go. (Joshua 1:9)

His Holy Spirit gives us the ability to be strong and courageous when we have no strength or courage of our own. We never have a need to be afraid nor discouraged. We may feel those things from time to time; we must reject them. If we act in fear or from discouragement, we are not trusting the Lord but listening to the lies of the devil. Hebrews 3:6b reminds us that we are a part of the Lord's household and family and to hold on to the courage and the hope He has given us.

Our hope is in Jesus, His shed blood, His death on the cross, and His resurrection. We have no other hope for forgiveness from sin and eternal life than Him. Our hope and faith in Jesus give us the wonderful ability to be courageous, standing firm in the storms of life.

A Beautiful Blanket, Kindness, Benefits....Friday, June 14, 2013

What a glorious day. I feel fabulous for a first day after chemo. I had a two and a half hour nap after coming home from the hospital and a long night of rest. Praise the Lord for the wonderful rest.

I did not hear my final blood counts, but know they were good. Dr. Gill keeps a close eye on them. As I think of Dr. Gill and her care for me, I want to share with you the incredible thing she did yesterday. As she came into the examining room, she was carrying what looked like a beautiful, fuzzy pillow, covered in butterflies. It was for me! But, it wasn't a pillow. It was a blanket that unfolded out of the inside of the pillow pocket. One side of it was a soft blue color she picked to remind me of heaven, the butterflies were to remind me of new life, and the other side is covered with puppy dogs, for Ellie Mae. How blessed I am to have a wonderful doctor with so much love in her heart.

Dad, Mom, my niece Abby, and my great-nephew A.J. all accompanied me yesterday. It was a blessing to have them all there. Abby and I had a great time taking pictures and playing around with her hair covering my head. I was able to see many of my new friends, too. They always greet me with smiles, encouraging words, hugs and good-natured teasing. I am very grateful the Lord sent me to St. Luke's for my treatment. The folks there are considerate, sensitive and kind. Hmmm... kind.

As I think about the kindness of the staff, I cannot help but think of the Lord's kindness to me (Psalm 100:5). God does so many good, loving and kind things, showing His faithfulness and generosity. Just as the Lord expresses kindness out of His love for us, we are to express kindness to others out of the love God places in our hearts. Kindness is part of the fruit of Holy Spirit (Isaiah 54:8b). When we allow Him to control and fill our lives, His fruit will flow freely through us (I Timothy 2:14a).

It is easy to be kind to those who are kind to us, but as others hurt us, we must remember all we have been given in Jesus. He was kind and forgave us as we sinned against Him (Ephesians 4:32). As we show kindness to others, the Lord will bring benefits. "A kind man benefits himself, but a cruel man brings trouble on himself." (Proverbs 11:17). To whom can you show God's kindness? Are you allowing His kindness to flow through you to everyone?

Attentiveness or Drifting... Saturday, June 15, 2013

It is nice to be on vacation and have the ability to slow down. It feels strange not to set the alarm as I go to bed. Strange, but wonderful! First of all, yesterday, I had almost no pain in my ankles. Secondly, I had enough energy and stamina to walk the subdivision twice with Abby. My favorite praise of the day is that my brother, Mark and his family will be here today. I can hardly wait. This will be the first time I see my great-niece. She was born last December. As I was writing, Mark called saying they will soon be here. So, I will leave you with a thought for the day.

"We must pay more careful attention, therefore, to what we have heard, so that we do not drift away." (Hebrews 2:1). Hmmm… I am reminded of the importance of paying close attention to God's Word, keeping it in the forefront of our hearts and minds. If we do not pay careful attention to all we know of God's Word, putting it into practice, the things of this world will draw us away from the Lord. Just as a boat in the ocean with its engine off, and no captain or navigational system constantly directing its way will drift off course, so will a Christian who does not constantly pay attention to God's Word. When we allow ourselves to drift, Satan draws us further, putting wedges and hurdles between us and the Lord, hindering our relationship with Him.

Are you drifting? If so, ask the Lord to help you get back on course. Spend time in prayer asking for His forgiveness. Then diligently get back into His Word focusing on His direction for your life. If you are not drifting, thank the Lord for His direction, and stay the course.

Heavenly Father... His Child...Sunday, June 16, 2013

Hello and Happy Father's Day! May we not only celebrate our earthly fathers, but most importantly, our Heavenly Father. As I think about Father's Day and how grateful I am to have the earthly father I have been blessed with, I cannot help but also think of my Heavenly Father and how grateful I am to be His child. When I gave my heart and life to Jesus, I became a child of God. He placed His Holy Spirit in me, sealing me as His own for all eternity. He adopted me and all who trust Jesus as Savior.

> Because those who are led by the Spirit of God are sons of God. For you did not receive a spirit that makes you a slave again to

fear, but you received the Spirit of Sonship. And by Him, we cry, "Abba, Father." The Spirit himself testifies with our spirit that we are God's children. (Romans 8:14-16)

Christians have been given special honor. They are adopted as God's children. Children of the King! A very special part of that honor is that we are not only able to call Him Father in reverence as King, but we are also given the ability to have an intimate relationship with Him as a little child would with their "Daddy." Thank your Heavenly Father for His love and all the ways He provides for you. Thank Him for adopting you as His child. If you do not know Him as your Heavenly Father, take time to seek Him, trusting Jesus to be your Savior. There is no decision more important.

Vacation, Weariness and Refreshment....Monday, June 17, 2013

Good evening! I started the day at the courthouse and when I returned home, my brother, Mark and I went shopping for some things I needed for my computer and spent time just hanging out. It was a really great to simply enjoy some time together. After picking up fried chicken for a house full of family for dinner, we returned home to lots of family fun.

The last couple of days, I have been dizzy and lightheaded. During worship service, if I had not sat down while singing, I think I would have fainted. At first, I thought it might have been dehydration, so I guzzled more water and a bottle of Gatorade. I got really fuzzy another time, too. Then, I thought it might have been low blood sugar since I had not eaten. I am just not sure. It was much worse than anything I have experienced to date. The good news is, even though I am still experiencing times I feel as if I might faint, today was much better. Hmmm... faint. "I will refresh the weary and satisfy the faint." (Jeremiah 31:25).

Just as God promised to refresh the Israelites, satisfying them as He brought them out of captivity, so the Lord desires to refresh and satisfy His children. In this difficult season, the Lord refreshes me when I am so weary I do not feel like I can go on. I thank Him and praise Him for it. I trust the Lord moment by moment to give me the refreshment and strength I need. He is worthy of your trust, dear friends and family. He will provide all that you need as you need it. He has done it for me time and time again.

Time Flies ...Thursday, June 20, 2013

This week it seems like the days are flying by. I am thoroughly enjoying my family and our time together. It saddens me to see the end of the week and their time to return to Denver coming closer.
Today is a chemo day. Hmmm... time. As I think about time and how it seems to fly by, I am reminded that our time on earth also quickly passes. We are here for a season and then gone.

> As for man, his days are like grass, he flourishes like a flower of the field; the wind blows over it and it is gone, and its place remembers it no more. (Psalm 103:15-16)

I think about flowers of spring; daffodils, tulips, and crocuses. They come up beautifully, we enjoy their bright pop of color, and they are quickly gone, making way for the next flowers. Our life is the same.

We are here for a short time, then the next generation comes and we leave the earth. I am soon to be gone. What am I doing of eternal value? I have only a short time. Tomorrow is promised to no one. What are you doing of eternal value? You will soon leave this earth as all before you.

We have only a short time to make a difference in this world and in the lives of those around us. What is the Lord prompting you to do today? Step out and do it. Time is short. We live in a society that bombards us with distractions. We must focus our eyes and hearts on the Lord. When we allow ourselves to be distracted and slow to respond, we miss opportunities the Lord gives us to make an eternal difference. Because of the brevity of our lives, we only have a limited number of opportunities. What are you doing with the time the Lord has given you?

Great Chemo Day and a Favorite Psalm...Friday, June 21, 2013

Today is the last day of vacation for me. I return to work tomorrow. Time with my family has been great. I started the morning yesterday with a walk with my niece, Alecia, and her six month old daughter, Kacie. I enjoy one on one time with my nieces. We have so many folks in the house that one on one time is not easy. I will have some one on one time with another of my nieces, Anne. She requested to have a quiet time with me this morning. What a loving request.

Yesterday was chemo day. As always, it was lots of fun. Mark, Loren, Anne and Dr. Porter all accompanied me. Mark and Dr. Porter worked on setting up his computer and the girls and I chatted and took pictures. Photo shoots with the staff created lots of fun. I added pictures of the staff in the lab where they draw my blood and some with the staff that take me back to see Dr. Gill. Then, I took a few of my cheerleading team that were with me today.

I had Jessica for my nurse today. What a precious young woman. We were able to pray with her just after I started chemo. And then we were able to pray with Heather, another of my caring nurses, when she shared some good news with us. We even had a short time to spend with Gen, my favorite volunteer, before she finished her shift for the day. The love God has put in my heart for the staff here at St. Luke's is wonderful.

My appointment with Dr. Gill went well. She looked at my blood counts and said they were good. She also checked my feet and ankles which looked great, too. We talked of the dizziness and she suspected that it was caused by too much medication from the water pill. She cut the dose to see how I do.

After chemo, we all went out to have Chinese food and enjoy more fellowship. God always takes chemo days and makes them wonderful with lots of love, encouragement and fun. I can only thank and praise Him.

I will share with you some verses from a favorite Psalm the Lord gave to me about a year and a half ago. I have returned to it time and time again, allowing the Lord to encourage me. Pray before you read, asking Holy Spirit to teach you. It is Holy Spirit's great joy to teach Christians to get quiet before the Lord, opening their hearts to hear as He speaks to them.

> I will extol the Lord at all times; his praise will always be on my lips. My soul will boast in the Lord; let the afflicted hear and rejoice. Glorify the Lord with me; let us exalt his name together. I sought the Lord, and he answered me; he delivered me from all my fears. Those who look to him are radiant; their faces are never covered with shame. This poor man called, and the Lord heard him; he saved him out of all his troubles. The angel of the Lord encamps around those who fear him, and he delivers them. Taste and see that the Lord is good; blessed is the man who takes refuge in him. Fear the Lord, you his saints, for those who fear him lack nothing. (Psalm 34:1-9)

Unconditional Love... His Pleasure... Saturday, June 22, 2013

Hello, friends and family. I am still tired from the busy week and chemo. Even though I was on vacation, the week was a full one. My family started back home yesterday. I miss them already.

I think Ellie Mae is tired, too. She has hardly raised her head since I first got up this morning. She loved having all the extra people around. It does not matter who you are, Ellie Mae always wants to kiss you, slathering you with her affections. She gives unconditional love to all, even those who do not necessarily want to receive it. Unconditional love... hmmm. As I think of Ellie Mae's unconditional love, my mind thinks of God's unconditional love for us.

Many people think that they have to clean themselves up and be good enough for God to love them. That is not true. God loves us at our worst, just as much as He loves us at our best. He saw us at our worst "while we were still sinners," and poured out His love for us by sending Jesus, His one and only precious Son, to die for us (Romans 5:8). I often wonder why God would love me that much. Why did He choose me or you to pour out His love on in such a sacrificial way?

> For He chose us in Him before the creation of the world to be holy and blameless in His sight. In love He predestined us to be adopted as his sons through Jesus Christ, in accordance with His pleasure and will... (Ephesians 1:4-5)

He chose to love us and to offer us salvation and adoption into His family for "His pleasure." Did you ever stop to realize that you were created for God's pleasure? I often wonder, "Why me?" The simple answer is that He loves me, just as He loves you. Spend time with Him, sitting quietly before Him, listening to Him speak to your heart.

Willing spirit, Weak body... Sunday, June 23, 2013

It is a beautiful Sunday! Ellie Mae and I are out on the deck enjoying the fresh air and warm temperatures. I just came home from church and am contemplating a nap. I feel more fatigue today. Working late last night, combined with helping with counseling, and getting up early this morning, has taken a toll on my body. As I think about the fatigue and my desire to do the things as I did before starting chemotherapy, a verse comes to mind.

"Watch and pray so that you will not fall into temptation. The spirit is willing but the body is weak." (Mark 14:38). Even though we desire to do the right things, when temptations come, our flesh is weak and does not always have the strength to withstand the temptations of the enemy. Despite the fact that Christians are given a new spiritual nature when they receive Jesus as their Savior, they still walk in the fleshly body given at birth, which wants to do things that will cater to their selfish nature. The new spiritual nature the Christian is given is a godly nature. The new nature and fleshly nature war against each other.

It is a conscious decision to put off and reject the old self and its sinful desires and to put on and embrace the new self and a righteous and holy life. It is not an easy task, but with reliance on Holy Spirit, the Christian can accomplish it. The verses in Ephesians 4:22-24 tell us the battle between the two natures is fought and won in the mind.

> Do not conform any longer to the pattern of this world, but be transformed by the renewing of your mind. Then you will be able to test and approve what God's will is... His good pleasing and perfect will. (Romans 12:2)

Just as keeping my mind focused on the Lord, His love, provision and promises for me strengthens me in spirit, giving me the ability to press on when the fatigue from the chemo is weakening me. We will be able to bring our weak body into submission to know and do God's will because we are transformed by the renewing of our minds.

Hmmm... are we renewing our minds by meditating, praying and worshiping, so that we will be able to stand firm in times of testing and temptation? Dear friends, after receiving Jesus as Savior, there is no more essential exercise than the renewing of your mind. As your mind is renewed, you will be able to stand against the temptations and schemes of the enemy. It is not a one-time occurrence. We are to remain diligent each and every day.

Ellie Mae's Fear... God's Peace... Monday, June 24, 2013

Good evening. I am still tired even after a three hour nap. I was supposed to work eight hours today, but went home after only four hours. The fatigue was strong today.

After awakening from the nap, I moved slowly around the house until I decided that exercise might help me wake up. I walked the neighborhood twice again tonight. After returning home from the walk, I took a shower and returned to my bedroom to find a scared Rottweiler. The neighbors were shooting fireworks, scaring Ellie Mae. Hmmm... fear... scared.

As I think of Ellie Mae and her fear of fireworks, I am reminded of how often we react in fear of things that will likely never happen. It is highly unlikely that Ellie Mae will ever be hurt by fireworks because I try to protect her from harm. It is also unlikely that many of the things we give mental and emotional energy to feeling fear will ever happen. Why do we waste our time being afraid? Satan works hard to instill fearful thoughts in our minds. He is skilled at putting "what if's" into our minds. How many times have you thought "what if" this or that happens, long enough to have yourself in full blown worry? Fear and worry cannot coexist with peace and trust. They are complete opposites. As Christians, we have authority over Satan. Jesus has given us His authority. Because we have Jesus' authority over Satan and his demons, we can exercise it and be safe from the harm the devil desires to bring us (Luke 10:19). We must not forget to exercise that authority.

God's Word is full of promises of provision, protection, hope, love and many more good things. Focus on the Lord's promises to you, reject the lies of the enemy, and step out in faith, trusting God. He is always faithful. Satan has been trying to feed lies to me the last few days. But, the Lord reminded me to trust Him and His peace would guard my heart and mind against the enemy (Philippians 4:7). Trust the Lord, dear friends. He will do for you what He has done for me.

Painful Feet... Judgment ... Tuesday, June 25, 2013

I made it through my whole work shift today, but fatigue is still with me. Yesterday's nap went a long way to help with renewing some of my energy. I took a nap this afternoon before taking a walk around the neighborhood. I hope the regular walking will increase my energy.

The swelling in my feet and ankles is still minimal. I have been wearing the compression stockings to work this week. They are helping with the swelling, but I am not sure if it is neuropathy causing all of the pain in the bottom of my feet and toes or if the compression is somehow causing pain. Today, the pain was considerable. All I wanted to do was get off my feet. For anyone watching me at work, I am sure I was a comical sight. I would regularly stand on one foot like a stork and shake the opposing foot like a cat who had just stepped into a puddle, in order to momentarily relieve pain in the raised foot. Then, I would lift the other and repeat the process. It would help for a second or two on the foot that was raised, but as soon as the foot hit the floor, the pain returned. I am grateful that foot pain and fatigue are the only two side effects experienced today. It could be so much worse.

Today as I read in John 8 the story of the woman adulterer whom the Pharisees wanted to stone, I was reminded of how often people judge each other, even when they have sin in their own hearts. Jesus did not condemn the woman for her sin (John 8:7). We may think we know what is in someone's heart, but only God truly knows each person's heart.

> Do not judge: or you too will be judged. For in the same way you judge others, you will be judged, and with the measure you use, it will be measured to you. (Matthew 7:1-2)

These verses show us the connection between our judgment and condemnation of others and the judgment and condemnation we will receive when we choose to judge another. The Lord is the ultimate judge. We will all stand before God's judgment seat to be judged (James 4:12).

Hmmm… who are you judging? We can see the actions of others, but we cannot see their heart as God can, so our judgment will be based on external appearance. I heard a pastor say something which has been of help for me in refraining from judging others. He said, "Hurting people, hurt people." In that light, my heart holds more compassion for those who are acting in hurtful and ugly ways.

Bringing me OUT… To Bring me IN!…
Wednesday, June 26, 2013

Hey there! I have had naps after work for the last three days. I needed them because the fatigue is strong. The naps perked me up enough to walk all three days so that is positively a praise. The rain this evening even cooled the temperature enough to take Ellie Mae with me. She only goes with me when the temperatures are cooler because she is a fair weather walker. If the temperatures are too hot, taking her with me is like dragging a bowling ball. She mopes behind, panting, and trying to stop under each shade tree.

I have to confess to you that the last week has been a struggle for me. I am "tired of being tired," and it has left me feeling a bit frustrated with the seeming slowness of this perplexing time in my life. As I hmmm it all, the Lord reminded me of a Bible study concept that really hit home and the Lord brought it to my mind to encourage me.

> But He *brought us out from there to bring us in* and give us the land that He promised on oath to our forefathers. (Deuteronomy 6:23)

The story tells of the Israelites' liberation from bondage in Egypt, their wanderings in the wilderness, and how the Lord brought them into the Promised Land. The Lord reminded me, just as He brought the Israelites out of Egypt to bring them into their promised land, He was also in the process of bringing me out of this difficult season to bring me into the promises He has for me. God always has a purpose for what He allows in our life.

When the Lord "brings us out" of something, it is never just for the sake of "bringing us out." It is always to "bring us in" to the next place where He plans to continue to do an even greater work in us than He did in the last. There is a purpose for where we are, a purpose for bringing us out, and then, for bringing us in.

Look back over your life. What has the Lord brought you out of? For what purpose and plan did He bring you out? If He brought you out, He wants to bring you in. Don't waste forty years wandering the wilderness as the Israelites did before they were ready to be brought in. Be prepared and willing for whatever He wants to bring you into today. He loves you too much not to bring you into the best, if you will allow Him.

Cancer Treatments, Waiting and Trusting, Thursday... June 27, 2013

I started the day at work and then went to the hospital. I now have only four more chemo treatments. The tentative schedule for time and treatments after chemo is finished will be, a rest of two to three weeks, surgery, two to three weeks of healing time, then radiation five days a week for six and a half weeks. I trust the Lord and know His timing is perfect. Hmmm... I must wait upon Him.

Today, it was just Dad, Mom and me at the hospital. I took candy for the folks in the oncology and transfusion areas and also for the ladies who draw my blood, Melinda and Charity. Today, Charity's sweet words blessed me. She told me that I always came along just when she needed a lift and the week was starting to get her down, and that I always helped put her week back on track. I am grateful that the Lord would allow me to lift her. The smiles, laughs, sweet words and lifted spirits of those partaking of the sweet treats always makes my day. What fun! No wonder the Lord tells us, "It is more blessed to give than to receive." (Acts 20:35).

As I contemplate the tiredness and fatigue of the week, I am reminded of something Jessica said as we were talking. She looked at my blood counts and mentioned the reason I might have felt so good last week while my family was here and so tired this week is because my white blood cell count was much higher last week than this week. She told me I had a great count last week because of the prayers the Lord answered for me to have a great week with my family. God is so good. Praise His Holy Name!

Any treatment I miss adds one more week to the treatment time. I desire to finish chemo in the next consecutive four weeks. Waiting is not easy. I am sure someone besides me needs a bit of encouragement to wait upon the Lord for relief from something difficult in their life.

> I am still confident of this: I will see the goodness of the Lord in the land of the living. Wait for the Lord; be strong and take heart and wait for the Lord. (Psalm 27:13-14)

As we wait for the Lord, we are to be confident that He has heard our prayers and petitions of our hearts. He is a good God and does good things. *Wait* can be translated as eagerly wait, expect, hopefully wait and to look. So, as we wait on the Lord, we are to wait in eager expectation. The word *strong* can be translated as courage, encouraged, or hold fast. As we wait for the Lord in eager expectation, we are to stand in His courage, knowing that He is working on our behalf. The phrase *take heart* also carries the connotation of courage, being determined, and being strong. As we wait, we are not to be moaning and complaining about our plight, but confident the Lord is working and that in His perfect timing, we will see His goodness.

Peach Fuzz.... Health, Joy, and Peace.... Friday, June 28, 2013

Hey there. I have a praise and prayer request I would like to share with you. The praise is, my head is showing signs of "peach fuzz." The color is quite a surprise. It is not the "blonde as I paid to be" I hoped for, nor the "dirty dishwater blonde" that I was naturally. It is really dark! I am not sure exactly what color it is because it is still short and thin. But, it is a color I have never had before. Many prayed I would not lose my eyebrows or eyelashes, and I haven't. My request is that my eyelashes and brows would not thin any further than they currently have and that some new would start to grow. I cannot help but think how odd it is that some parts of my body never lost hair, some lost all, and some only thinned.

"Pleasant words are a honeycomb, sweet to the soul and healing to the bones" in Proverbs 16:24 points to the importance of true, wise, good and uplifting things being spoken. Our words are vitally important to our health and to the health of those to whom we speak. "Do not be wise in your own eyes; fear the Lord and shun evil. This will bring health to your body and nourishment to your bones." (Proverbs 3:7-8).

God's Word tells us that the condition of our heart is important. "A cheerful heart is good medicine, but a crushed spirit dries up the bones." (Proverbs 17:22). The word *cheerful* can also be translated as joyful. We must constantly and intentionally place ourselves in Him through obedience, prayer and meditation on His Word. Knowing God's love gives great joy as well as confident peace. "A heart at peace gives life to the body…" (Proverbs 14:30a).

The focus of our hearts and minds is of utmost importance to our health and well-being. When we make the Lord, His Word, and His will and His way our focus, we can never go wrong. It is even more important to our well-being than eating well and exercising.

His Eyes… Sunday, June 30, 2013

Hello and Happy Sunday. As you know, Sunday is my favorite day of the week. I always love going to my Father's house, worshiping, and spending time in fellowship with my church family. I spent the rest of the afternoon resting and napping. One encouraging email I read reminded me of several important truths. Here is what it said: "His eye is ever on you to bless you and guide you into His perfect will." Hmmm... God's eyes. His eyes are always on His children. As a matter of fact, He sees everyone and everything (Hebrews 4:13). He sees our hearts, minds and emotions. Nothing is hidden. He looks for those whose hearts are fully committed to Him to strengthen them. His desire is always to strengthen, support, and bless His children.

> For the eyes of the Lord range throughout the earth to strengthen those whose hearts are fully committed to him. (II Chronicles 16:9a)

God not only watches us with a desire to bless us, but wants us to see His perspective so He can guide us into His perfect will. For us to see as He sees, we must think as He thinks. To do so, we are given His mind in Holy Spirit to follow for instruction and leading (I Corinthians 2:16).

For us to be guided into the Lord's perfect will for our lives, we must look with His perspective. He knows what lies ahead, behind, to the side, and around each turn. Our fleshly and sinful natures lead us into death while Holy Spirit leads to life. When we allow Holy Spirit to lead, we show we are truly God's children (Romans 8:13-14).

Whose eyes and mind are you using, yours or the Lord's? Are you allowing Holy Spirit to lead or are you doing what your flesh desires? A quote you may have heard before says, "Sin always takes you farther than you want to go, keeps you longer than you want to stay, and costs you more than you want to pay." As your eyes open to each new day, ask the Lord to lead you with His.

Chapter 8

Countdown to Finish Chemo

July 1, 2013 – August 2, 2013

Eternally Secure and Surrounded…Monday, July 1, 2013

Hey there! Today was a long day. Quitting time could not come soon enough. The fatigue was stiff. I also had more numbness in my feet and fingers than I have experienced before. The praise is, I made it all the way through work. Last night the pain was back in my ankles. Previously, I thought it was from the swelling. I speculate it is caused by neuropathy, as is the numbness in my fingers and feet.

I am ready for sleep, so my hmmm time will be short. I want to share a couple of verses that are special to me from the Psalms.

> Those who trust in the Lord are like Mount Zion, which cannot be shaken but endures forever. As the mountains surround Jerusalem, so the Lord surrounds his people both now and forevermore. (Psalm 125:1-2)

Because I trust in the Lord, I am completely secure for an eternity. Nothing can shake me from His eternal salvation. Nothing, ever! I can live life with peace and confidence, knowing that whatever difficulties come my way, I am secure. He not only goes before me, but comes behind me. I am completely surrounded by His protection and love.

In the stormy seasons of life, these are wonderfully encouraging and uplifting truths. They have been especially comforting for me as I have walked through the storms of the last year. The Lord is faithful. No matter how tired I am this evening, these truths make my heart sing and leap for joy.

There is no other...Tuesday, July 2, 2013

Good evening! I spent most of the day with my parents running errands. The fatigue was still very strong, today. I took a two hour nap when we arrived home. After I got up from my nap, I did a few things around the house and played with Ellie Mae to give her a little exercise. Now I sit, sharing my favorite part of the day.

Today, I spent time in the book of Isaiah. Chapter 45:5-22 is where my hmmm begins. God continually reminds us that He is the only true God. People may set up idols or choose to worship other gods, but they are all false. There is no true God except the Lord.

Looking at the world today, I see why the Lord would find it necessary to repeat this truth. People set up many different things as idols in their lives, giving them a higher priority than the Lord. Idols can be almost anything: money, sports, fashion, another person, a job, a hobby, etc. Look at the other religions of the world. All through history, people have created their own gods. Whether it be Allah, Buddha or any other in the multitudes of gods people have chosen to create and worship, they are all false. The Lord is the only true God. In today's world, the belief is prevalent that there are many ways to God and to heaven. The Bible makes it clear that there is only one God and one way to heaven. Do not be deceived. Jesus is the only way to God and heaven.

> Jesus answered, "I am the way and the truth and the life. No one comes to the Father except through me." (John 14:6)

Hmmm... are you placing something or someone higher than God? Is anything else of greater importance to you than the Lord? Have you believed the lie that there is more than one way to heaven? Have you chosen the one true God? He desires life for you and not death. "Now choose life, so that you and your children may live." (Deuteronomy 30:19).

God has given us the truth of who He is and what it takes to have a relationship with Him, gaining life in abundance here on earth, eternal life, and heaven. Have you chosen the one true God or a false god, who has no ability to save and bless you eternally?

Well, I must head for the bed. Morning will come early. I work tomorrow and then go to the hospital for chemo. It is scheduled a day earlier this week because of the 4th of July holiday. I am a little concerned that my blood counts may not be all that I would desire them to be because I have been experiencing so much fatigue. I pray that the counts are good and that I will be able to have the treatment as scheduled.

Be Still... Cease Striving... Wednesday, July 3, 2013

Hello, dear friends. I got an email from one of my nieces, Anne, in Denver with a picture attached. She had some of her hair dyed pink for me. How loving! The swelling in my feet and ankles is in good shape, and the headache has been minimal. The numbness in my feet and hands is no worse today. Hot flashes mainly hit at night. I still have the dark peach fuzz on top of my head. I am still able to go to work. And, most wonderfully, I have the love, prayers and support of many.

I started the day with work, and then I went to the hospital. I had the usual first stop at the lab to have my blood drawn. Melinda and Charity were there waiting on me, with hugs and words of encouragement. Next, I went to the oncology department with some sweet treats to share. It is amazing how a little sugar will bring a smile. I had my appointment with Dr. Gill and found that my white count was too low to take chemo today. She said she could give me a lower dose of chemo today, but thought I might be stronger if we just waited until next week to take treatment. So that is what we will do. I should begin to feel better and have more energy, which will be welcomed, because I have been challenged with strong fatigue these past couple of weeks.

I garnered my usual teasing from Colby and Katrina and Dr. Gill evaded my camera again. She did tell me that she would eventually let me get a picture. I will positively hold her to it. Before I left, Jessica came to see me and get a hug since I would not be getting chemo today. Her smile and beautiful countenance always lift me.

Since arriving home, I have been resting. It is nice to relax and be still for a while. Hmmm... "Be still" (Psalm 46:10a). The words *be still* can also be translated as cease striving. The Lord tells us to stop struggling and striving in our own strength and "know that He is God." When we know that He is God, we are aware of His attributes and trust Him because we know who and what He is.

He is Jehovah, the Lord God Almighty, and He has many attributes, but just to give you a few. He is omnipotent, omnipresent, all knowing, perfect love, holy, righteous, without error, creator, sustainer, provider, protector, all wise, teacher, Savior, comforter, healer, and truth. When we know this is who and what He is, and fully put our trust in Him, we will cease our strivings because we know He is working on our behalf. As we stop our struggling, we are to wait patiently for Him to fight for us. As our Father, it is His joy to fight for us. "Be still before the Lord and wait patiently for him; do not fret." (Psalm 37:7a).

These words are a comfort to me this evening. Missing another chemo treatment means that the treatment time is extended another week. I would like to be done with all the treatments already and back to what I consider normal living. Hmmm... but, do I really want normal living? Normal living in this world often means relying on yourself and what you can do, and trying to make things happen in your timing, not God's. No, I suppose "normal" is not what I really want. I want to be still knowing that He is God, trusting and waiting while He fights for me. The Lord is always the winner.

Are you struggling with something the Lord told you to be still and wait about? Do you trust Him, knowing who He is? His Word tells us that we are to have faith in Him. Without faith it is impossible to please Him. I want to please Him, so I must be still, knowing He is God.

A photo shoot and freedom...Thursday, July 4, 2013

Happy 4th of July! Even as I write to you, I hear the neighbors continuing to shoot off fireworks. The last few hours have been solid with crackling, popping, and booming. Ellie Mae has not been fond of it at all. She tried to crawl up in the bed with me twice. As of now, she is sound asleep in her own bed, tired from a busy day. She and I started the day early. We met Valerie, one of the ladies I go to church with, to have some pictures taken. Valerie is a photographer and graciously volunteered to take some photos of Ellie Mae and me to help chronicle this season of life. Valerie takes great pictures and I am excited to see how they all turned out.

After Ellie Mae and I had our "photo shoot," I came back home just in time to go to lunch with my parents. Today is my Mom's birthday, and she wanted to go to Taco Bell. After lunch, my energy was depleted, so I took a nap. Ellie Mae was worn out from posing for the camera so she took a nap, too.

As I think about the 4th of July holiday, and the freedom I am blessed to have by living here in the United States, I remember the freedom I have been given as a citizen of the United States was not free. There were many who fought and died for me to have the freedom I have today. Then, I think of the spiritual freedom I have been given, the freedom from the ultimate consequence of my sin, which is eternal death. That freedom was not free either. Jesus paid for it with His life. Once we give ourselves to Jesus as Savior, Lord and Master, gaining spiritual freedom, we must realize the freedom we are given in Christ Jesus is to be used to serve one another in love (Galatians 5:13).

We are not to use our freedom as a license to sin and cover evil in our lives (I Peter 2:16-17). We may be free from the eternal consequence of spiritual death, but we are to be changed from what we were and renewed to live in the freedom we are given, loving and serving one another and the Lord.

Fireworks & Ellie Mae...Fear & Trust...Saturday, July 6, 2013

Hey there! It is me again. Yesterday was a workday for me. I was definitely ready to go home at quitting time. The fatigue is the worst side effect for me to deal with. I do have a fairly new side effect I have not shared before. My fingernails and toenails are sore. They feel like I have been scraping with them. I asked Dr. Gill about it and she said it was caused by chemo. She also told me, the fact that my big toenails looked somewhat like I had dropped something heavy on them was also a side effect. They have purplish and red streaks underneath them. Even though the feeling of the nails is annoying, the praise is, I am getting accustomed to it. I think a lot of the side effects are that way.

The weather is great this morning, so Ellie Mae and I are out on the deck. Somebody just shot off some loud fireworks which startled Ellie Mae. She came over and tried to climb up in the glider with me. Ellie Mae finds security in being close to me. I told her it was okay and to lie down, which she did. She trusts me and knows that I will protect her.

Hmmm... that is just what Holy Spirit does for Christians. Holy Spirit is our indwelling comforter and protector. "The One who is in you is greater than the one who is in the world." (I John 4:4b). Holy Spirit resides inside a Christian, while Satan is in the world. The Lord's power is always infinitely greater than Satan's. As Christians, we have the Lord's power residing within us because His Spirit resides in us.

Hmmm... Ellie Mae trusts my ability to protect her when she is feeling fear, just as Christians should trust Holy Spirit to protect them when they feel fear. Protection is God's promise for His children. "But the Lord is faithful, and he will strengthen and protect you from the evil one." (II Thessalonians 3:3). One of the ugliest tools Satan uses against God's children is fear. He craftily does his best to place it in the minds of Christians to convince them that God is not faithful to protect and provide for them. Keys in our relationship with the Lord are faith and trust. By encouraging us to act in fear and not in faith, Satan tries to drive a wedge in the relationship Christians have with God. When we cower in fear we won't step out in faith, doing what the Lord instructs.

When Satan tries to implant fear into our hearts and minds, we must reject fear, choosing to place our faith in the Lord and His Word. Even though we feel fear, we must not act on it nor focus our minds on it. Just as Ellie Mae would let fear control her if she did not place her trust in me for protection. If she focused her mind on the fear of the fireworks and not on me, she would be panting, pacing, and shaking and not quietly resting in peace. Where we place our focus is of utmost importance to our ability to walk in faith and trust, not fear.

If we allow Holy Spirit to control our hearts and minds, we will have peace (Romans 8:5-6). When you walk in faith, you will have peace no matter the chaos around you. Search your heart, as I will mine. What do you find there? Perfect peace and trust in the Lord, or fear, uneasiness, anxiety, and frustration? Is your heart troubled or at peace? Jesus died to give us His perfect peace (John 14:27).

Hmmm... time spent on God's faithfulness in contrast to fear is always beneficial for me. Satan controlled many years of my life with fear. Now, I want to be certain to always reject it, never giving it a foothold in my life again. As you might imagine, I would be a mess right now if I focused my mind on all the things Satan tries to implant fear in me about rather than on the Lord's promises. God has been faithful to me and I never want to let my eyes be drawn from the truth of His complete love and devotion to me.

Blameless... Blessing... Sunday, July 7, 2013

Hello, dear friends and family. I like to slip in extra rest on Sunday afternoons after coming home from church. Unfortunately, today did not allow that. I had lots of jobs that kept me from it. I will be short this evening because I work early in the morning. But, before going to bed I want to share a verse with you.

> For the Lord God is a sun and a shield; the Lord bestows favor and honor; no good thing does He withhold from those whose walk is blameless. (Psalm 84:11)

The Lord provides all the light, truth and direction we need for each and every moment of life. He is also our protector. He shields us from harm and the attacks of the evil one. If it were not for God's protection, we would be dead already, because Satan is out to destroy and kill all of humankind, especially God's children. We have no better protection than what the Lord gives. There is no power greater than the Lord's.

God's promises are for "those whose walk is blameless." The word *blameless* used to bother me a lot, because I thought it meant that I had to be perfect and sinless, which I knew was impossible. Then, I learned that living blamelessly really meant to live without willful or intentional sin. If we are doing our best to be obedient to the Lord, we will be living without willful sin in our lives. In doing so, we will fulfill the condition for the Lord to withhold no good thing from us. Obedience is always the key to receiving the Lord's best.

God's favor in our lives is a welcome gift, as is the honor He places on us. Could you receive any greater glory or honor than that which is given you by the King of kings and the Lord of lords? How many times has God given you favor? Money you didn't earn, but was just given to you? A promotion that you were not the most qualified for? A discount that you did not know was available? When have you seen God's favor? Always seek to obey the Lord. I want His best. I am sure you do, too.

Weariness, Strength, and Rest... Monday, July 8, 2013

Happy evening. The temperatures are quite warm today. I made it all the way through my work shift. It is no fun to feel weary as often as I do. I have to push myself much harder now to keep up some semblance of normality in my lifestyle. I know this is just for a season. For that, I am grateful. The weariness I feel is much different from anything I have experienced before. As I was discussing it with one of my customers today, I told her I would rather have the tired feeling that I experienced after spending all day in the hot hay field, sweating, picking up and stacking square bales of hay on the trailers and then in the barn, than the physical weariness that comes from chemotherapy. Hmmm... weariness.

We often grow weary in the hustle and bustle of everyday life expending energy on things that have no eternal value or even life sustaining purpose. We can find ourselves carried away with hobbies, perfectionism, obsessions, maintenance of a lifestyle above our means, pursuits of desires, etc. As we weary ourselves on these things, we are left with little or no strength or time for the things of the Lord. God prepared things for us to do in our lives and we must be careful to balance our lives appropriately in order to have the energy and strength to do them. The Lord even goes on to remind us not to weary of doing the good things He has for us. "Let us not become weary in doing good for at the proper time, we will reap a harvest if we do not give up." (Galatians 6:9). This is a promise. We will gain a harvest from the good things we are doing if we do not give up or quit. That is good news. Knowing there is a payday coming makes it easier to press on. But, how do we press on and keep from getting weary?

When we keep our eyes on Jesus, remembering the price He paid that we might be free from the consequences of our sin, asking and trusting Him for His strength, we are able to persevere and press onward (Hebrews 12:2-3). When we are weary and come to Him, not only does He promise to give us rest (Matthew 11:28), but He also promises to give us strength and increase our power.

What great promises! We can easily grow weary while doing good things when we are working in our own strength. But as we focus our eyes on the Lord, doing the things He has prepared for us, in His strength and not our own, we will cease from struggling and be at rest even as we labor. That is truly good news.

The Lord has been so good to give me His strength when I have felt weak in this season. Even though I may not have my normal physical strength, the Lord has given me His strength to stand spiritually and to continue to do the work He has prepared for me. I can only thank Him and praise Him.

Never Weary... Never Sleeps... Tuesday, July 9, 2013

Hello, dear friends. It is another hot July day. Ellie Mae and I limited our time outdoors today. I had hoped to have the time and energy to walk the neighborhood. But, today was not the day. When I went outside with Ellie Mae, the heat confirmed the fact that I was not yet up for a walk. Instead, I took an hour and a half nap. I did have plenty of energy to make it through the workday. The nap refreshed me. The day proceeded without headaches, minimal foot discomfort, ankles that were feeling fine, and swelling was still under control in my feet and ankles. Praise, praise, praise!

As you all know, I had asked for prayer in regard to keeping my eyelashes and eyebrows. The Lord graciously allowed me to keep them these last four months and I am so very grateful. But, they are now slowly falling out. My right eyelid has very few lash hairs remaining. The left eye has a few more than the right, but they are also diminished. The eyebrows are still there, but have developed bald patches and are thinning, too.

I am also getting a little better with new makeup techniques. I have been experimenting with eyeliner, eye shadow, eyebrow pencils, and false lashes. I found a few things that make my face look a little less… hmmm. What is the word I am looking for? A little less odd, I guess is how I would express it. The lack of eyebrows and lashes radically changes the look of one's face. But, makeup can enhance the appearance once they are gone. I am thanking the Lord for "Cover Girl" and "Miss Maybelline." Using eyeliner makes my face look much different than normal for me, but, much better than with no eyeliner.

I am grateful that the lack of hair on my body is only for a season. As I expressed yesterday, the weariness I am experiencing is only for a season as well. Hmmm… a little more on weariness.

> Do you not know? Have you not heard? The Lord is the everlasting God, the Creator of the ends of the earth. He will not grow tired or weary, and His understanding no one can fathom. (Isaiah 40:28)

Among other things, this verse reminds us that even though we may grow tired or weary, God never does. His strength is inexhaustible. As we rely on His strength to work in and through us, there will never be a time that it is tapped out or unavailable. Not only is His strength inexhaustible, but it is anywhere and everywhere we would need it, even to "the ends of the earth." His strength is everlasting because He is everlasting. There will never be a day or time when it is unavailable to one of His children. Not only does the Lord never grow tired or weary, He never sleeps (Psalm 121:3-4).

The Lord is constantly watching over His children. There is never a moment they are not in His loving, watching, and protecting sight. What a comfort that is. He never sleeps, so it is continual. As a child, when we knew our father, mother or another adult loved one was watching over us, we had the courage and confidence to try things that we would never have tried without knowing we were under their protective and watchful eye. God gives us that same gift. He is always with us, watching, encouraging, and strengthening.

When we have Jesus, we have all we need. "And my God will meet all your needs according to His glorious riches in Christ Jesus." (Philippians 4:19). What a great promise! I have positively found this truth to be a great comfort, especially in this particular time in my life. Jesus has truly been all that I need. I thank Him and praise Him. He is so very good to me.

Looking for Wisdom ... Thursday, July 11, 2013

Good morning. Yesterday was busy from the time I got up at 4 a.m. until the time my head hit the pillow last night about 10:30 p.m. As you know, the morning started with eight hours of work, and then I spent time counseling with Dr. Porter. A common need for the folks we counseled was wisdom.

> If any of you lacks wisdom, he should ask God, who gives generously to all without finding fault, and it will be given to him. But when he asks, he must believe and not doubt, because he who doubts is like a wave of the sea, blown and tossed by the wind. That man should not think he will receive anything from the Lord; he is a double-minded man, unstable in all he does. (James 1:5-8)

God promises to give us wisdom, but we must do our part. We must ask in faith. If we do not ask with faith, we are walking in disbelief of the Lord and His promises, which is most assuredly not in obedience to Him. Remember, with obedience comes blessing, and disobedience brings consequences.

Chemo, Thirst, and Living Water... Friday, July 12, 2013

Happy morning to you! I had a great night of rest with only one trip to the smallest room in the house. Praise the Lord for that. The need for rest has been much greater lately, so my heart rejoices, especially in those nights that I sleep all the way or most of the way through.

Yesterday was a really good day. I started it with work and then chemo. I had my usual stop at the lab for blood to be drawn. It is always a joy to be greeted with hugs and caring words from the nurses there. When I went to get my chemo treatment, I received the same welcome from the folks there. Gina was my nurse today and when I arrived, she had a special gift for me. It was a cushion that slides onto the seatbelt that helps keep the seatbelt from irritating the port used for administering the chemo. My port is located on the front of my left shoulder, right where the seatbelt goes across my body. Gina remembered that I mentioned the discomfort of the seatbelt and got the cushion for me. That was incredibly thoughtful.

The nurses double checked my blood counts. When my blood counts came back, they were still very low. It was a borderline decision whether or not to give me the treatment. I have taken it before when my counts were this low. They left it up to me to decide whether or not to take it. Since I felt much better the last few days, I decided to take it. Now, there are only three more chemo treatments to go. My prayer request for today would be for my blood counts to come back up for the next treatment. With each knock down my body takes from chemo, it is harder for it to get back up. Through prayer, God has given me an abundance of grace, blessing me with the ability to continue working and doing many other things even when the fatigue has been strong and the blood counts low.

Dad, Mom and Dr. Porter all accompanied me today. I love having them all there with me. It is a great comfort and encouragement. My Dad is so thoughtful. He gets up to take me to work at 6 a.m. and then he and Mom pick me up from work and drive straight to the hospital.

As I settled in my chair for chemo, I met Ray, the gentleman in the chair next to mine, who was accompanied by his wife. Ray was taking his first chemo treatment for lung cancer. What a card Ray was! He was lots of fun and his wife, Becky was a delight. Ray, Becky and my group visited and teased each other the whole treatment time.

Would you believe that Denise and Shirley (the lady I gave my cell phone holster to a few weeks ago) were on the other side of me taking their treatments, too? I had a wonderful time visiting with them. I even had the opportunity to pray with Shirley before the two left. We exchanged phone numbers and they both wanted to know when I am having surgery so that they can come and visit me. How delightful those two ladies are.

I added a few more photos to my collection for the future scrapbook. Gina, Ray and Becky as well as Shirley and Denise were all featured in some of my snapshots. Gen and my cheerleaders also got in on the pictures. As usual, our chemo party was lots of fun. I am grateful to the Lord for bringing such joy to my chemo treatment time. I do not dread going to take the treatments. The only downside is the way they make me feel afterwards. But, they are doing what they are intended to do by killing the cancer. Feeling lousy for a little while is a small price to pay.

As I write to you, I cannot seem to keep away from my water bottle. The time after chemo always dehydrates me, making me thirsty. Any of you who see me on a regular basis know I always carry a water bottle. The doctor told me it was important for me to stay hydrated especially right after chemo. The water rehydrates my body and flushes the chemo through my system.

Hmmm... thirst... water. Of course, you know, those two words kick-started me to hmmm. Our bodies physically thirst, becoming parched and dehydrated without water, just as our souls are dry and dehydrated without the Lord. Our inner longings for satisfaction and filling can only be quenched by Jesus. "I spread out my hands to you; my soul thirsts for you like a parched land." (Psalm 143:6).

Our souls thirst. It is important for us to realize that only the Lord can quench our inner thirst. He fills us full to overflowing with His joy, peace, love, wisdom and more. When we give our lives to the Lord, accepting the free gift of His salvation by asking for forgiveness for our sins, turning away from those sins, and believing in Jesus, placing our faith and trust in His sacrifice on the cross for us, we receive Holy Spirit, who fills us with "living water." With His Spirit flowing through us, we will never run dry as recorded in John 7:35-39.

When we try to live our lives without Jesus, we are spiritually dehydrated. Jesus and He alone is the only source who can satisfy our thirsty and weary souls.

Attributes of His Love... Saturday, July 13, 2013

Good Morning. I am writing to you even before I crawl out of bed this morning. It feels nice to stay beneath the covers and start my day with you. I am feeling just a bit lazy. Ellie Mae has not even stretched yet, so she is contented to rest in her bed a little longer too. I am working 9 a.m. to 5 p.m. so I have the ability not to have to jump and run so quickly this morning.

I spent yesterday at church sitting in on counseling sessions with Dr. Porter. I always enjoy seeing the Lord work to encourage and set people free. I was even able to spend a bit of time hanging out with a couple of young fellows while their Dad was busy. That was fun, too.

Do you all remember me sharing with you about Ellie Mae and my "photo shoot" on the fourth of July? Well, I was able to see Valerie, the photographer, today. She brought me a couple of prints and a disk with the best of the shots that were taken. I have been excited to see how they all turned out. I could not be more pleased. They are great! Valerie had great ideas for the photos and picked the perfect location. There are so many good ones that I am not sure which ones I want to print.

There is one verse I want to share with you. It was in a devotional I read. "But you are a forgiving God, gracious and compassionate, slow to anger and abounding in love." (Nehemiah 9:17b). This is encouraging to me, because I have often blown it and had to go to the Lord for His forgiveness. He understands our weaknesses and is gracious and compassionate as He draws us back to Himself. When we would have lost our patience and grown angry with another because of the way we were treated, God remains patient. His great love for us is what causes Him to respond to us with forgiveness, grace, compassion, and patience.

Hmmm… He loves us. We are called to love others with His love. As Christians, are we sharing and giving the love of the Lord by forgiving others when they have wronged us? Do we give them grace? Are we compassionate, treating them with understanding? Or, do we respond in anger or impatience? Jesus set the example for us to follow.

Considering Him and Present Sufferings…
Monday, July 15, 2013

Good Morning. It is early as I join you. I love starting my day with you, even when the time will be short. I have to work from 7 a.m. to 3 p.m. today. As I get closer and closer to the end of the chemo treatments, the need for rest is getting much greater. The fatigue is getting tougher to deal with. It is why I took yesterday to almost exclusively rest, with the exception of time spent at church with my church family in worship and Bible study. When I came home, I napped almost all afternoon. I am very tired. I know the increased fatigue is an indication that my blood counts are low. And, I know that if they stay too low, the chemo treatments cannot be taken on schedule. This knowledge gives me the opportunity to exercise the patience the Lord continues to teach me. It is not easy to be patient. I want to be finished with the chemo part of my treatments. Praise the Lord that I am down to the last three!

The Lord gave me a verse the day after I started my first chemo treatment. I have it highlighted, underlined, and dated in my Bible as a remembrance of how the Lord used it to encourage me on that day. It was a blessing and encouragement to me then and still is today.

> I consider that our present sufferings are not worth comparing with the glory that will be revealed in us. (Romans 8:18)

What a great reminder and comfort. The things I am presently suffering are minor in the whole scheme of things when they are looked at with God's eternal perspective. He crowns me with His glory and honor, which will be for eternity. The sufferings of today are only temporary. They are just for the present time. His glory and honor for me will be forever.

Jesus suffered and died for you and for me. He endured the suffering for the "joy set before Him" (Hebrews 12:2-3). That joy was the ability to bring all who would trust in Him to heaven to spend eternity with Him. When I look at all He suffered for me, my present sufferings are positively not worth comparing to that glory.

Hmmm... what are you facing today? Whose perspective are you using as you look at the difficult things in your life? Do you trust the Lord to carry you through? Or, have you grown weary and lost heart? Keep your eyes on Jesus, dear friends. Face the difficulties of this life with the strength of His Holy Spirit.

Giving Account...Wednesday, July 17, 2013

Hello! I know that some have been praying for my energy and strength. The Lord answered and gave me more yesterday than the day before. I still suffer fatigue, but I made it through all eight hours of work yesterday. Praise the Lord!

After coming home, I decided to take a short walk whether I felt like it or not, just to get out. I did so and am glad that I did. A little fresh air and sunshine always makes me feel better. The walk was short and slow. But, praise the Lord. I was able to do it.

It feels like, no matter what I do, I can't get enough sleep. No matter how much sleep I get, my body always wants more. I have another early work shift today. My body did not want to move again this morning as the alarm went off, so my hmmm will be limited to one verse that I read this morning.

> Nothing in all creation is hidden from God's sight. Everything is uncovered and laid bare before the eyes of Him to whom we must give account. (Hebrews 4:13)

The truth that struck a chord in my heart this morning is that each and every one of us must give an account for our lives to God. No one is exempt. As I hmmm a little bit further, I think of the folks who claim there is no God. As a man attempts to avoid accountability for his life in order to do just as he wants, he will claim there is no God. We can claim anything we want, but our claiming it does not make it true. God sees each and every one of our thoughts, actions, motives and even our inaction. We will have to give an account to Him for all of it.

That is a heavy thought. It gives me pause to stop and think. Is there anything in my life that should not be there? Am I doing things I should not be doing? Watching things or looking at things I shouldn't? What about the things I am listening to, whether it is music, talk shows or gossip? Am I thinking thoughts that are pure and clean? Are they thoughts of truth or lies? I cannot hide any of it from the Lord and will stand before His throne to give an account, just as you will.

Approaching with Confidence…Wednesday, July 17, 2013

Happy Day. The first praise of the day is that I felt much better today than the last three days. Praise the Lord for more energy. I am still not running marathons, but I can feel the energy rising. The second praise of the day is that the hair on my head continues to grow. Yea! It does not appear to be as dark as it was when it first started growing. It is still brown and not the blonde I had before, but a lighter brown than it initially appeared to be as it first began making its appearance on my head. I am still wondering what it will be like as it comes in more fully. One of my coworkers, Carrie, rubbed it today and said it was so soft and that it reminded her of the fuzz on a peach.

Today, as I was preparing to leave for work, I began having a hot flash, so I decided to wait until I got to work to put a scarf on my head. When I got to work, I carried it in and then decided not to wear it today. The scarves are hot and are beginning to make my head itch because of the heat. I am tired of wearing them, too. Today was the first day I chose not to wear a scarf at work, since the buzz cut when the hair first began falling out in clumps.

My customers and coworkers are thoughtful. They gave me lots of encouragement. Some told me I looked great and that they were glad to see the hair starting to come back in. Others told me I had a great shaped head or they wished they could carry off the shaved head look like I did. Their encouragement was very much appreciated. I suspect there are days when I will still wear a scarf, but it is nice to start breaking out of them a little bit more, and not just when I am around the house or walking the neighborhood.

I have a comical story for you from today. This morning as I was working the checkout, I turned off the light at my cash register to make a pit stop. When I returned, I forgot to turn the light back on. JoAnn, my coworker working the register next to mine, said to me, "You are not going to get any attention with that off." Of course, I thought she meant the scarf and told her I wasn't trying to get attention. She immediately blushed and realized what her comment must have sounded like since I did not realize I had forgotten to turn the light on. We both laughed till we were red in the face and the customers and other coworkers thought we were a little silly. Laughter really is good medicine and makes you feel wonderful.

I noticed a new side effect from the chemo. If you remember, a few weeks ago I had a pedicure and noticed bloody streaks under my big toenails. Well, today I went to get my fingernails redone and noticed that one of my fingers had a nail that looked as if I had lightly smashed it. The nail had a faint purple spot underneath. The Vietnamese gentleman painting my nails also noticed another nail that was beginning to show some signs of discoloration. I am a bit disappointed because I like having my nails done with a French manicure, but it allows the discoloration to show. If they continue to get worse, I may have to start painting them with a darker color to hide the discoloration. Hopefully, my nails will not discolor much more or at least not until I can get them painted again.

A friend of mine said in an email to me that he was feeling so bad about himself that he felt as if he shouldn't even ask the Lord for anything or even speak to Him. I have felt that way in the past, as I suspect most of us have at one time or another. Satan will tell us lies to convince us that these feelings are truth when nothing could be farther from it. The Lord wants us to come to Him in prayer concerning everything. He loves us with a love that is unconditional and everlasting. Our failure doesn't change His love for us.

Not only are we to pray to the Lord concerning all things, but because of who Jesus is and all He has done for us, as Christians we can come before the Lord's throne with freedom and confidence. We can only do this because of what Jesus has done for us. His righteousness covers us and His blood cleanses us from our sin, making us acceptable to come before God's throne with boldness. We are to pray with faith, believing that He hears us. Not only are we able to approach the throne of God with confidence, but we are encouraged to do so.

Jesus has been tempted in every way as we are. Therefore, He understands our weaknesses. I am glad to know He understands me and my weaknesses. He understands yours, too, dear friends and loves you. As we come to Him, He stands ready to give us the grace and mercy we so desperately need.

I am scheduled for chemo tomorrow. It is my prayer that my body will have rebuilt the blood cells needed to have a treatment.

Believing the Truth, Rejecting the Lies…Friday, July 19, 2013

Hello, my friends. It is the day after chemo day. Praise the Lord. My blood counts were good. I was able to take the treatment this week. I know that the improved blood counts were an answer to prayer. The count they are looking for is a 1.2. Last week I had a 1.1 and it took me two weeks to get there and they reluctantly gave me the treatment. This week the count was 1.4. Yea! Now there are only two more chemo treatments to go.

I also have another bit of good news about my blood counts. Dr. Gill is going to have me get a shot today and another one tomorrow which will help my body to kick start making the cells needed. I may very well be on track to finish the chemo treatments in the next two weeks. Hip! Hip! Hooray! The only part that saddens me is that I will miss my weekly trips to St. Luke's to see all of my new friends there. God has been is so good to give me many folks there to hug, love, and encourage me all along the way.

It brings tears to my eyes even as I think about it now. No matter where we are in life, God knows just what and who we.

For all of you who are wondering, Dr. Gill held true to her word and let me snap some photos of her for my scrapbook. She realized I was persistent and not going to give up. They are great photos. (Dr. Gill, even without the extreme makeover, you take a beautiful photo. When I cannot see that wonderful face of yours, weekly and in person, I can at least go back to my scrap book and remember. Thank you!) Mom was my co-photographer of the day.

The chemo party was a little quieter today. All the chairs in the middle of the room were taken and I ended up with a place at the far end. With the busyness of the room, the nurses were really scurrying to get things accomplished and had less time to visit. Heather was my nurse today. She is always a blessing. Brian came down and got me started by putting the needle in the port and taking the second blood pressure and temperature readings of the day. After the treatment was finished, I got a quick chance to visit with Jessica. And, during the treatment, we got to visit with Gen. Others said quick hellos as they hustled by. It brings a smile to my face even now as I remember. I truly do love those folks.

I got my usual hug and loving greeting at the lab from Melinda. Charity was on vacation this week, so I missed her. But, she had left some thoughtful words with Melinda to deliver to me along with a reminder that she would look forward to seeing me next week. The Lord was good to bring the technician from the back, who counts the blood to have a quick visit with me as well. What a precious lady she is. I have seen her passing through on several days but never got a chance to really talk with her until today. God gave me the opportunity to share with her just how good He is and how well He is taking care of me. It seemed to be just the encouragement she needed because it brought tears to her eyes. God knows what we need and always brings someone along to deliver it. I had no idea that was what she needed, but her Heavenly Father did. Yup! It was another great day at the hospital.

On our last outing, Elmer, one of the neighbors was out on his tractor mowing and drove down for a visit. He is always an encouragement to me. He never fails to tell me that I am a beautiful lady no matter how much hair I have or don't have on my head. He almost always sees me with no scarf. I rarely wear one around home, especially in this heat.

A very important truth that I had missed knowing and appropriating into my life in the past is that Satan is always trying to speak lies into our minds. He knows when he controls our minds, he controls us. So, we know Satan is a liar and a deceiver who speaks lies to our minds (John 8:44b). In Revelation 12:9, *lead astray* is also translated as deceive in other translations. It is imperative that we are aware of the difference between Satan's voice and lies and Holy Spirit's voice and truth.

Carefully listen to what I tell you next. Hmmm on it until it becomes a normal and natural part of your everyday thinking and living. I cannot overstate the importance of this simple but unbending truth. Holy Spirit's voice will never put you down and make you feel less than who God says you are. He will always lift you up and draw you closer to the Lord. Satan's voice puts you down causing you to feel less than who God says you are. He will say things like, "You are not good enough. You are not pretty or handsome enough. You are not smart enough. Nobody really loves you, not even God. How could God love you? Look how bad you are. Why try? You can't do that." Those are just a few examples of the lies Satan slips into our minds. Before I learned this truth, wholeheartedly accepted it, and made it an integral part of the everyday battle in my mind, I thought the voice I heard in my head telling me these lies was my own. Even worse, I accepted the lies, rehearsing them in my head so often that I believed them. You must speak the truth of who God says you are, out loud if possible and to your heart and mind.

Holy Spirit's job is teaching us truth and reminding us of what the Lord has taught us. He will encourage and guide us. The Bible tells us that Holy Spirit will guide us into all truth (John 16:13). Holy Spirit's voice will always lift us. Even when He corrects us or disciplines us, He will do so in a way that directs us away from destructive things in our life and draws us closer into the Lord (John 14:26). My encouragement for you today is to spend some time in God's Word. It has radically changed my life. It will change yours as well.

Watching, Seeing, and Joining... Saturday, July 20, 2013

Good Morning! I am "up and at it" early again this morning. I have another shot to get at the hospital before I go to work for the late shift this afternoon. I go to the same place where I take chemo. I like that because it gives me a chance to see the folks I have come to know and love. Jessica gave me my shot yesterday. She is absolutely precious. When she gave it, I bled more than she thought I should have, so she checked into my platelet counts from Thursday and the week before. The platelet count for this week was 149,000. Last week the count was 179,000. The count has to be at least 100,000 for me to take the treatments. So, I pray for not only the infection fighting cells in the blood to work, but for the platelet count to stay positive, too.

After the shot yesterday, I stopped at Hobby Lobby and picked up a couple of things for the "Stones of Remembrance" scrapbook I plan to make to remind me of God's goodness and faithfulness to me through this stage of life. It will be a remembrance for me, just as the stones the Lord instructed the Israelites to erect when He brought them across the Jordan River into the Promised Land were a remembrance for them. I know there is still much more to come during this time in my life. It is still far from complete. I have two more chemo treatments, surgery, and radiation yet to face. I look forward to all I will see God do in the coming days. It is fun to anticipate. There are wonderful surprises in the people He sends, doors He opens, and circumstances that come. I know He orchestrates them.

Anticipating all the things I will see the Lord do in the days ahead, before this season is complete, a set of scriptures came to mind.

> Jesus gave them this answer: I tell you the truth, the Son can do nothing by himself; he can do only what He *sees* his Father doing, because whatever the Father does the Son also does. For the Father loves the Son and shows him all he does... (John 5:19-20a)

Just as Jesus watches the Father to see what He was doing, so should we. As Christians, we are in Jesus and He is in us. Are we watching? We must not only train our spiritual ears to hear the Lord's voice, but also our spiritual eyes to see the Lord's working. As you pray, ask Him to open your spiritual eyes that you might see where He is inviting you to join Him. You will be blessed.

Covenant of Love... Sunday, July 21, 2013, Monday, July 22, 2013

Good evening. Sundays and Mondays are getting to be two of the most difficult days of the week in regard to energy levels and feeling well. After church this morning, I took a four hour nap and decided to continue to rest this evening rather than go back to church. The energy just wasn't there. I knew Ellie Mae needed a bath and brushing to eliminate some excess hair. That was the accomplishment today. My Aunt Connie and Uncle Harold are coming to visit on Tuesday afternoon. I want Ellie Mae to be clean and fresh for their visit. I am really looking forward to it since I do not get to see them often.

Today was my first Sunday to go to church without a scarf. My church family was incredibly kind this morning, as they always are. Their love and encouragement blessed me beyond what words can express. I cannot thank the Lord enough for His gift to me in my church family. I have been humbled and amazed by their love and care.

Walking through this season, the Lord has opened my eyes to see so many, what one might call, "little blessings" all along the way. There have been big ones, too. But, it seems like the little ones come one right after the other, day in and day out. And, the ones that seem little sometimes end up being even bigger blessings. As I think about all the blessings, my heart swells because I see how very much the Lord loves me. With each blessing, He is reminding me how He pays attention to every intimate detail of my life. It may be an email of encouragement on a day when I am feeling discouraged, or a hug from a coworker when I am feeling a little low (Carol, you have been great in this area. Thank you!). Or it may be words of care and concern from one of my customers when I needed a boost to continue because the fatigue was heavy on me.

Those are just a few examples of the many ways the Lord blesses me through others on a daily basis. I must diligently keep my eyes focused on the blessings, keeping a grateful heart, in order to keep a joyful and positive attitude. It is also necessary for me to keep the hands of my heart holding tightly to God's promises.

Satan is always doing his best to distract God's children from the many blessings God has given them. He often tries to focus my mind on the fatigue and more unpleasant side effects of the chemo and the uncertainty that appears to be ahead of me in the future. If I were to let it, it would swirl me into a pit of depression, feeling sorry for myself. God blesses me in too many ways and gives me too many wonderful promises to let Satan have that victory.

> If you pay attention to these laws and are careful to follow them, then the Lord your God will keep His covenant of love with you... (Deuteronomy 7:12)

His promise to keep His covenant of love is a great encouragement. There is no love greater than God's love and no greater promises than His for salvation, provision, protection, blessing, honor, glory, mercy, grace, peace, joy, and so many other things. He fulfilled His ultimate covenant of love by sending Jesus to die for us.

Are you and I being obedient, allowing the Lord to fulfill His covenant of love to us? Hmmm a little while on that question and ask the Lord to show you what you need to do in order to allow Him to fulfill all that He has promised. I guarantee it will be time well spent.

Beginning of Wisdom...Monday evening, July 22, 2013

Hey there, dear friends. I am going to try to spend some time with you this evening rather than in the morning. Sleep is becoming a more precious commodity these days. Even with yesterday's four hour nap, I still did not want to get up for work this morning. And, I found it difficult to get through the workday. I hate it, but I could feel tears of exhaustion threatening to make an appearance near the end of my shift. Grrr... but praise the Lord; I made it all the way through the full eight hours.

Next, I went to my chiropractor's office. I am blessed to have a chiropractor who will allow me to bring Ellie Mae into his office while he adjusts me. (Thank you, Dr. Pappas! You are the best!) It was much too hot to leave her in the car. She loved the outing. I have not had her out much since I started chemo and I know she has been missing our times out together.

God positively gives wisdom, but the beginning of wisdom comes from the Lord. "The fear of the Lord is the beginning of wisdom; and knowledge of the Holy One is understanding." (Proverbs 9:10). God is not a magic genie whose lamp we can rub, praying and expecting Him to answer, giving us what we want when we are not coming to Him in the manner He requires. He is a sovereign God who promises us blessing as we seek and reverence Him. The dictionary defines the word *reverence* as awe, combined with respect. The way to respect Him is to give Him love the way He defines it. The way He defines love is obedience in I John 5:3a.

The first step is to acknowledge that you are a sinner and place your faith and trust in Jesus as your Savior and Lord. Until you have taken the first step, your other efforts are futile. The Bible continually tells us that the Lord hears and answers the prayers of the righteous. But it does not promise that He will hear the prayers of those who do not know Him (Proverbs 15:29).

What does it require to know someone? It requires having a relationship, talking and spending time with them to know what they think, how they feel, what they desire, what they love, and what they hate. If you do not spend time with the Lord, accepting His invitation of relationship, and then studying His teachings, praying and waiting before Him, listening for Him to speak to your heart, how can you expect to know Him?

We are in desperate need of the Lord's wisdom in order to live this life well. Let us do the things the Lord requires to receive His wisdom and blessing. We will never regret it.

Forgiveness, Love, and Prayer... Wednesday, July 24, 2013

I slept in a little bit and then visited with my relatives before they left for the day. I had a rough day yesterday. I felt much better as far as fatigue was concerned, but dizziness was a bigger problem. When I went to work, I felt really good, but after a couple of hours, began to feel very dizzy, especially if I turned my head down and then looked back up again. A few times I had to grab hold of the checkout stand to steady myself to keep from losing my balance. I checked my blood pressure to make sure it was all right. It was. That was not the problem. They were able to cover me at work, so I only worked a half day.

On the way home, I called Dr. Gill's office to tell them of the problem I was having. Dr. Gill and her nurse both called me back. Dr. Gill speculated it might be a sinus infection causing the problem. She had me take Zyrtec and told me to take a nap, rest and drink plenty of fluids. That is what I did. At bedtime I was still not feeling quite right, so I called and had them cover me at work again today. I am glad I did because when I got up this morning and took Ellie Mae out for the sniff over the yard, I felt the need to sit and rest a bit before I did anything else.

Fortunately, we had no plans other than to visit with my aunt and uncle who were here for a short time. If we had plans that would have included moving about, I am not so sure I could have done it. As it was, I took a nap in the recliner in the living room while the family visited. I did not want to miss out on any time I had with them.

My family and I spent time reminiscing of days past and of people and events that we remembered. It was nice. I always enjoyed, even as a little girl, sitting and listening as my parents, aunts, uncles, and grandma talk of the days when they were young. As I sit here writing to you, past remembrances come to my mind, some pleasant and some painful. As I remembered things that were done to hurt me, Holy Spirit reminded me of my responsibility to the Lord in respect to those who hurt me. "But I tell you: love your enemies and pray for those who persecute you." (Matthew 5:44).

God's Word reminds us that our response to those who hurt us is love and prayer. When we earnestly seek the Lord, His will, and His way, He will give us the ability to do as He commands. He will give us His love for those who hurt us, when we have none of our own to give. The most natural response, when we love others as the Lord has taught us, is to forgive them for the hurts they inflict. Jesus is a perfect example. Even from the cross, as He was being crucified, He spoke words of forgiveness and prayed that the Father would forgive those who were killing Him (Luke 23:34a). There is no greater prayer or greater love ever given.

We are to imitate Jesus, doing the same for others. No one ever said forgiveness was easy. It isn't. The Lord promises us blessing and reward as we follow Him. Jesus paid the ultimate price that we may have forgiveness. We must also be willing to sacrifice ourselves and our feelings to give forgiveness. We are blessed not to be asked to pay the price that Jesus did. Generally, all we are asked to give is our self-proclaimed right to feel angry and bitter. If we are to imitate Christ, we must be willing and ready to forgive.

Hmmm... is there anyone whom you hold bitter or angry feelings toward? Do you want to get back at someone? We have no right to hold those feelings. Vengeance is not ours to take. It is the Lord's.

> Do not take revenge, my friends, but leave room for God's wrath, for it is written: "It is mine to avenge; I will repay," says the Lord. (Romans 12:19)

The Lord will take care of the repayment of those who harm His children. Our job is to forgive those who hurt us, to love and pray for them. It is very difficult to remain angry and bitter toward someone when you earnestly pray for them. Trust the Lord. He knows exactly how to handle them, just as He does you.

Praising Him, Remembering His Benefits.... Friday, July 26, 2013

Woo! Hoo! One more chemo treatment down! I only have one more to go. Praise the Lord! My blood counts were good and even higher than last week. Yesterday was a really good day. I felt good as I got up for work. The worst thing I dealt with was a headache

The day at the hospital started with the three ladies in the lab. When I arrived, I received hugs and encouraging words from all of them. After the lab, I headed up to the oncology department. I spent a little time teasing Stephanie, who works at the reception desk. She is good-natured and a lot fun, too. Dr. Porter had the pleasure of delivering the sweet treats to those in the waiting room and office areas. Dad, Mom, and I went to the exam room to wait to see Dr. Gill. During our visit, she called the office of my surgeon, Dr. Patricia Limpert, to check on the length of time I will likely need before going back to work after surgery. It looks like I will have two to three weeks off after surgery. I am looking forward to having time for more extended rest.

After my time with Dr. Gill, my cheerleaders and I headed back to the infusion area for our usual chemo party. There were hugs all around and lots of love and cheer shared as we entered. I had the pleasure of having Jill as my nurse today. I have been so blessed by the love and care I receive from the ladies and man, (I can't forget to include Brian) while receiving chemo. Before chemo was started in my IV, Dr. Porter prayed. Jill joined us in our prayer time. I thank him for being so faithful to pray for me before starting each chemo treatment. What a blessing that has been.

During our time there, Mom had the chance to visit with and encourage a retired couple she met earlier in the lab waiting room. The husband and wife were both there for treatments for cancer. I can only imagine how difficult it must be for both of them to be dealing with cancer at the same time. I hung out with Dad and Dr. Porter for most of the treatment time and visited with the nurses and other patients. When I arrived at my seat, Gen was there to greet me with her hug and magnificent smile. She will not be there next week for my last treatment. I am so sad for that. She is a precious lady and takes great care of our group. She brings Pepsis for my cheerleaders and apple juice with no ice for me. She also brings Cheez-Its for all four of us. She knows what we like without even asking. Can you tell we are predictable? When I need warm blankets she always takes care of that for me, too. (Thank you, Gen! Your sweet love and care is a precious gift to me.)

Before we left, we made the rounds for a few more hugs and for Dr. Porter to say his goodbyes. He will not be able to be with us next week for my last treatment. I think he will miss the folks at St. Luke's almost as much as I will. We are already planning at least one return trip, just to visit with the folks during my radiation treatment time.

After leaving the hospital, we all had lunch together. Then, Dr. Porter and I headed to church for counseling time. I have an appointment to get a shot this morning at the hospital and one again tomorrow. This is the shot to kick-start my body into making the needed infection fighting blood cells.

As I think over yesterday, I praise the Lord for the many things He has done for me. Really, it is every day that He is so good and faithful.

Psalm 103 is a favorite of mine. It starts and ends with the writer, King David, reminding himself to praise the Lord, being careful not to forget all the benefits and blessings that He gives. At the very least, we should stop and praise the Lord at the beginnings and endings of our day for who He is and all He does. Ideally, we should be doing it all day long.

Truth, Confession, Forgiveness, Freedom…
Saturday, July 27, 2013

Good morning, dear friends. I will be off to the hospital this morning to get the second shot. Yesterday was spent counseling. It is always a favorite time for me. I never tire of seeing the Lord work in peoples' lives, encouraging, giving wisdom, and setting them free.

As I think about the freedom the Lord gives, I am reminded of how important truth is to freedom. In order for us to be free from the bondage of sin in our lives, we must face the truth of our sin. We may not always know when the sin we are struggling with came into our lives, but Holy Spirit can guide us to see what has caused us to continually sin or even what has caused us to deny a particular sin. As we open our hearts to the Lord, His Spirit will show us the truth. "But when He, the Spirit of truth, comes, He will guide you into all truth…" (John 16:13a).

As Holy Spirit guides you to see the truth about the sin in your life, however recent or far in the past, it is absolutely necessary to confess it. Until you bring the darkness of the sin into God's light, you will not be free from it. It will continue to plague you, bringing destruction into your life. When Holy Spirit brings truth to you, and you embrace it by acting upon it, you will be set free.

> If we confess our sins, he is faithful and just to forgive us our sins, and to cleanse us from all unrighteousness. (I John 1:9)

Because of His great love for us, God provided the way for us to be free from the burden of our sin. Jesus paid the ultimate price with His death. Our part is to trust and believe Him, then to confess sin and turn away from it. He wants to set you free. When Holy Spirit shines the light of truth on sin, confess it. Then, if He instructs you go to the one you offended to make it right, do so. Is it worth losing freedom in order to hold onto pride by continuing to cover the sin that plagues you? Hmmm... God wants to set all of His children completely free if they will let Him. Trust Him to do that work in your life.

I am off to the hospital, then to counseling, and finally to work the late shift until 10 p.m. I have a busy day ahead.

Good Gifts, Holy Spirit, and His Fruit... Monday, July 29, 2013

Good Morning. Yesterday I did not have the energy for writing. I thought I would have more energy after church, but I didn't. A nap helped a little, but not nearly enough. I am propped up in bed on my pillows just now, thinking about work. I already feel tired and have a good sized headache. I keep reminding myself, this is just a season and it too shall pass. The Lord is, has been, and continues to be faithful to me. I am just feeling "so very tired of being tired." I have been up a little while and have been trying to evaluate whether or not I can make it to work this morning. Wisdom told me not to even try. I called work just to tell them that I would not make it in today. I hate calling in. I know how much it inconveniences others who have to try to cover the shift.

Saturday was tougher than it has been for a while. I experienced more fatigue than usual and my skin ached, which I had not experienced for a while. But it was back in full force. It is weird how the skin itself can ache.

My knees also ache and feel much weaker, especially as I go up and down stairs. I surely do not bounce up and down them like I was accustomed to doing. As I think about it all, it makes me appreciate the times I have felt better and been able to do what I wanted to do, when I wanted to do it. It is kind of like the old saying, "You never know what you have till it is gone." God has given me an even greater appreciation for all that He continues to allow me to do. I could be much worse off. I thank Him and praise Him for giving me the strength I have. Without Him, I would have none.

Hmmm... all the good gifts the Lord gives me. They are too numerous to count. They range from all he has given me in nature. Sunrises, sunsets, animals, plants, stars, a gentle cool breeze on a hot day, then there are the people he gives me: family, friends, church family, coworkers, customers, doctors and nurses. They all bless me abundantly. Then of course, there is Ellie Mae. I have the ability to live in the USA. I have food in my belly, a roof over my head, clothes on my back, a vehicle to get me back and forth to work and many more things than the simple necessities of life. I still have energy and strength to do many of the things I desire to do, even though not all.

I am down to my last chemo treatment. With each day, I am closer to being finished. More importantly, in the spiritual realm, He has given me more things than I can enumerate: Salvation, love, protection, comfort, wisdom, and peace, joy, courage and many more things. God's Word alone is a precious gift. Unfortunately, sometimes we have to be reminded of our blessings. We begin to take what we have for granted, sometimes even our health and the relationships we have with those around us. Holy Spirit is one of the greatest gifts we have been given (Luke 11:13). The great news is that God will give Him more fully to those who ask. As a believer, if you allow Holy Spirit to control of your life, He will produce His fruit in you. "But the fruit of the Spirit is love, joy, peace, patience, kindness, goodness, faithfulness, gentleness and self-control." (Galatians 5:22-23a). The evidence of a Christian who is walking with the Lord, yielded to His Spirit, is exhibited by the fruit His Spirit produces in and through their life.

Hmmm... am I yielding each part of the fruit Holy Spirit produces? What about you? Where are we lacking? My encouragement to you is to look closely at the fruit Holy Spirit produces. Do you see each part of the fruit He produces in your life? Where are you lacking? Ask the Lord to show you what He would have you know, see, and do. God has given His children no greater gift than the gift of His Spirit through Jesus Christ.

I hope you will join me in thinking about these things for yourself. After I sign off, I will be crawling back under the covers for more rest. The headache I woke up with is getting stronger and fatigue is drawing me back toward sleep. Be filled with His peace, His love and His joy.

His Molding Hand... Tuesday, July 30, 2013

Hi there! It is me again. Yesterday was a day of rest. I needed it, however. I did take care of one good sized chore. All the scarves and bandannas that had been worn and were pinned to the special rack my parents made for them got taken down today, un-knotted, washed, dried, folded and put away. The wall where they were hanging looks rather bare. I love to wear scarves and will still use them, just not on my head anymore. I haven't worn a scarf on my head since the first day I went to work without one. My hair is growing really fast and is beginning to lose the baby fuzz soft feel. I still look very much like a brunette and not a blonde. Who knows, I may like the new color well enough not to highlight it. Saving a little money on the beauty shop bill would not be a bad thing. Besides that, the Lord has the right to give me the color He desires no matter what my preference is. His plan is perfection. Hmmm... this line of thought ties into some verses I read this morning.

> But who are you, O man, to talk back to God? Shall what is formed say to Him who formed it, "Why did you make me like this?" Does not the potter have the right to make out of the same lump of clay some pottery for noble purposes and some for common use? (Romans 9:20-21)

As I read this, I was reminded of how many times I have second guessed God concerning how He made me. I have been guilty of wishing I was blonder, prettier, smarter, and shorter, had different gifts and talents, etc. This verse reminded me that God made me as He chose. He is the Creator. I am the clay to be formed by Him, the potter, as He pleases. My place is not to question how He has made me. I am to accept it and to know that He made me just as He desires me to be. To complete the plan of all He desires for me, I must be pliable in His hand, just as the moist clay is pliable in the potter's hand. My duty is to be all that I can be in His hand. His Word reminds us that we can do all things through Christ who strengthens us (Philippians 4:13).

God made us with the ability to grow and change, and to draw closer to Him. If we live each day yielded to Him we will be molded with expert craftsmanship and intricate detail, perfectly prepared for the purpose for which we were created. There is no happier place than when a person is doing what he or she was created to do. There is perfect peace and contentment, great joy and satisfaction.

Search your heart and ask the Lord to help you see anything that would make you a more willing vessel in His hand, one that is soft and pliable for His molding. Being molded is not always comfortable, but the final result is worth the temporary discomfort of the process. Trust Him for it. He loves you more than you will ever know and has a perfect plan for you.

For Such a Time as This… Wednesday, July 31, 2013

It is me again. I am happy to say I feel immensely better. Praise the Lord for renewed energy and strength. Having Monday off work positively helped me make it through the Tuesday work shift with flying colors. The morning started off a little sluggish and with some nausea. My upset stomach was readily settled with a Coke and some pretzels. I had a headache most of the day. I am grateful it is mild headache and not severe. I am also grateful and praising the Lord that the ache in my skin has gone away. With each day that passes, I am closer to the end of the chemo treatments and the end of the side effects. I am looking forward to feeling normal and good again. As I spoke with one of my customers who had been through chemo treatments, she said when she got back to feeling normal; she had forgotten how good it felt. I am absolutely looking forward to that time.

I think about the times I had complained about being tired prior to starting the chemo treatments. I now realize I had no real concept of the deep tiredness I have experienced in waves for months now. As I thought about it, I realized I have been seeing doctors for the diagnosis and treatments for over five months. The 8th of August will be five months since my first chemo treatment. It is amazing how quickly those months have passed. Much of it seems like a blur. I am glad I have been regularly sharing my experience with you so that I will be able to look back and remember many of the wonderful things the Lord has done during these days and weeks.

I think about the time that has passed and the ways the Lord prepared me for the past and the present time. This is His plan to mold and make me. I am reminded of Mordecai's words to Esther from the book of Esther.

> "For if you remain silent at this time, relief and deliverance for the Jews will arise from another place, but you and your father's family will perish. And who knows but that you have come to royal position for such a time as this?" Then Esther sent this reply to Mordecai: "Go, gather together all the Jews who are in Susa, and fast for me. Do not eat or drink for three days, night or day. I and my maids will fast as you do. When this is done, I will go to the king, even though it is against the law. And if I perish, I perish." (Esther 4:14)

These verses are favorites of mine. They are taken from the story of Queen Esther. She finds herself, amazingly, as queen in a land where an edict has been sent out to destroy her people. She alone is in a position to seek the king's ear and heart to save them. To do so, she must risk death, by going against the law. Only by the king's mercy will she be saved from the law demanding her death as she approaches the king, without invitation, to seek his favor. Before she endeavors to approach the king, she has the people and her maids pray and fast, as well as doing so herself. She knows she will need God's help and favor to gain the king's favor.

Esther is reminded that she is in the position of queen, "for such a time as this." And, despite the possibility of losing of her life, she must go before the king, in order to save the lives of her people. She decides she will go in spite of the possible consequences, even if she perishes. In the end, her people are saved and she and Mordecai, her cousin who encouraged her, are greatly blessed by the Lord, through the king.

Hmmm... I cannot help but apply some of the lessons in these verses to my own life and ask myself some questions. First, do I have the realization that God has put me here "for such a time as this?" Not every one of us has a calling with as seemingly large of an impact as Queen Esther did, but we all have an important calling nonetheless. Each one of us is important in God's eyes and is given specific things to do for the Lord. No matter how large or small, they are important to the Lord's work and master plan.

Dear friends, we must be aware that we too, are a special and intricate part of God's master plan. He has put you and me where we are "for such a time as this." He has important work for us to do. It is important that we seek Him, asking what He would have us do, and then do it.

I do not want to miss out on the blessings the Lord has for me. If I do not step out in obedience to do the things He has prepared for me, I will miss the blessing He promises (Ephesians 2:10). He gives each and every one of us multiple opportunities to serve each and every day. Are we taking them? Ask the Lord to open your eyes and speak to your heart that you might know what He is calling you to do.

Who I Am, Was, and Will Be... Thursday, August 1, 2013

Good morning, dear friends. I rose early this morning and contemplated the upcoming events of the day. I am excited as I look toward my last chemo treatment. If my blood counts are good, today this will be the last chemo. Praise the Lord! I will be pleased to have this leg of the journey behind me. I am anxiously anticipating feeling better and getting back to doing some walking and exercising, not having to take medicine for swelling or keeping my body's plumbing in order or keeping my stomach happy, seeing all my facial hair return just as the hair on my head is returning (I am still watching for curls.), controlling my diet more easily (No steroids and feeling tired, which both make me want to eat.), and re-losing the 15 pounds that re-found me during the chemo treatments. Those are just a start on my list of things I am looking forward to. I know I will not have more time yet because there is still a long road ahead with surgery and radiation, but the road to finishing is much shorter than it was.

I felt pretty good yesterday, with lots more "spit and vinegar" than even the day before. As I was cleaning out some old emails, I ran across one I had written to a friend. In it, I shared a truth the Lord was sinking into my heart at that time. He was taking a truth I already knew in my head and sinking it deep in my heart as well. When God's truth gets from our heads into our hearts, it becomes truly ours. Heart knowledge is experiential knowledge. We have experienced it and know that we know it. Head knowledge is good, but it is only in our head. It is nowhere near as solid as heart knowledge because it has not yet fully become a part of who we are.

I will share with you the truth I shared in the email to my friend. The Lord is the One who is, who was, and is to come. "I am the Alpha and the Omega, says the Lord God, who is, and who was, and who is to come, the Almighty." (Revelation 1:8). I focused on the truth that not only is He, the

One who is, was, and is to come, but, as He looks at me, He sees who I am, who I was, and who I will become. He is not limited to knowing who I am today and who I was yesterday. He sees who He is growing me to be. I like that picture even better, even if I am not sure yet what it looks like. Before He formed us in our mother's womb, He knew us and all the things we would or wouldn't do in our lives (Psalm 139:13-16). Each of my days was already written in His book of history before even one of them came to pass.

From the beginning of all creation the Lord knew us. He set each and every one of us apart for His special purpose, before we were even conceived. He knew me and loved me even before I was born (Jeremiah 1:5a). You, too! That boggles my mind, but my heart knows it is truth.

Hmmm... have you ever stopped to realize, God knows and sees who you will be when He is finished growing you? He knows who we are in the process of becoming and already sees the finished product. Oh, how I thank Him and praise Him for that knowledge. It comforts my heart because I am surely not yet who He desires me to be. But, as I continue to submit to His molding hand, I will be. He sees me in my perfected state already. He sees you as you will be, too. He is the master craftsman, molding us to perfection. Trust Him for His perfecting work in your life.

Last Chemo and Many Praises!... Friday, August 2, 2013

Good morning all. I slept in. It was wonderful! Yesterday was a wonderful day full of praises. As of yesterday, the last of the twelve treatments in this cycle and the sixteen total chemotherapy treatments are *done*! Praise the Lord for His wonderful faithfulness to me.

The blood counts were even higher this week than last. The only thing that showed up as a negative in the blood work was that my liver function was not all that Dr. Gill would have hoped for. But, it is still not of great concern. She said it is common for the liver to have a difficult time since it is working so hard to filter out the numerous chemo chemicals.

As I arrived at the hospital, I made my usual first stop at the lab for the blood work. I was greeted by Charity and Melinda with hugs and smiles. As we visited and my blood was drawn, they gave me a bag with gifts and a beautiful card in which they had both written thoughtful words of love and appreciation for me. It made me cry, good tears of course. Oh, how I will miss my regular visits to those two.

I proceeded to Dr. Gill's office for my visit with her. After I passed out candy to all the folks in the office and waiting room, Katrina did the usual weigh in, blood pressure and temperature check. Then, she tucked me in an exam room to wait for Dr. Gill and went to track down Colby so she could say "Hello." What fun those two are! When Dr. Gill walked into the exam room, she put beautiful lei of two colors of pink ribbon with green leaf-like ribbons around my neck. It looked like the flower ones you see put around the necks of people in Hawaii. How wonderful was that! She is so thoughtful. (I love it and you, Dr. Gill!) Then, she examined me and answered the million questions I had written down to ask her. She was very patient, answering each and every one. It was good to have a better idea of what is yet to come.

She said that it was possible that I might lose my big toenails since they had so much damage and pain from the chemo. Even if I do, with time, they will grow back. She said it was still possible that I could lose the hair that has grown back. I will pray I get to keep the hair the Lord has already given me back. Even though the color is different, "it is beginning to grow on me." (I even tickled myself with that one.) She also told me that the numbness in the hands and feet, as well as the fatigue, should all be gone in a year or less. The damage to the veins that causes swelling in my feet and ankles should heal and no longer be a problem in about a month.

With some breast cancers, patients need long term hormones or medicine. I am blessed. That will not be necessary for me. I have an appointment today to get a shot to boost the production of infection fighting cells in my blood and then another one tomorrow. I also have an MRI scheduled for today.

After all treatments are done, I will need to keep check-up appointments with Dr. Gill every three months for two years and then four to six months for the next three years. At the five year mark, I will go once a year thereafter. Not that I get excited about going to a doctor's office, but I will be glad to see Dr. Gill each time. She has a very special place in my heart.

When time to receive my chemo came, Jessica was my nurse. What a precious young lady. She and Heather always greet me with their smiles and hugs as do some of the others. Quite a few of the other nurses wished me well as I received treatment. Bonnie and Heather both came by my chair and chatted for a while. Dr. Porter and Miss Linnie were on the phone for our usual prayer time before chemo was started. I put the speaker phone on, so all in our circle of prayer could hear as he prayed. When the last treatment was finished, Jessica brought me two bells to ring as the nurses cheered for me at the finishing of the last treatment. How fun!

Those were just a few of the blessings and praises of the day. There is one more I want to share with you. As some of you know, I have been working to get a new vehicle since the one I am currently driving has almost 250,000 miles on it and needs around four thousand dollars' worth of work. I have been seeking to get court approval because of the bankruptcy since last December, when I found out how much work the Blazer I am driving needed. Well, the financial attorney called and gave me the news that the court agreed to let me buy the car. I also received the trustee's letter agreeing to allow me to keep the tax refund to use toward the new vehicle. The biggest praise in it all is that, even though the vehicle I am currently driving needs so much work, the Lord kept it running since December. I did not have to put out any money for repairs since that time.

God knows our each and every need and attends to them with perfect precision. I can only thank and praise Him and give Him my love and obedience in return. And, really, that is all He asks from us, despite all He gives to us. Hmmm… He wants to hear our praises. As I was read in Psalms this morning, I was reminded of that very fact. "My mouth is filled with your praise, declaring your splendor all day long." (Psalm 71:8).

Hmmm… do you and I tell of His wondrous works, praising Him all day long? Do we even do it once a day, every day? Or just on those days when He gives us what we want? Even in the times when God allows trouble into our lives, we are to praise Him knowing that He will restore us. His promise is to work for our good as we love Him and submit ourselves to Him. We either believe His Word is true or we don't.

Hmmm… can you and I praise Him even during the difficult seasons and struggles of life? If you have a difficult challenge in your life, bring it before His throne, submit yourself completely to His will and way for your life, thank Him for His promise to work all things for good for you.

I hope you will take a little time and hmmm on the questions I have posed and read all of Psalm 71. See what else Holy Spirit would reveal to you as you ask Him to show God's truth to your heart and mind. He is always faithful to do so as we are obedient, focused and quiet before Him and listen. I love you all! Many blessings to you today.

Writing and Taking Chemo.

My Cheerleaders: Dad (Paul), Mom (Shirma), and Dr. Curtis Porter

Chemo Time with nurses, Heather and Jessica

Blood Drawing Time with Melinda and Charity

My Favorite Volunteer
Geneva (Gen)

Colby and Katrina
Come for a Visit

Wrapped in the Blanket Dr. Gill made

Getting Ready for Chemo with Dr. Porter

Matching Bandannas for my Brother, Mark and Me

The Girls of the Family: Anne, Amanda, Mom, Kacie (on my lap), Alecia, Loren, and Abigail

Ellie Mae and the Wig

Enjoying the 4th of July Photo Shoot

Photo Shoot with Ellie Mae

Check Up Time with My Oncologist, Dr. Julie Gill

Celebrating the Last Chemo Treatment with
Heather, Jessica, Gina, and Bonnie

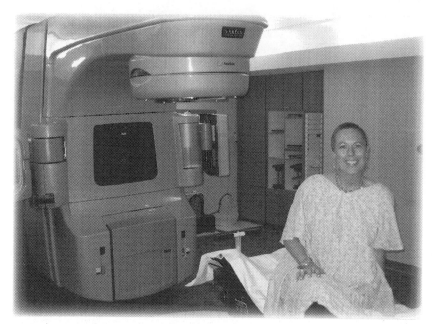
Radiation Time

After Chemo with Dr. Gill and Dr. Porter

With My Surgeon, Dr. Patricia Limpert

Out to Lunch with Miss Linnie, Dr. Porter, Mom, and Dad

God taught me, my value is not in my hair nor my appearance, but in who He created me to be!

Chapter 9

Surgery

August 3, 2013 – August 14, 2013

Trust and Strength… Saturday, August 3, 2013

Hey there! I am a bit tired. Yesterday, I went to St. Luke's to get the shot to boost the infection fighting cell production in my blood and to have the MRI done. I suspect it will show the effectiveness of the chemo and determine which surgery is recommended. I look forward to the MRI results and hearing whatever Dr. Limpert, the surgeon will tell me.

One of the hospital staff mentioned that I might be concerned about the outcome of the test. But, I am not. The Lord has given me peace about it all. He has assured me, He has it under control. On my way home from the hospital, I was contemplating how good God is to give me His peace. I know I only have peace because I trust Him. I stopped at a Christian bookstore and the Lord pointed out a verse on one of the products there and placed it in my heart as I pondered the peace and strength He has given me.

> This is what the Sovereign Lord, the Holy One of Israel, says: In repentance and rest is your salvation, in quietness and trust is your strength… (Isaiah 30:15a)

I have had folks tell me how strong I am. But, I know, I am not strong. The Lord is. He gives me His strength as I trust Him. If I were to fret and worry, I would not have His peace nor be able to rest in the quietness of soul that He offers to those who trust Him. His Word promises us that when we are weak, we can be strong in Christ's power.

> But He said to me, "My grace is sufficient for you, for my power is made perfect in weakness." Therefore I will boast all the more gladly about my weaknesses, so that Christ's power may rest on me. That is why, for Christ's sake, I delight in weaknesses, in insults, in hardships, in persecutions, in difficulties. For when I am weak, then I am strong. (II Corinthian's 12:9-10)

I do not have the ability to live this season of life without fear, worry, and anxiety, but with Jesus' strength I can. One of the best things about His strength is that it comes to us in our weak moments. Hmmm… so, as I trust Him and remain quiet before Him, no matter the circumstance, He will be with me. With each trial and hardship, He will teach me and you, how to more fully walk in His strength and trust Him.

In the second verse, the writer, Paul, chose to be glad about his weaknesses in order for Christ's power to rest on him. He even goes so far as to tell us that he boasts and delights in his weaknesses and difficult seasons of life because of Christ's strength given in his weakness.

I am not quite sure that I have reached the point that I delight in my hardship, but I can truly say I delight in all the good things I see God doing in this prevail of life. There have been many more blessings than I can count. I shared with you a few, but they are just the tip of the iceberg. The things He has done in me have been far beyond what He could have done if this last year had been a quiet, happy, and smooth one. My pastor recently preached on the truth that it is in the difficult times in life that God can grow us the most.

Remembering, Obedience, Promised Lands, Monday, August 5, 2013

After working late Saturday night, being up early Sunday morning for church, an afternoon full with friends, and church last evening, the energy and time to write and hmmm with you was gone. I was pleased to have energy enough to do those things. The last two Sundays were difficult because of fatigue. I had anticipated going home after church and napping until evening church time, but I did not nap at all yesterday. I went to lunch with some old neighbors and friends instead. It was fun to catch up with each other.

My feet and hands were bothering me more than they had for a while and still are to some degree. My fingernails and toenails are hurting and the bottom of my feet have that "been walking around at Six Flags all day on the hot pavement and can't wait to get off them" feeling. At least, that is the best way I know how to describe it. I still had a headache and my stomach was very uncomfortable. I was having a hard time figuring out why until it dawned on me, I had forgotten to take the Omeprazole the last few days. The last few weeks, I noticed that my memory has been affected by the chemo. I forget some things and then remember them much later. But, I praise the Lord, it hasn't bothered me much and I still function well despite a little forgetfulness. Another thing I forgot and remembered later was a question I had for Dr. Gill. I was wondering when I would be able to have my port removed. Jessica hunted down Dr. Gill and asked her for me. Her answer was, "After radiation is complete."

The verses in Nehemiah 9:16-17 show us that when we refuse to listen to the Lord and remember His hand in our life, we become stiff-necked, arrogant, rebellious and disobedient. Those are some ugly consequences. But, they are exactly what we will reap when we refuse to listen to the Lord and remember all that He has done for us like the Israelites did. It tells about the Israelites after the Lord brought them out of captivity in Egypt, but applies to us as well. Instead of remembering all of the ways the Lord had provided for them and rescued them, they refused to listen to His commands and did not remember His miracles and the ways He had provided for them. As a result, they spent forty years wandering in the desert and their generation was not allowed to enter the Promised Land. Think about that a minute. The Lord had a land "flowing with milk and honey," rich beyond their wildest dreams, prepared for them. He was in the process of leading them there. Before they arrived, they became rebellious by refusing to obey the Lord. The journey to the Promised Land was not many miles away and would not have taken them very long, but they rebelled. The Lord would have taken them straight there. They sacrificed their ability to have all that God desired to give them by their rebellion. The next generation was brought into the land, but not the current one.

That realization makes me think long and hard. What are we sacrificing by not being obedient to the Lord and refusing to remember His faithfulness to us? When we are rebellious and disobedient, we sacrifice God's best and suffer consequences.

Fortunately for us, God is forgiving, gracious, compassionate, and slow to anger and abounding in love. Because He is all those things, He will never forsake His children. Even when Christians choose to be in a pit of disobedience, the Lord is with them. His promise is to "never leave nor forsake" His children. And, He doesn't. Only we can stop His blessing with our disobedience. Hmmm… am I stopping His blessing because of disobedience? What about you? I am ready for my promised land. Are you?

Great News! Chosen, Strong, Working… Tuesday, August 6, 2013

Whoopee! I will start my time with you with a great big praise. The MRI results show no sign of cancer whatsoever. Praise the Lord! The tumor itself is gone and the spot that was next to the tumor that they were not sure what it was is also gone. Dr. Gill called me this evening to personally share the good news with me. I am glad the Lord sent me to her to be my doctor. Her genuine care and concern warms my heart.

I now have a more solidified plan for upcoming treatment. The surgery with Dr. Limpert, is scheduled for Tuesday, August 13, 2013. The only thing that might change that is if my blood counts are not sufficient. Dr. Limpert looked over how my counts ran throughout the chemo treatments and feels confident they will be fine. I will go the day before surgery to have blood drawn to check the counts. The plan for surgery is to remove the tissue that was marked with titanium clips when the biopsy and ultrasounds were done. They will also inject a dye to discover the closest draining lymph node which will be biopsied. The tissue removed should be very small and not noticeable after the surgery is done. The surgery will be outpatient and the pathology report on the lymph node and removed tissue should be back in four to five business days.

I anticipate three weeks off work. Two to three weeks after surgery, radiation should start. It is planned for five days a week for approximately six and a half weeks, thirty-three treatments. I plan to take radiation at St. Anthony's Medical Center rather than St. Luke's Hospital because of the closer proximity to home and work. Dr. Limpert and Dr. Gill both believe I will do well through surgery and radiation. They both have expressed that I am an unusual patient. Praise the Lord for that. They agreed that I had been able to go through chemo much differently from most by continuing to work and to do extra things, too. I know it was only by God's grace and the prayers of so many. Thank you, dear friends, for your prayers and support. The Lord has used you mightily to bless me. There is a verse that I would like to share with you.

> Consider now, for the Lord has chosen you to build a temple as a sanctuary. Be strong and do the work. (I Chronicles 28:10)

This verse is taken from King David's words to his son Solomon as he was giving him instructions for building God's temple. As I read it, the Lord quickened my heart and reminded me that He had work for me, work that He had specifically chosen for me to do. His encouragement to me was just what David's was to Solomon. "Be strong and do the work!" His promise is to give us the strength, the courage, the wisdom to do what He asks. God will never call us to do anything He will not equip us to do. We often think that we cannot do what the Lord is asking. In a sense, we are right. We cannot do what the Lord is calling us to do. But, in Him, in His strength, His courage, His wisdom, His ability, we can.

Nowhere in the Bible does it tell us we are to do what God has called us to do in our own strength. Our fleshly nature often causes us to want to procrastinate. We think, "I'll do it tomorrow, I will get to it when I am more prepared, I am too tired right now, or I want to do this other thing now, so I will do that later." If we put off until tomorrow the work He has for us to do today, we cannot do what He has for us to do tomorrow. Windows of opportunity are not permanently open.

God's encouragement to us is, "I have chosen *you*. Be strong and do the work." What work is He is asking you to do? Whose strength are you doing it in? Is it His or yours? His desire is for you to succeed, accomplishing all that He has called you to do. Remember, He will not call you to do anything that He will not enable you to do.

Don't Give Up!... Wednesday, August 7, 2013

After all of yesterday's good news, I feel like I do not have as much to tell today. I had the usual workday. My energy was really good for the first three quarters of the day, but fatigue started to rear its ugly head the last couple of hours. But, I made it through the workday. Praise the Lord.

I have to work from 6 a.m. until 2 p.m. today. I really like the early shifts. But, with the fatigue, I am not enjoying opening my eyes when the alarm goes off. At least after surgery, I will be able to turn off the alarm for several days. I am positively looking forward to that! As I think about gaining needed rest and refreshment, my thoughts return to what Dr. Limpert said about folks giving up and quitting part way through their cancer treatments because it gets hard. They don't feel well and they have to make continual trips to the hospital day after day. Because some do not follow through, giving up before they have completed all the treatments, the cancer is not completely destroyed and returns. This reminds me of a command the Lord gives to us. He tells us to not give up, tire or grow weary when we are doing what is right in His eyes (II Thessalonians 3:13).

> Let us not become weary in doing good, for at the proper time we will reap a harvest if we do not give up. (Galatians 6:9)

The Lord knows how difficult it is to continue to do what is required when we are not yet seeing the results. He gives us these verses not only to remind us that no matter the circumstance we are to continue. Jesus came to earth and lived a life as a man. He knows and understands all the challenges and difficulties we face because He faced them. It comes as no surprise to Him that we often find it difficult to continue doing what is right when we are not seeing any or very few positive results. That is why He reminds us of His promise to "reap a harvest."

Just as it takes time for the farmer to reap his harvest, so it is with us. Many steps and days are required. He must till, plant, cultivate, fertilize water, weed, protect the plants from pests and wait. If he should grow weary anywhere along the way and quit, he will not reap the full benefit of the harvest. The growing of the plant and production of the fruit is work that can only be done by God. This applies both in the earthly realm by planting actual gardens and in the spiritual realm. The gardener does not expect his harvest at the time of tilling or sowing. He knows, in due season, he will reap the fruits of his labor. So it is with us. In God's time, we will receive the benefits of our labor.

God's timing is not always our timing. However, His timing is perfect. Trust Him for it. Do not give up, dear friends. Do what is right.

Stand Firm… Thursday, August 8, 2013

I know I've told you before, but I truly do enjoy our time together. The energy was good for most of the workday. I felt tired toward the end, but made it through. The biggest annoyance was the discomfort in my feet from neuropathy. I came up with what I think is an even better description of what it feels like. Add the feeling of spending all day on the hot asphalt, on your feet, at Six Flags to the feeling of your feet having fallen asleep and beginning to wake up with that, all over, pins and needles feeling, and that is pretty close to what I have in my feet. I was glad to get home and get off them.

This morning, the Lord reminded me of the importance of standing firm in His truth. Satan does all he can to discourage us and to keep us from seeing the evidence of God's truth. He lies and tries to blur the truth, hindering us from receiving all God has promised. It is important that we wait, being patient, and standing firm in the truth as we face the trials of this life (James 1:12).

Our perseverance is required; continuing to do the good work God has called us to do. God's Word encourages us to "wait upon the Lord." After we have done all, we are to stand firm in God's truth, knowing He will bring His promises to pass.

> Therefore put on the full armor of God, so that when the day of evil comes, you may be able to stand your ground, and after you have done everything, to stand. Stand firm then, with the belt of truth buckled around your waist... (Ephesians 6:13)

I am very guilty of feeling like I have to continue working, doing things to obtain His promises. Often, He wants me to wait upon Him as He brings His plan and promises to pass. My struggling and striving hinders rather than helps what He is doing in my life. Hmmm... that is tough to do sometimes.

Are we standing firm on His truth or do we believe lies? Are we continuing to struggle and strive, trying to bring about results after the Lord instructed us to wait upon Him? God and His truth are the only things we can truly depend on. They are unshakeable, unbreakable and unstoppable. Trust the Lord for His promises and work in your life, dear friends. He is faithful.

Kimberly McGary

Great Promises and Humility... Friday, August 9, 2013

Hey there. It is good to be with you this morning. I have had more energy the last few days. I am praising the Lord for it. I am excited as I think about the energy rising. I still, however, did not want to move when the alarm went off. Well, I suppose that is not just a chemo problem. The only extra difficulties I dealt with yesterday were an unhappy digestive tract, a few moments of dizziness, and a headache.

The morning hours at work were a pleasure. I received an unexpected blessing. As I stood, waiting for another customer to come, a couple that I did not recognize came in and walked by me. I greeted them and they said hello and kept on walking. In just a moment or so, they turned around and came back. They proceeded to tell me that they had been praying for me. How good God is! I did not even recognize them. They told me they do not regularly shop in the store, but do so occasionally. They had seen me a few months back and talked with me. They have been praying for me since that time. I was able to thank them and share with them the many ways the Lord was answering their prayers for me. What a delightful time. Then, later as they checked out, they came through my line. As we chatted, we discovered that the wife and I are distantly related. What fun! That is just like God to add extra fun and blessings to my day.

The blessings continued as I went to the church to spend time with the folks counseling. I always enjoy watching the Lord encourage and free folks in our time spent together. All it takes is for us to humble ourselves before the Lord, submitting to Him, and He does great things in, through and for us.

Hmmm... humble. I looked up the word *humble* in Webster's dictionary and the definition is of a low or unpretending character, lowly, meek, or modest. Dr. Porter and I talked about humility yesterday and one of the things he said about a humble person is that they always think another can do a better job at something than they can. And, if a person is truly humble, they will never say they are humble because it would be a sure sign that they are not.

The Bible stresses the importance of humility. The scriptures in Ephesians 4:2, James 4:10 and Luke 14:11 give us the command to humble ourselves and He will lift us up. If we humble ourselves and are obedient to the Lord, He will reward us. Obedience always accompanies humility (Philippians 2:8).

If you hmmm on that thought, I am sure you can come up with a time or two when you were humbled through circumstances. It was not pleasant was it? God promises grace to the humble. "This is the one I esteem: he who is humble and contrite in spirit, and trembles at my word." (Isaiah 66:2).

Jesus is the best example of humility and a humble heart. "Take my yoke upon you and learn from me, for I am gentle and humble in heart, and you will find rest for your souls." (Matthew 11:29). If you are truly humble, you understand the Lord knows what is best and you know you do not.

Love, Discipline, and Blessing... Saturday, August 10, 2013

Good morning, dear friends. My energy level was good almost all day. By the end however, I was pooped out. But, that is okay. It meant I was ready to sleep at bed time. Praise the Lord! My feet and ankles look much better this morning. The best praise of the day was the ability to watch the Lord work in folks lives setting them free from strongholds and the control the enemy had gained in their lives. There is nothing like watching the joy on their faces when they gain freedom that only the Lord can give. I was helping with counseling all day. I will do so again this morning before I go to work. I only have two more workdays before I am scheduled for surgery. It will be nice to have time off and a rest from the disciplined schedule of work and treatments for a few weeks.

Hmmm... discipline. The word *discipline* means to train up well or to chastise. It can also mean training or subjection to laws, punishment, and correction. There are two basic meanings to consider for discipline. From God's perspective, one is something given to us to correct and encourage us to obedience, the other is a strict obedient adherence to the Lord.

Hmmm... the Bible has lots to say about both types of discipline. The one I will focus on today is the discipline the Lord gives His children to correct them. He does so because He loves them. His disciplines are to turn them from their sin to repentance (Revelation 3:19). Discipline is never fun or easy to take. If we are not careful, we can be angry and rebellious when we are disciplined. The Lord knows our fleshly tendencies and reminds us we are not to despise nor resent His discipline. Love is always the motivating force behind the Lord's discipline (Proverbs 3:11-12).

Dear friends, we can expect God's discipline when we are outside of His will. Just as a parent disciplines a child because they love him and want the very best for him, so does God discipline His children. The parent knows the child will not be blessed or safe when they are not following the rules the parent has given them. The same is true with God's children. "No discipline seems pleasant at the time, but painful. Later on, however, it produces a harvest of righteousness and peace for those who have been trained by it." (Hebrews 12:11).

Hmmm... righteousness and peace, isn't peace one of the things we are all searching for? And, righteousness leads to life. No matter how uncomfortable the Lord's discipline is, it is always worth it when we allow the Lord to correct and direct us.

I encourage you to think back on some of the times the Lord disciplined you. Did you repent and accept the correction and learn from it? Or did you rebel and despise it? What consequences did you reap? I have learned to thank the Lord for His discipline, not that I like or enjoy it by any means. But I have learned it always brings spiritual growth when I allow myself to be corrected by it. Submit yourself to His discipline, dear friends and reap His blessings.

Self-Discipline... Monday, August 12, 2013

Today is an early workday for me. As soon as I get off work, I will go to the hospital to have my blood drawn, so they can check my blood counts to be confident I am ready for the surgery.

After I shared scriptures concerning the Lord's discipline, one of my brothers in Christ, Kerry, wrote back to me and shared with me some hmmms of his own on discipline. My heart was in complete agreement with what he shared. His words said it so well that I will share with you part of what he wrote.

> We can either discipline ourselves to exercise and grow our spiritual muscles or the Lord will discipline us for trying to live our own way. The end results are not the same. Self-discipline produces spiritual fruit from the beginning. God's discipline produces spiritual fruit only after a lost season of rebellion, and only if our brother or sister accepts His discipline. Therefore, if we discipline ourselves, rather than risking God's discipline, it results in much more fruit with much less waste. The problem is, it usually takes God's discipline to teach us to be self-disciplined. Hmmm...God

is our Father and just like He teaches us through the Biblical roles of parents and families, the primary purpose of parental discipline is to teach immature children to become self-disciplined in order to avoid God's discipline for sin. There is an old adage that says, "Discipline yourself or God will do it for you."

God tells us in His Word how we are to conduct ourselves. If we heed His instruction, we will miss the discomfort of the Lord's discipline. And, as Kerry's words remind us, we will produce more fruit because we wasted less time undergoing the Lord's discipline brought on by our rebellion. Rebellion is sin and brings judgment and the Lord's discipline (Romans 13:2).

I want to avoid bringing the Lord's judgment and discipline into my life. Don't you? Obedience and self-discipline bring that freedom. When we become God's children by trusting in Jesus Christ, we are given His Holy Spirit. As we allow Holy Spirit to control our lives, He produces His fruit in us. Self-control (self-discipline) is a part of His fruit (Galatians 5:22-25). We must discipline ourselves to be obedient to the Lord.

Surgery Day, Good Enough?... Tuesday, August 13, 2013

Today is surgery day. I am ready and looking forward to it. Surgery is one more step closer to the finish line. Besides that, the thought of the extra rest and refreshment, following surgery, is very appealing. I have to be at the hospital early. I am scheduled to have the dye injected to determine the closest draining lymph node. Then, I will have a procedure where they insert wires into the tissue, pinpointing the exact spots where the surgeon needs to cut and remove tissue. Finally, I am scheduled for the actual surgery. Between the surgery and the other procedures, it will be an all-day affair.

I have surgery today and my Dad has hernia surgery tomorrow. My Dad is a worker and it is difficult for him to slow down to take time to heal.

Yesterday was incredibly touching for me. Many of my customers and coworkers wished me well and let me know they would miss me while I was out recovering. After work, I went to the hospital for the blood counts to be checked, making certain the surgery was a "Go" for today. The counts were all satisfactory with the exception of my white blood cell count, which was a bit low. Dr. Limpert said if I were a regular patient she would not be sure about proceeding with the surgery, but since we knew chemo caused the low white count, she was positive about proceeding, as long as I was. She knew without asking my answer was: "Let's do it!"

    I arrived at the lab and quietly stepped in. Charity was out of sight drawing blood on another patient and Melinda was working at the counter. As she turned and saw me, she let out a squeal and ran over to hug me. She said God knew how much she needed to see me today. She had just dealt with a very difficult situation over the weekend and had a heavy heart. As we hugged, tears began to flow down her cheeks as she told me about it. I did my best to comfort her and prayed over her for the Lord's comfort. As soon as Charity was done with her patient, I got a big hug from her. She, Melinda, and I all joined hands before I left because they wanted to pray over me before my surgery. What precious ladies those two are. When Melinda finished praying, I offered a prayer of my own for the two of them. What a wonderful time that was. I am pleased that I will get to see them every three months when I go back for checkups.

    After I left the lab, I had to make a stop at Dr. Gill's office to see about getting the water pill prescription refilled. As I talked with Stephanie about it, Katrina came out of the back and saw me. She came running for a quick hug before she went to finish the task at hand and then came for another before I left. I would have loved to walk the whole office and transfusion area to see all my new friends, but had an appointment with Dr. Limpert, so it was not feasible today. Another day, I will.

    After dinner, I shortened Ellie Mae's toenails and rested a bit while Mom brushed her. After she was sufficiently brushed, I gave her a bath. I may not have felt up to it for a few days after surgery, and she was in need, so a bath last night was in order. I did not have energy for anything else, so I rested. When I sit down, the fatigue is often so strong that my body shuts down.

    But, after the sleep of last night, I am chipper enough to share with you this morning before heading to the hospital. As I read this morning, I came upon these verses.

> But if we walk in the light, as He is in the light, we have fellowship with one another, and the blood of Jesus, His Son, purifies us from all sin. If we claim to be without sin, we deceive ourselves and the truth is not in us. If we confess our sins, He is faithful and just and will forgive us our sins and purify us from all unrighteousness. If

we claim we have not sinned, we make Him out to be a liar and His Word has no place in our lives. (I John 1:7-10)

To "walk in the light" means we must believe and act on the truth. We are deceiving ourselves if we think we are without sin. The truth is we are all sinners. Therefore, we are not "good enough" to be in the presence of a righteous and holy God. You must come to Him in repentance (sorrow over your sin with a desire to turn from it) and faith (trusting Jesus to be the one to pay the debt you owe because of your sin).

It is Jesus' blood and death that cleanses us from sin as we come to Him in repentance. If we come to Him confessing, He is faithful and just to cleanse and purify us. Oh! That is good news! God loves us so much that He made a way for us through the sacrifice of His Son, Jesus. Our faith and trust are to be in Jesus. He is the only one "good enough." Neither you nor I are. God wants to save us from the ultimate consequence of our sin which is death, spiritual death (Romans 6:23). He gives us the gift of eternal life when we confess and put our faith and trust in Jesus' death on the cross, not when we work real hard and try to be "good enough" on our own.

> That if you confess with your mouth, "Jesus is Lord," and believe in your heart that God raised him from the dead, you will be saved. (Romans 10:9)

Only through Jesus can we can be saved from the ultimate consequence of our sin, go to heaven, and gain eternal life. Who do you trust to get you into heaven? If you haven't trusted Jesus to be your Lord and Savior, I encourage you to do it today. If you have accepted Jesus as your Lord, Savior and Master thank Him for the great sacrifice and great price He paid. He is worthy of all our gratitude, love and praise.

Surgery Day, Wonderful Hmmms ... Wednesday, August 14, 2013

Good morning. It is the beginning of my first official day of feeling like I can rest and refresh. And, guess what? I am up just as early as I am most other days. It is 4 a.m. Mom and Dad are getting ready to go to the hospital for Dad's hernia surgery. I would love to go with them, but I am not sure I am up to it. Besides that, I know they would not let me go anyway. I appreciate the prayers on behalf of my Dad for his surgery today and for my Mom as she ends up as nurse-maid to both of us.

The Lord answered prayers for me with a good surgery day. Dr. Limpert told my parents the surgery went well. She told them that she removed two lymph nodes from under my arm. I am curious as to why she took out two lymph nodes. That will be on my list of questions to ask at my next appointment. The pathology report on all the tissue removed should be back in approximately five business days. Tissue was removed from the tumor site, as well as the location of the unidentified spot in the breast.

Before surgery, when I talked with Dr. Limpert, she told me that she would have to take a bit more tissue than originally thought because the chemo had caused the two titanium clips to move further apart than they were at the time of the biopsy and ultrasound. She said it was necessary to take out the tissue between the two spots and not just the spots marked by the clips. But, the good news is, she said it was still not enough tissue that I should notice a difference. I have two incisions, one under the front part of the armpit where the lymph nodes were removed and the other is at the tumor site. Both are about an inch and a half long. The neat thing is there are no stitches. The incisions are glued together. I speculate that will make smaller scars. It also means no aggravating prickly sticking from the ends of stitches under the armpit. And, there are no bandages over the incisions. Best of all, I can bathe today. How great is that!

I am definitely sore this morning, both where the incisions are and where they injected the dye to determine the closest draining lymph nodes. I am also sore where they inserted the guide wires. The injection of the dye was yesterday's most painful part. It felt like being stung by a wasp. That was even after the nurse anesthetized it. The test to determine where the closest draining lymph nodes were was the first procedure of the day. After that was finished, they wheeled me over to get the guide wires put in. The guide wires were two thin little wires that went from several inches outside the skin, all the way down to where the titanium clips were. It gave Dr. Limpert the exact spots to work from. After that, I was wheeled over to the surgical holding room to wait surgery time. The surgery lasted just over an hour.

The day at the hospital was positively an all-day affair for my parents and me. We did not get home until around 7 p.m. That included a stop at the pharmacy to get prescriptions. Well, along with a pain killer, Dr. Limpert prescribed a Z-pack (antibiotic) to get rid of the rest of the sinus infection.

So far, I have not needed to take any of the pain killers. I don't like taking anything I do not have to take and am generally good at tolerating pain. Hmmm... pain, which reminds me of one of my favorite promises given by the Lord.

> He will wipe every tear from their eyes. There will be no more death or mourning or crying or pain, for the old order of things has passed away. (Revelation 21:4)

What a great promise. I enjoy thinking about what that day will be like. That day will come when God has finally dealt with Satan and his demons permanently, and all God's children are gathered to Him. He will be dwelling with us in His fullness. Wow! That is a mind boggling thought. Can you imagine what it will be like as God Himself is with us in the entirety of His glory? I can't, but I surely enjoy thinking about it. Because He will be dwelling with us in the fullness of His glory, we will have no need for the sun. God, himself, is light. (Revelation 21:23).

When one makes Jesus Savior, Lord and Master of their life, their name is written in the Lamb's book of life and they are sealed with His Holy Spirit. Nothing can pluck them from God's hand at that point. Only those whose names are written in the Lamb's book of life will enter the place that God has prepared for His children (Revelation 21:2).

I am so grateful that Jesus' purity and righteousness has been credited to me. Otherwise, I would not be able to enter God's city, heaven, and His glorious presence. My encouragement to you is to read all of Revelation 21. It gives a marvelous description of the Christian's eternal home. My mind cannot completely comprehend it. But, it sure is a joy to imagine. Join me in contemplating the things the Lord has in store for those who love Him and accept Jesus as their Savior.

I am grateful for all the prayers that have been lifted on my behalf. I am incredibly blessed to have so many as part of my life and circle of friends and family.

Chapter 10

Days of Recovery

August 15, 2013 – September 3, 2013

Changing Seasons... Thursday, August 15, 2013

Hello. Here it is, 4 a.m. and I am again awake. The mind knows I have time off and the ability to sleep in but the body doesn't. Oh, well. I like spending this early morning time with you and the Lord. The rest of the house is quiet and no one else is up moving which makes it easier to focus. Ellie Mae hasn't even raised her head or turned over. She is so good to know not to bother me in this time. I am sure after our time together I will lie back down and gain more rest and sleep.

Dad's surgery went well. Praise the Lord! I am feeling well, all things considered. I am sore, but that is to be expected. I felt up to going to church and then visiting a friend in the hospital. And, I have not taken any pain pills. Praise the Lord! The incision under the arm causes more annoyance simply because the arm continually moves over it. But, the area where the dye was injected has more pain than the incision areas. I looked at it last night and it looks almost like a rash may be developing. The area still stings a lot when water hits it or even when I lightly rub my hand over it.

I talked with the Dr. Limpert and heard from Dr. Gill as well concerning the lymph nodes. Removing two nodes is pretty standard procedure. Often, more than one lymph node is a sentinel node and the first to be affected by anything coming from the breast. If those two are clear, which I believe they are, then the rest would also be clear.

I noticed one new effect from the surgery. The majority of the back of my upper arm and the portion of the armpit just above the incision are numb. I noticed it last night, but assumed it just had not lost the numbness from being deadened at the time of surgery. I talked with the doctor's office about that, too. It is also normal. A nerve was cut when the lymph nodes were removed which is causing the lack of feeling. In time, the feeling should return.

"He changes times and seasons; He sets up kings and deposes them." (Daniel 2:21a). This verse reminds me that the Lord is in charge of the seasons of our lives. None of us ever want to go through the dreary, harsh and bitter winter seasons of life when the world seems to be treating us so coldly. But those seasons of life are just as much a part of God's overall plan for us as the completely bright, warm and sunny ones. He knows just exactly when to allow the storms and winters in our lives to teach us, grow us, and draw us nearer to Himself. That in turn, brings about the most awesome springs and summers in our lives. However, we must be patient, trusting the Lord as we wait for the change of seasons in our lives. Just as the seasons must run their course on the earth, so must the seasons of our lives run their course. We cannot hurry them any more than we can hurry spring time when we are in the dead of winter.

If God can set up kings and bring them down again, don't you think He can change your travail of life and bring you back up again after one of those difficult seasons? Seek Him for whatever He desires to teach you in difficult seasons and trust Him to do all He has planned for you. As you do so, the spring He planned for you will be even better than you can imagine. After this season of storms, I can hardly wait to see the springtime He has planned for me.

Building up or Tearing Down?.... Friday, August 16, 2013

Good Morning, dear friends. I slept longer last night than usual. I was not awake at my customary 4 a.m. Yea! Maybe my body is beginning to recognize it has a little time off from work and does not have to awaken so early.

I did quite a bit of resting again yesterday along with starting to sort through the mountain of papers that had accumulated on my computer table. While going through treatments and working, the time, energy and willingness to sort, file and deal with them was not there, so now is a great time to catch up on that chore and the other lighter duties that have been neglected. I felt up to a walk yesterday evening. Mom, Ellie Mae and I walked the neighborhood together. If Mom had not gone with me, I am not sure I would have gone. I needed the extra encouragement of her being with me. The walk was slower than in the past and I could tell my stamina was nowhere near what it was even a few weeks ago, but, now that the chemo is over, I can hopefully start rebuilding the energy level and muscle tone.

I am not sure what is on today's agenda except more work organizing. It is a strange feeling not to have a regimented schedule of work and treatments to follow. Strange and Wonderful! I know I will get back to that in a few weeks when radiation treatments start along with work, but I will enjoy the reprieve while it lasts. I think I will try to work in another walk today. I have to be careful not to do too much with the upper body, so walking is the perfect exercise. Dr. Limpert said that reaching over my head may be difficult for a while, but I have been able to reach over my head with no problems. Praise the Lord! I can feel a bit of soreness when I do, but not enough that it would stop me from doing it. I still have not needed any pain pills. Pain pills often carry undesired side effects. I will be grateful to miss out on those.

As I spent time with God's Word this morning, the Lord highlighted several thoughts and ideas, but this verse really started me to hmmm.

> Do not let any unwholesome talk come out of your mouths, but only what is helpful for building others up according to their needs, that it may benefit those who listen. (Ephesians 4:29)

We must be careful what we speak about and to others. Even if what we are saying is true, we must think before we speak it and ask ourselves, and the Lord, if what we are about to say is helpful in building others up or if it will tear them down. We all have a great need for encouragement. Unfortunately, very few of us give it to others in great measure. It is natural for our fleshly natures to focus on the negatives and not the positives. And, if we allow our flesh to lead, we will speak discouraging words to others instead of the encouraging ones that Holy Spirit would have us speak.

Holy Spirit always speaks the truth in love. He encourages, corrects, and teaches truth and so much more. As He does, it is always done in a way that lifts us, reminding us of His great love for us. When Satan speaks and puts thoughts into our head, they are discouraging, putting and tearing us down. Hmmm…we are to be conformed to the image of Jesus by His Holy Spirit. Therefore, our words must be spoken in love, encouraging, lifting and beneficial in building others up. When our words tear another down, bringing hurt and discouragement we are not being like Jesus, but like the devil.

Hmmm...think about your words. Are they spoken in love? Are they encouraging? Are they truthful? Is it on the strengths in others or on their weaknesses? The old adage, that I am sure most of your mothers have taught you, is a pretty good rule of thumb. "If you don't have anything nice to say, don't say anything at all." It is better to remain silent than to speak hurtful words, but it is better yet to speak encouragement to one another.

Well, that is one of the things the Lord had me hmmm about this morning. If you know you have not been using your words the way the Lord would have you to, ask His forgiveness. He is faithful to forgive as you confess it to Him and repent. Then ask Him to guide you into His truth, putting His Words in your mouth.

A Blonde Ellie Mae, Mighty Warriors, Victory....
Saturday August 17, 2013

Hi there. The weather has been absolutely fabulous the last few days. And, I am off work to enjoy it. Ellie Mae and I took another walk last evening. We did the whole neighborhood again. I felt stronger. I like that feeling a lot. Praise the Lord! Ellie Mae and I even got to meet some more neighbors as their chocolate lab, Sanford, ran to greet us. Ellie Mae was thrilled to meet a new four-legged neighbor. She watches each one she sees with great intensity in hopes of a meeting. The neighbor was none too thrilled Sanford did not listen when he told him to stop, but it gave the neighbor and me the ability to meet and a thrill to Ellie Mae's day.

While we are speaking of Ellie Mae, I thought you all might enjoy hearing about the picture of her in all her glory. Many of you have asked me or mentioned to me about wearing a wig when my hair was all gone. Well, once you see the picture you will know why I never did. Ellie Mae was willing to share her scarves and bandanas with me, but not the wig. I thought you all would gain a chuckle from her and the wig. Even though I never wore the wig, several friends and I have had great fun with it. Laughter truly is wonderful medicine.

Yesterday was spent scheduling doctor's appointments. I have a post-op appointments with Dr. Limpert and Dr. Gill and I also had to make an appointment with the radiologist to prepare for the radiation treatments.

The Lord reminded me that we are in a great spiritual battle as we walk this earth. Many are unaware of the battle that rages for our very lives and souls. Just as much as the Lord and His angels desire to save and protect us, drawing us to Jesus, Satan and his demons want to destroy us, tearing us as far away from the Lord as possible. The Lord calls Christians to be mighty warriors in this battle. Just as He called Gideon, who was timid and fearful to be a mighty warrior, so He calls us (Judges 6:12).

Hmmm...so what gives a Christians the ability to be a mighty warrior in the Lord's army? The Lord is with them. He is not only with them but His Holy Spirit is in them. Jesus promised in John 14:16-17 that His Holy Spirit would live in those who believed in Him, giving them the Lord's mind and heart. When we have faith in Jesus, we have Him, His mind and His heart, giving us His peace, His love, His wisdom, His strength, His power, and His authority. Therefore, the things Jesus did, we will do.

> I tell you the truth, anyone who has faith in me will do what I have been doing. He will do even greater things than these, because I am going to the Father. (John 14:12)

As God's children, we have nothing to fear. As a matter of fact, His Word constantly tells us not to fear nor let our hearts be troubled. Only our trust in and reliance on Him and His Spirit gives that ability. Only in obedience to Him will we have the ability to exercise His authority. The battle is not ours to fight as we want to. The battle is the Lord's and we are His warriors. As we submit and obey Him, He will bring the victory. So, if we are not being obedient, we cannot expect Him to bring the victory nor can we expect to walk in His power or authority (II Chronicles 13:12).

Where do you find yourself today? Are you being obedient to the Lord? The Lord is always true to His Word and promises. Dear friends, I want success and the victory, don't you? Seek the Lord and His instruction, dear friends. Trust His promises. The road to His victory is a road well worth traveling.

He is Happy! ..... Monday, August 19, 2013

Hello again. It is good to be with you. I have had a headache most of the day, possibly because I did not sleep well. The neuropathy in my feet and ankles was bothering me. My joints ached, especially the knees. I am sure that is a chemo side effect, too. And I had some pains shoot down my arm. I suspect that is referred pain from the surgery. With all that said, I am still in pretty good shape for the shape I am in. The incisions seem to be healing well. That is a praise! I can do most of the things I want to do. Fortunately, most things I want to do right now do not involve lifting. I have lifting restrictions for the time being. I would surely hate to have an incision break open. The one under the arm gives me the most pain, but the surgeon gave me fair warning that would be the case. That is enough about the symptoms and side effects of the day. I have much happier thoughts to share with you.

When you think of God, do you think of Him as happy? How do you think of Him? Is it angry and stern? Is it merry and joyful? Close your eyes and picture Him in your mind's eye. Is He smiling or is He frowning? There is a verse that refers to "the blessed God." (I Timothy 1:11). Have you ever wondered what that means? In the original language, the word *blessed* in this context, means happy. Happy is a part of who He is. Hmmm that thought for a minute. God is pleased to give His kingdom to His children (Luke 12:32) and He takes great delight in them and rejoices over them with singing (Zephaniah 3:17).

Doesn't that sound like a Father who is happy, taking great joy in His children? It is important for us to realize that happy and joyful are an important part of who God is in His fullness. Absolutely, He has anger and indignation over sin. He knows the pain and destruction it brings.

Think back to when I asked you to close your eyes, imagining God. Was the picture you envisioned a true representation or a misconception of God's true nature? If you envisioned Him happy, great. Rejoice! If you envisioned Him frowning and stern, I challenge you to change the image you have in your mind. You will be glad you did.

Patient, Slow Breath... Tuesday, August 20, 2013

Good morning. Yesterday, I continued to work, sorting, organizing, and cleaning up my living quarters. I still have more to go through, but made a lot of progress. It will be good to have all that done before I have to go back to work. I did not leave the house yesterday and it was wonderful! I rarely have that pleasure.

Today, I have my first radiologist's appointment. It is the initial appointment to start preparing for my daily radiation treatments. I am curious to see what they will do. This is a new chapter in the cancer treatments. I will get to meet a whole new group of people. Even though I miss all the folks I love so much at St. Luke's, it will be fun to get to know a new group of folks.

I read a verse in Exodus that reminded me of more of God's attributes. We must truly know God to worship Him in truth. If we do not know Him by knowing His attributes, how can we worship Him in truth?

> The Lord, the compassionate and gracious God, slow to anger, abounding in love and faithfulness... (Exodus 34:6b)

This verse tells us He is compassionate, gracious, full of love, and faithfulness. The attribute that I hmmm this morning is patience. This character quality causes Him to be slow to anger. That fact of being slow to anger shows compassion, mercy, and grace given in patience. As human kind, we have snubbed, disobeyed, disrespected, rejected and showed disdain for God. We have lied to, hated, disbelieved, and turned our backs on Him. *Slow to anger* can also be translated as longsuffering. Hmmm... what it means in the original language is patient and slow of breath.

Many people see God not only as not happy, but as huffing with anger most of the time. Nothing could be further from the truth. How does a mother not lose her patience with a child who is throwing a temper tantrum? The same reason God is slow to anger with us; it is *love*. He loves us, even more than a mother loves her child. He wants His very best for us. He is willing to continue in patience, encouraging us, and drawing us to Himself that He might continue to teach us His truth and give us His salvation if we will accept it.

If the child continues to have a fit, he will eventually evoke anger in the mother and suffer discipline and consequences. The same is true with God. However, He remains patient with us much longer (II Peter 3:9). He desires for each and every one of us to come to repentance and not have to perish, suffering eternal death and separation from Him.

God is slow to anger because His desire is for us to be with Him, happy, and blessed. God's kind of happiness is permanent, not fleeting like the world's happiness. It is dependent on Him alone and not on our circumstances. I find myself thanking the Lord for being who He is and for being happy, loving, compassionate, gracious, faithful and patient with me.

No Sign of Cancer… Tuesday, August 20, 2013

Hello, dear friends. I am writing you this evening instead of in the morning because I have good news to share and did not want to wait till tomorrow. I got a call from the surgeon, Dr. Limpert, today. The pathology reports show no sign of cancer. Praise the Lord! He has answered my prayers and those of my prayer warriors.

> I will extol the Lord at all times; His praise will always be on my lips. My soul will boast in the Lord; let the afflicted hear and rejoice. Glorify the Lord with me; let us exalt His name together. I sought the Lord, and He answered me; He delivered me from all my fears. (Psalm 34:1-4)

The appointment with the radiologist went well. It was just a, "get to know you and give you a little bit of an idea what to expect" type of visit. I like the radiology doctor. He seems really nice and knowledgeable. He explained all the research on why they do radiation even though there are no visible signs of cancer and answered the questions I had. He also said my incisions looked great, especially for only being a week out from surgery.

I have another appointment next week. Then, he will do all the measuring and calculations in preparation for the start of radiation treatments, which will last for six and a half weeks, five days a week, for a total of thirty-three treatments. They are given Monday through Friday. The reason for radiation, even though I have no signs of cancer, is insurance. They want to make sure they kill any possible little hair-like roots that might be left and were undetectable at the time of surgery. Radiation decreases the likelihood of any recurrence of the cancer in the future.

He reiterated the fact that radiation should be a cake walk compared to all I have already been through. I am glad to end with radiation rather than chemo. This way, I know the worst is behind me. The only two side effects that I am likely to experience are skin irritation and fatigue. He said fatigue caused by radiation was much less than with chemo. Praise the Lord! I am ready to have my old "spit and vinegar" back.

My surgeon's appointment got moved to next week because the doctor had to do another surgery, putting a port in. I speculate that person is dealing with an aggressive cancer because of the rush to get the port in. I was glad to move my appointment to accommodate them. Somebody probably had to change theirs for me when I was first diagnosed. Next Monday and Tuesday, I will have to see all three doctors, surgeon, oncologist and radiologist. I am glad to be off work, healing from surgery. Otherwise, I would have had a difficult time trying to get all the appointments worked in around my work schedule.

I close with thanksgiving in my heart this evening. God is good all the time and worthy of our praise.

> Enter His gates with Thanksgiving and His courts with Praise; give thanks to Him and praise His name. For the Lord is good and His love endures forever. (Psalm 100:4-5)

Unshakeable Fortress... Thursday, August 22, 2013

Hmmm... have you ever noticed when we get good news, as I did with the pathology reports, or as great things happen we have been waiting and praying for that Satan does his best to immediately shake the joy from our hearts and refocus our minds on other things that are not going well? He does not want us rejoicing in the good things God has done and is doing in our lives. He immediately wants to refocus our minds on things that are not going as planned.

For me, the devil's attack and ploy to divert my heart from rejoicing in all that God had done, and is doing for me, came with new legal hurdles and obstacles I have to jump over and weave my way through to get past all the financial mess caused by the bankruptcy and the need to short sale the home my husband and I lived in. The difficulties were compounded by the fact that a car, with the agreed upon options and price, which the court agreed to allow me to purchase, seems to be illusive thus far. The salesman is looking for one, fitting the description we had agreed upon a few months back. I had to take the need for a new car, along with a purchase price and details, to the courts to gain their approval before I was allowed to purchase the car, elongating the time between deciding on a vehicle and the purchase date.

Satan also knows when we are tired; we are easier targets for him to topple. Even though I am not working and recovering from surgery, I am far from full strength and energy. He knows it and is hitting me hard at this point. If I were to let all Satan is hitting me with divert my focus from the Lord, I would be shaken. I would be fearful, worried, and angry. The

Lord knew the frustrations of my circumstances and the enemy's attack and lovingly reminded me this morning that my security is in Him, no matter the storms, frustrations, and uncertainty around me. These are the verses He used to comfort my heart.

> Find rest, O my soul, in God alone; my hope comes from Him. He alone is my rock and my salvation; He is my fortress, I will not be shaken. (Psalm 62:5-6)

As I look closely at these verses, I am reminded that my soul, my mind, will, and emotions, find their rest and peace only as I subject them to the Lord's truth. He promises to supply all my needs and give me His wisdom. Even as I write to you, He reminds me that He always has and always will, as I place my trust in Him. My hope and expectation, not only for this moment in time, but for eternity is to be in Him. Without Him, I have no hope. There is no one else in this world that is the unshakeable rock, solid and completely firm. The Lord alone is.

Think of a house in the tremors of an earthquake. The house that has a solid and firm foundation stands secure through the tremors while the house whose foundation is not firm crumbles when tremors come. So it is with us and the storms of life. When we make Him our foundation, we will stand firm because our foundation is firm.

Another great comfort the Lord gave me as I studied and meditated on this verse is the fact that He is my *fortress*. As I looked at the original meaning, I found it means, secure height, retreat, stronghold, and refuge. Hmmm... as I place myself in Him, He gives me refuge as the storms of life rage around me.

As I hmmm and think about a fortress meaning also that it has a secure height. The Lord knows that we will be hit with storms in this life, but wants to teach us to walk above them, with Him, at a secure height. We can go *through* the storms of life, but if we allow Him, He will teach us to walk *above* them, rather than in them. He is still teaching me how to do this. I do not have it perfect, but I know the only way to do it is by placing complete trust in Him.

I hope you will take some time to hmmm on the Lord and His truths with me. If you are not currently in a storm of life, it will not be long before you hit one. Now is the time to place yourself in Him, making Him your foundation. Do you fully trust Him to be true to His Word? Or are you allowing the storms of this life to shake you? Trust Him and you will find rest for your soul and peace as you wait. Walk with Him above the storms that rage. The Lord alone is our only unshakeable fortress.

This morning's hmmm time did wonders for me. It was exactly what I needed today. I was so very glad to have you with me.

Asking and Having ... Friday, August 23, 2013

Hi there! It is me again. Challenges are a normal part of everyday life. Some are more difficult to deal with than others. Some challenges are so minor, we only think about them once as we deal with them. Sometimes they are bigger and take more time to overcome. The Lord has blessed me, reminded me of His promises, and gave me comfort as I felt the frustration of the continued stream of problems. In time, these difficulties and trials will pass. Until then, I trust the Lord with them.

Hmmm... the Lord wants us to bring and lay our problems and difficulties before Him. He knows the answers we need and can give the help, wisdom, strength, comfort for each challenge we face in life. "Let us then approach the throne of grace with confidence, so that we may receive mercy and find grace to help us in our time of need." (Hebrews 4:16). What does it mean to approach Him with confidence? It means, as we boldly lay our requests and concerns before Him, we are to do so with the expectation He will answer. Because He loves us, He wants His best for us. We must believe He is working for, through and in us.

> But when he asks, he must believe and not doubt, because he who doubts is like a wave of the sea, blown and tossed by the wind. That man should not think he will receive anything from the Lord; he is a double-minded man, unstable in all he does. (James 1:6-8)

Our belief and trust in the Lord is important. It is the key to opening the door to the answers, help, wisdom, strength, comfort, and peace He has for us.

If you do not ask, you do not have (James 4:2b). God could not make it any plainer than that. He has promised if we will come to Him and ask with belief that He will give it. If we look a little deeper, we will see that this verse tells us our prayer causes things to happen that would not otherwise happen. Our prayer causes action. Prayer is a magnificent privilege, given by a sovereign God. Our prayers change things. God gives us the opportunity to open the door for Him to work in marvelous ways. He desires to do wondrous things and waits for us to ask. If the things we ask for are in His will, He gives us a great promise. "You may ask Me for anything in My name, and I will do it." (John 4:14). So, ask Him. Believe Him for it!

Thanksgiving and More! ... Saturday, August 24, 2013

Good Morning. I am awake early this morning. The body still wants to wake up as if I were going to work. I am grateful for a quiet time with no noise in the house and no distractions. Well, there is a little noise. Ellie Mae is in her bed beside me, snoring and softly yipping, as she dreams. I often wonder what she is dreaming as her feet move as if running and she softly yips.

Yesterday was a good day. I shared with you the difficulties of finding the right vehicle to satisfy the requirements of the court and fitting what I desired. Well, the Lord solved that problem for me. He found a car of the right kind and color, the right year, and with all the options I had agreed to and wanted. However, this one had more options than I had wanted to pay for when the salesman and I originally agreed upon a price for the car, which the court needed in order to give me approval to purchase. But, guess what! This car, which has more options than originally agreed upon, will cost me $20 less than the car originally planned, once all the incentives and rebates are applied. That is God! He often gives me much more than I imagine. Hmmm... more than I imagine.

> Now to him who is able to do immeasurably more than all we ask or imagine, according to His power that is at work within us. (Ephesians 3:20)

If you recall, I shared with you concerning prayer and confidently asking the Lord to work on our behalf. Well, I laid the car situation before Him, and not only did He take care of it, He did more than I imagined or even asked. I only asked for Him to find the right car, fitting the description initially agreed upon, preferably without a delivery cost. He provided all that plus He gave me more car for less money. And, through all these months, waiting on the court system to rule, allowing me to purchase the car, He kept my current vehicle running like a top, since December, even though it needed four thousand dollars in repairs. To top it all off, the court agreed to allow me to keep my tax refund check to use for taxes and license!

I did not think the process would take this long, nor would I have thought a vehicle that needed as much work as mine could hold out this long without needing me to spend some money to keep it running. I asked the Lord to keep it running and without me having to put money in it. He answered. Doing more than we ask or imagine is God's specialty. But, we must ask. If we trust Him, we will not be anxious or worried about the things we are laying before Him.

> Do not be anxious about anything, but in everything, by prayer and petition, with thanksgiving, present your requests to God. (Philippians 4:6)

We are not to be anxious concerning our requests of the Lord, but we are to lay them before Him with thanksgiving. Not only are we to thank Him for all the ways He is and has worked in and through our life, but I believe this verse is encouraging us to do something more. It is encouraging us to thank Him *in advance* for all He will do. We are to thank Him even before we see His hand at work. As we do this, we show Him that we trust Him and believe He will do the things He has promised.

The Lord wants to do more for us than we can ask or imagine. Do you believe He can? Do you believe He will? The Lord desires a grateful heart and one that trusts Him and believes Him for great and mighty things. He is waiting for us to ask in faith and with thanksgiving.

Wisdom and Wise Counsel... Monday, August 26, 2013

Hi there. I am glad I am not going back to work yet. It will be nice to get another week of rest.

I have doctor appointments tomorrow. I have a few questions that I look forward to getting the answers to, especially concerning the pain down the back of my upper arm. It is worse now than it was right after the surgery. I am sure it has to do with the nerves damaged when the lymph nodes were removed. It is just really annoying. When I run my hand down the skin on the back of the arm, it feels much like your skin does when touched, after you have burned it on the hot stove or pan. My niece also mentioned that I should ask, since I had lymph nodes removed on that arm, if I should abstain from having blood pressure taken on that arm or blood drawn from that arm because of the risk of lymph edema. That is new information to me and I will ask.

It is always good to seek the wise counsel of your doctors when desiring to take the best care your body. Hmmm... wise counsel. There are many times in life when it is needful to seek wise counsel. We deal with unnecessary frustration, consequences, and possible failure when we don't.

"Plans fail for lack of counsel, but with many advisers they succeed." (Proverbs 15:22). I am reminded of how I heeded the counsel of the doctors in treating cancer and the wise counsel to deepen my relationship with Lord. If I had not paid attention to the counsel of the doctors, my physical body would not be healing. If I had not heeded Dr. Porter's wise counsel, I would not have the same walk with the Lord I am experiencing today.

It is all too easy for us to think we are smart enough to make decisions without the help of wise counselors in our lives. As I look back over my life, I can see many times where I refused to seek the wisdom of one who had more experience and knowledge than me. I suffered the consequences of making wrong decisions based on my limited knowledge.

When we receive Jesus as Lord and Savior, we are given Holy Spirit, who is the Spirit of wisdom and revelation (Ephesians 1:17b). So, how do we receive the wisdom the Lord has promised? Ask and believe Him for it.

> If any of you lacks wisdom, he should ask God, who gives generously to all without finding fault, and it will be given to him. But when he asks, he must believe and not doubt, because he who doubts is like a wave of the sea, blown and tossed by the wind. That man should not think he will receive anything from the Lord; he is a double-minded man, unstable in all he does. (James 1:5-8)

The Lord makes His wisdom readily available to His children if only they will ask and believe. The Lord's wisdom is pure wisdom and can be trusted. His wisdom is full of great benefits (James 3:17). I do not want to miss any of the benefits He has for my life. Do you?

Kimberly McGary

Lip Service or True Trust? ... Tuesday, August 27, 2013

Good morning. As Ellie Mae and I were out, we saw Elmer, one of our neighbors picking his garden. He is feeling sad and lonely. His Boxer, Jenny, died a week ago. She was his shadow and he is missing her greatly. I hoped Ellie Mae and I could bring at least a small smile to his day. While we were there, he filled my shirt tail full of tomatoes from his garden. Yum! There is nothing like homegrown vegetables, tomatoes especially. I am missing my garden this year. I normally did about a 900 square foot vegetable garden. Even if I still lived in the country, I would not have had the energy to have worked a garden this summer. As I think about the lack of energy and my great desire to have my old "spit and vinegar" back, I am reminded of some of the things Dr. Gill and Dr. Limpet told me. Dr. Limpert said it will take about six months for me to begin to feel like I am starting the process of feeling better and Dr. Gill told me it normally takes about a year after completing chemo to be back to feeling normal. Positively, more patience is required.

When I saw Dr. Gill, I asked her about the side effects I was still experiencing and the fact that I now have more joint pain. She reminded me that I was no longer on the heavy duty steroids they were giving me each week. They were responsible for helping me not feel the effects of the chemo as strongly. I had not thought of that. My mind was thinking, "Okay, the chemo is over, so I should at least be feeling some better as each week passes." I did not expect to feel worse some days after finishing chemo than I did during it. Grrr...the exercise of more patience is needed again. I don't have it in myself. He is gracious and continues to provide it for me as I trust Him.

I found out yesterday that not only did they remove two sentinel lymph nodes during surgery, which is what I was originally told, but a total of seven lymph nodes. There were six very small nodes in the tissue surrounding one of the sentinel nodes that was removed. From what Dr. Limpert and Dr. Gill both said, I should not have blood pressure taken, shots given, or blood drawn from that arm any longer. I also need to be careful not to allow any trauma, cuts, scratches, sun burn, or even bug bites, if possible, to that arm. Wow, what an obnoxious thought that is. My risk of lymph edema is statistically small, only five percent. But, Dr. Limpert told me, once you have it; there is no medical cure for it. I was told even if I work in the garden I must wear a glove on that hand. Scratching it and getting infection would increase risk. Maybe not having my usual garden is not such a bad thing. I hated wearing gloves if I could help it. I will also no longer be picking up hay in the summer since I no longer have horses. I suspect that is a good thing, too. My arms were always scratched up after a day in the hay field.

The burning sensation on the back of my arm, as well as the numbness, should go away with time. At least most of it should. Dr. Limpert said it was the compression of the nerves, where the incision under the arm is, causing them. She also told me it was normal for the pain to have increased at this point in time. That is good to know.

The best news is, after talking to both doctors, they agreed I had the best possible results from the treatments I have been given. I had what is termed as a complete pathological response. Neither doctor could be any more pleased with the results. Me either. Praise the Lord! In my conversations with both of them, they talked with me about my faith. And, in their own way, asked me where my faith would have been if the results had been different. What if I had not gotten the results I wanted? I shared with them, either way, I would have been fine. Would it have been more difficult? Absolutely, but I am going to heaven one way or the other. Now or later. It is up to the Lord when that day is.

I am His and was created for His good pleasure and purpose (Philippians 2:13). I cannot just trust Him in the good times when I am getting everything I want and then not in the more difficult ones when things are not going my way. I told one of the doctors, "I did not want a divorce, bankruptcy, haggling with the court to buy a new car, losing my home, having to move back in with my parents, nor cancer. But, none of those things have shaken my trust and faith in the Lord and a different prognosis would not have changed it either." As a matter of fact, the Lord has used all the difficult challenges of these experiences to deepen my faith and trust in Him in a way that would not have happened otherwise. I have seen His hand at work protecting me, healing me, and providing for me in many ways. Just as patience is like a muscle you must use to strengthen, so are faith and trust. Hmmm… they must be used and not just given lip service.

My faith is not perfect yet, but the Lord continues to grow and complete it in me. With each step of obedience, I show Him I trust Him and believe His Word and promises. I am grateful He continues to teach me and grow me. The growth He brings as I walk through difficult times, trusting Him, is well worth the pain. I wouldn't ask for the difficulties, but I have learned to embrace them. I pray about them, ask others to pray, do as the Lord asks, and then wait for Him to work. That is all He expects from us. I know, it sounds easier than it is sometimes. But, oh, the benefits are well worth it.

Take a moment. Search your heart. Do you have faith in the Lord? Do your words and actions agree?

Humor, Lord's Continual Comfort ...
Wednesday, August 28, 2013

Hello again. I had my appointment with the radiologist yesterday to start the preparations needed before the first radiation treatment. For those of you wondering, no, I did not get tattooed. Praise the Lord! Those who were asking me about being tattooed so they could line up the radiation equipment had me praying that was no longer how it was done. Whew! Thank you, Jesus. I did not want tattoos. However, I have royal blue body paint drawn all over my torso. I can no longer wear a blouse that is open at the neck without it showing. I have lines and dots down both of my sides and all over my chest. You would think I had a child and had gone to sleep and gotten doodled on by one of their markers.

With radiation, I have another new set of rules with things to do and not do. I have to wear special deodorant under the one arm or none at all for the whole treatment time. I think "none at all" is not an option. I know those of you that see me often will be glad to hear that. I plan to shop today for the special deodorant. I have special lotion to use on the area that receives radiation. I am not to wear perfume on radiation days. I am to use mild soap without perfumes and can only use lotion at certain times on that particular area. I must be careful between now and the first treatment to try not to wash off the body paint. They will redo it as needed throughout the treatment time.

And here is the worst part. I cannot shave that armpit. And, it is summer. The nurse and I talked about options. She assured me the treatments were done in the dark and they would not be looking at my hairy armpit. They see so many hairy armpits, what would one more be anyway? Well, as the nurse and I talked about options, we both got so tickled that we were laughing as the doctor walked in while I was lying on the CT scan table. You could tell he was amazed to see me laughing so hard. We shared with him the discussion we were having, but he missed the humor in it.

As I think about humor and laughing, I realize I have not yet shared with you more of the fun I had with the wig I would never wear. Well, as you know, Ellie Mae got in on the wig wearing. The wig has graced lots of other heads and had many photo ops, too. A couple of weeks ago when Dr. Porter was in town, we were talking about the wig and I was able to sweet talk him into letting me put it on his head and take a picture. He made me do the same. One of our friends from church was rolling laughing right along with us. It all started when Dr. Porter reminded me he had never even seen me in the wig. That prompted me to bring it to show him. He had encouraged me at the beginning of the chemo treatments to get it, even though I told him at the time I would never wear it. And for the fun I have had with it, I am glad I got it. Monday, before I took the wig back to the hospital, Mom and Dad got in on the fun and I have photos of them in the wig, too. Then to add to the collection for the scrapbook, Dr. Gill very graciously let me snag a shot of her in the wig, too. (You make a beautiful blonde, Dr. Gill, especially with the brunette bangs!) Oh, what fun I have had with the wig I never wore. It brought so much laughter and good-natured humor to the loss of my hair. Before returning it to the cancer center, I set her, "the wig," on one of the forms and took a few pictures of her by herself and said my goodbyes. She will go on to grace another woman's head. Maybe with another woman, she will be able to get out and see the town a little more than she did with me.

As I had my appointment with Dr. Limpert, she apologized for having to change my appointment when she had to put a port in on another patient. I told her it was no big deal since she probably had to move somebody else when she put my port in. We scheduled my port to be put in the day following my first appointment with her, which was the day after my cancer diagnosis. As it turns out, Dr. Limpert was able to use my story and the success the Lord has given me to encourage this particular lady. She is dealing with the same kind of cancer. It is always comforting and encouraging, knowing another has been where you are and has been victorious.

Hmmm... the Bible is full of stories of folks who have gone through challenges, tragedies, temptations, and difficulties. I am grateful the Lord recorded them so that we might be encouraged as we read them and can relate them to our lives. God has given each one of us the ability to minister to another who has been through similar circumstances that we are going or have gone through. I am reminded of the many of you who have gone through what I am experiencing and have offered words of comfort and encouragement.

> Praise be to the God and Father of our Lord Jesus Christ, the Father of compassion and the God of all comfort, who comforts us in all our troubles, so that we can comfort those in any trouble with the comfort we ourselves have received from God. For just as the sufferings of Christ flow over into our lives, so also through Christ our comfort overflows. (II Corinthians 1:3-5)

When we allow ourselves to be under the control of Christ's Holy Spirit, we will overflow with the comfort of the Lord continually. That is not only good news for us, but it is also good news for the world around us. We live in a hurting world, desperately needing the comfort only God can give.

We are always blessed when we give to others what the Lord has given to us. I encourage you to receive all He is offering you, and then to share it with the world around you. God not only offers you Himself, but also His comfort, His peace, His love, His joy, and so much more. They are yours to receive and to share.

Well, those are the things the Lord has for me. I always enjoy the time spent digging into His Word and truth. I am supposed to pick up my new car this morning. They should be cleaning it up, checking it over, and topping off all the fluids. Thank you to all who have faithfully prayed over the car situation for me.

Road Trip…And a New Vehicle… Thursday, August 29, 2013

Hello friends. I have my new vehicle. It is packed and I am going on a road trip. If you don't hear from me for a couple of days, you will know I have skipped town and Wi-Fi was not readily available.

I want to take a trip before I have to start back to work and radiation treatments. Between work and treatments, I will be tethered to home base starting Monday.

Our needs... His Provision ... Monday, September 2, 2013

Hello there! I missed you! It was nice to get away for a few days, but it is always nice to get back home, too. Nothing sleeps as well as your own bed. I did not go too far on my road trip. I went to Cape Girardeau. That is where my Aunt Jean and Uncle Lee live. It was really nice to be able to spend some time with them. With all the craziness of my life recently, doing extra fun things has not been a possibility. This was a great treat. We mostly just hung out and visited. My Aunt Jean and I spent quite a bit of time just sitting on the swing under their carport and talking. Uncle Lee would join us, too. Sitting and talking was about all I had the energy for anyway.

I emailed Dr. Gill about the fatigue being worse than it was before surgery. She said it was a "chemo/surgery hangover" of sorts. I had hoped and imagined my energy would be better at this point and not worse. But, it is what it is. I will just have to be patient. As much as I wanted to make more trips and do more fun things while I was off recuperating, I did not have the energy. Hopefully, later in the year, with any vacation time I have left, I can make a trip or two. Hopefully, by then, I will be feeling better and all the treatments will be behind me.

I suffered nausea the last four days. I asked Dr. Gill about that, too. I took myself off the Omeprazole a couple of weeks ago. I guess I should have stayed with it. She told me to start taking that again and to lay off my vitamin packs for a month. Even before chemo, they could make me nauseous if I did not take them with food. Oh, well, the radiology oncologist told me that I needed to make sure not to take too much Vitamin C during radiation anyway. Excessive Vitamin C can decrease the effectiveness of the radiation.

The new vehicle is great. I enjoyed it the last few days. I don't think I told you what kind it is. It is a Chevy Equinox. I have a lot to learn to be able to use all the bells and whistles it has. I had my last vehicle, the Trailblazer, for over eleven years and never learned all the "do-dads and whatcha-ma-call-its" it had. With this one, I am determined to learn them all. It is almost like learning a new computer. I have my cell phone paired up with the Equinox and it automatically links as I get in. My phone book, music, and podcasts from the phone are in the car's computer when the phone is placed inside. Then, it is gone from the computer in the Equinox when the phone leaves the car. It has voice command, remote start, and lots of other goodies.

I gave the Equinox her first bath at the house already. It was a family affair. Mom and Dad joined in the car washing fun, too. It is always more fun to do things together. Besides that, I might not have made it through the job on my own. Between fatigue and the heat, it was almost too much for me. Even though I have fatigue and other symptoms, I am still doing very well, all things considered. I may not be able to do all I want, but that will come with time. When you go through seasons like this, you find it easier to realize the difference between what you truly need and what you just want. Hmmm… need. The Lord knows all my needs even before I ask for Him to provide (Matthew 6:8b).

During this time in my life, I prayed, asking the Lord for things I needed. I have seen the Lord provide for other needs I was not yet aware of. When I received the cancer diagnosis, the Lord already had the doctors I needed lined up for me. He knew before I did that I would need them. I did not have to search them out. He placed them before me and gave me His peace that they were the right doctors. And, they are the best. I could not have asked for more excellent care. He placed me in my parent's home, knowing that I would need extra help to walk this difficult road. When I moved, I did not know I would have to deal with cancer. The Lord had also placed the perfect support system of people around me for this time in my life. I did not know I was going to need them, but He did. I also saw His hand providing for my insurance needs before I knew I needed them, too. When I moved into my parent's home, I looked into renter's insurance to cover my things in case of loss or damage of any kind. Well, unbeknownst to my parents or me, there was already a rider on their insurance policy which covered my belongings. I did not even have to take out renter's insurance.

Then, as I sought insurance for the Equinox, I saw how the Lord had already provided. Because of the bankruptcy, my credit was ruined. And, because of the impending divorce I needed to drop my husband's name from the policy. These things would have increased my rate substantially. I knew my rate would increase because I had a new car, but I had not thought of the other reasons for rate hikes. The Lord knew in advance and gave me a great insurance agent who immediately went to work to see how he could save me money and cover me and the Equinox for less. He found a way and saved me around thirty five dollars a month. How great is that! Those are just a few of the ways I have seen the Lord providing in advance of my realization of the needs I've had. He is so good to me. I cannot thank Him or praise Him enough! God knows what we need and reminds us not to worry.

> And do not set your heart on what you will eat or drink; do not worry about it. For the pagan world runs after all such things, and your Father knows that you need them. But seek his kingdom, and these things will be given to you as well. (Luke 12:29-31)

That is a great promise. When we seek the Lord and His kingdom, He will give us all we need. We will not go hungry nor lack clothes to wear. Not only does His divine power provide for everything we need for life itself, but His power also provides everything we need to live a godly life as well (II Peter 1:3). We cannot live a godly life on our own. We need the help of His divine power. He gives it through Holy Spirit and His divine power provides for all we need for life and godliness.

Do you know Him as Savior and Lord? If so, do you take the time and energy to know Him on a personal and intimate level? My encouragement to you today is to take the time and the effort to know the Lord. He loves you. I have much more I would love to share, but am out of time and must prepare for work. It is my first day back after surgery.

He Understands Me.... Tuesday, September 3, 2013

Hey there. I am glad to be getting back into my regular routine of time with you and the Lord. I always enjoy sharing the things about the Lord. Hmmm... it is a great start or end to the day, no matter when I find the time to do it. Sometimes, I start my time with you before bed and quit when I can no longer hold my eyes open and then finish after the alarm goes off in the morning.

As I write, I am propped up in bed, looking down at Ellie Mae who is sprawled across her bed. Her whole body is on the bed, with the exception of her head, which is lying on the floor. All four legs are sticking up in the air because she is lying on her back. I have always wondered how that could be comfortable. She does it all the time, so it has to be comfortable for her. I get a smile just looking at her in that crazy position. The way her head is laying, her ears are both falling open on each side of her face and one upper lip is flapped back and hanging open. She is a comical sight. I am so glad the Lord gave me Ellie Mae. He understands my love for animals and gave me a special blessing when He placed her in my life. Not only does she provide love and comfort, but a little bit of humor as well.

I am praising the Lord because I made it all the way through my first day back at work. It was tiring and not easy, but I made it. Promptly, at the end of my workday tomorrow, I will head straight to the hospital for my first radiation treatment. In one way, I am looking forward to radiation because at the end of it and the surgery to remove the port, all the cancer treatments are done. In another way, I am not looking forward to it because I am required to take it five days a week. Besides that, fatigue is a side effect of radiation and I am already tired. I am grateful the Lord understands all the things I feel. He understands me even when I do not understand myself.

Hmmm... the Lord's understanding of us is limitless (Psalm 147:5). It brings my heart much comfort to know that the Lord knows me, inside and out, and understands everything about me. He does you, too. He knows our hearts (Acts 15:8a). He understands all that we are going through and what we are feeling. Jesus, our High Priest, is able to sympathize with us no matter the temptation or trial we face, because He has been tempted in every way we are.

> For we do not have a High Priest who is unable to sympathize with our weaknesses, but we have one who has been tempted in every way, just as we are, yet was without sin. (Hebrews 4:15)

I don't know about you, but one of the deepest desires of my heart is to be fully and intimately known and understood, and then loved, as it is said, warts and all. There are very few people in my life, who I believe, have a thorough understanding of who I am deep inside. I especially cherish the love and friendship of the folks who truly understand me. And, as well as those particular people understand me, it is not nearly as well as the Lord understands me. He understands every little detail of who I am, and why I am the way I am, the good, the bad, and the ugly. Despite it all, He loves me totally and completely. Only in Him do I find the deepest longings of my heart satisfied.

Chapter 11

Radiation Treatments

Five days a Week
September 4, 2013 – October 17, 2013

First Radiation Treatment... Wednesday, September 4, 2013
A Favorite Verse... Thursday, September 5, 2013

Hello friends. It is dark and early as I write to you. I slept well last night, even after an hour and a half nap yesterday evening. It seems like every day now, since going back to work, I need a nap. The morning part of the workday seems to go smoothly, but as I hit the halfway mark, fatigue rolls in and the feet start hurting.

The only other side effect to really bother me is the pain in my toenail beds. While I was off work, I wore almost nothing but sandals, which put no pressure on the big toe nails. I wear tennis shoes each day now to work and my toes' constant rubbing against the shoes makes them tender. I have also noticed that when I have been still a while, my joints stiffen up. When I first begin to move, I am stiff. The praise here is, as I continue to move, I limber up some.

Radiation time yesterday was quick. The nurse took me back, I put on my classic and stylish hospital gown, received the treatment, redressed and was out the door in fifteen minutes. Fabulous! As tired as I was, all I wanted to do was go home. Praise the Lord for fast radiation treatments.

As I write to you this morning I can hardly keep my eyes open. They keep shutting despite my insistence to them to remain open. I will leave you with a favorite verse and encourage you to contemplate on it. Hmmm... I am in need of a little "persevering" encouragement today.

> You need to persevere so that when you have done the will of God, you will receive what He has promised. (Hebrews 10:36)

I will try to gain maybe another half hour's rest before rising the final time this morning. It will be good for my body. Blessings to you today, dear friends.

Eternal Hope... Friday, September 6, 2013

Good morning, friends. I slept in this morning. It was a good and long night's sleep. My body desperately needed it. It was one the longest nights of rest I have had in a long time. When I dressed for work yesterday, I decided not to wear the compression socks. And, praise the Lord. I had no extra swelling last evening when I returned home. I did wear diabetic socks which are very loose and do not hinder the blood as it flows back up the leg. Changing the socks helped the neuropathy in my feet. Any relief from the foot pain is a plus.

As I worked these first four days following time off for surgery, I have been incredibly blessed by my coworkers and customers. I treasure their care and concern for me. They all want to know how I am, how the surgery went, and what kind of treatments I have left. It warms my heart to know and feel their love. I have a prayer request for one of my customers. His wife has been battling cancer for quite some time and died the day before yesterday. He does not know the Lord, therefore; does not have His comfort. A few days ago, he brought me a pretty pink hat for the winter time. I think his wife may have crocheted it. I am especially saddened as I know that many are without the hope the Lord provides.

Hmmm... hope. When we know the Lord, we have hope. We have eternal hope. A hope that knows, no matter what this world dishes out to us, our future and eternity are secure. Nothing can change that. God set into motion His plan for hope, salvation, and eternal life for mankind even before time began.

> ...A faith and knowledge resting on the hope of eternal life, which God, who does not lie, promised before the beginning of time. (Titus 1:2)

Our hope of eternal life is found in our faith and trust in Jesus as our Savior and Lord and the belief in His resurrection from the dead. "We have this hope as an anchor for the soul, firm and secure." (Hebrews 6:19a). I cannot help but think of my own life and the great upheaval that has come upon it in the last year and a half. As I have put my hope in the Lord, despite all the waves of turmoil and difficulties washing over me, the Lord has anchored me firmly. Because I have trusted Him, placing my hope in Him, I know I am secure no matter what comes. Have I always done it perfectly? No, but the Lord is faithful. He continues to walk with me through these challenging days, giving me His peace and comfort. He is so very good to me. That is His promise. If we seek Him, placing our hope in Him, He is good to us (Lamentations 3:25).

Hmmm... as I continue to think about the Lord and the great hope He has provided, I cannot help but ponder some questions. What or who are you trusting and putting your hope in?

> But those who hope in the Lord will renew their strength. They will soar on wings like eagles; they will run and not grow weary, they will walk and not be faint. (Isaiah 40:31)

The only true and unshakeable hope is found in Jesus Christ. The Lord wants to give us His hope and strength.

New Vehicle, New Creation.... Saturday, September 7, 2013

Hello. I am glad to be joining you again. I slept in late again today. My body is not at all thrilled about me asking it to get up and go to work. It complies, but very begrudgingly. I know that I cannot expect to be at my best, considering all that I have been through physically in the last six months. I would really like to be, at least, at the level of energy I had before the surgery. Patience, Patience, Patience.

Yesterday consisted of sleep, naps, rest and more rest. The only things I did beyond resting were the daily radiation treatment and washing the new vehicle God blessed me with. I knew I needed a little fresh air and sunshine, and that it would be wise to burn at least a little energy, so washing the Equinox provided all of the above. Besides that, it had dirt on it. It is funny how dirt on an old vehicle is not seen in the same way as it is on a new one.

Hmmm... that is similar to the way it is with sin to those who have given themselves to the Lord. When we place ourselves in Christ, we are made new. Sin is no longer acceptable in our new life in Christ as it had seemed in our old life (II Corinthians 5:17).

The old, filthy, and sinful person is gone, and we are made new. We are no longer the old person, but a new creation which has been given Jesus' righteousness and holiness as recorded in I Corinthians 1:26. We have been made new and covered with the righteousness of Christ. When we give our lives to Christ, our old and sinful selves are crucified, and dead to sin. This means that we are no longer slaves to sin. (Read Romans 6:6-7, 11-13). We are no longer to be dominated by it. We have been freed.

Wow! Do you realize that once you accept Jesus as your Lord and Savior, you are no longer the dirty, filthy sinner you once were, but you are now "the righteousness of God?" You have been made new and righteous. As a sinner, sin is what you did, but as one who is now in Christ, saved by His death and resurrection, you are forgiven. Are you living a life befitting who you are in Christ, the righteousness of God?

I hope my hmmm has been an encouragement to you. He brought to mind a few areas in my own life that were not befitting who He has made me to be. I have asked His forgiveness and asked Holy Spirit to lead me that I might follow His guidance and not my own selfish way.

Radiation, Fingernails, Toenails, Grace...
Monday, September 9, 2013

Good morning. I am excited to share with you that I felt much better the last two days. My Saturday night work shift was easier to get through, but I was still ready to call it a night before quitting time rolled around. I felt better on Sunday. I had a nap between church services which helped refresh me enough to have energy to go back to church for the evening service.

I even had enough energy to stop and have a manicure and a pedicure. A friend of mine has been spoiling me with that nice treat. I have been extra glad for it because several of the nails show quite a bit of damage from the chemo, and the paint helps cover the ugly damage beneath the nails. As I looked down at my toes before they were repainted, they looked much worse than the last time I had seen them without dark paint. At least three quarters of the big toes' nails appear to be detached from the nail bed. The nail beds are discolored, dark red and purple, as if I had smashed them. It is no wonder they are so tender if I bump them or a shoe rubs the top of them. I almost always wear sandals when I am not working because it is much more comfortable. I have a few fingernails with the same detaching damage. But, the fingernail damage is considerably less than the big toes. The praise is, I still have all the nails, at least partially attached, and the added blessing of having them professionally done so that they look pretty. As I talked with the young lady who was doing my nails, she shared with me that most of the chemo patients, whose nails she has done, lost the nails completely. I consider myself blessed to have minimal damage.

I usually would not have my nails done on a Sunday, but I sensed that is what the Lord was prompting me to, so I did. When I arrived at the nail shop, I was waited on by a young woman who had done my nails before. God opened the door for me to share His goodness and His grace with her and to tell her about Jesus. She asked many questions. I pray that she will accept my invitation to come to church, as well as accept the grace God is offering her.

As I think about this young woman and her hunger to hear about God, His plan of salvation in Jesus, and the truths of the Bible; I was saddened to hear all the misconceptions she had about Christianity and God. She was truly interested to hear the truth of who God is and what the Bible teaches about Him, but had never been told. She was surprised to hear that she did not have to work her way into heaven by being good. As we talked, I saw myself in her eyes.

Many years ago, before I truly understood the Lord and His truth, I too believed that I had to be good enough to get into heaven. We were different in the fact that I knew Jesus died for me, but, I also believed I had to be good enough. Well, I tried and tried to be good enough but knew in my heart I was failing miserably. I was frustrated and feeling ready to give up when someone shared the truth with me. I could never be good enough. I was a sinner and nothing I could do would ever earn my way into heaven. But, God in His infinite love and grace gave His Son Jesus to be the payment for my sin.

> For it is by grace you have been saved, through faith –and this not from yourselves, it is the gift of God– not by works, so that no one can boast. (Ephesians 2:8-9)

When I learned this truth of God's grace, His unmerited favor, I could not wait to accept the free gift of salvation the Lord was offering me. Thank you Jesus!

Hmmm... I think of the prevalent belief in today's world that being a "good person" will get you into heaven. Nothing could be further from the truth. The Bible makes it clear that only God's grace given through Jesus will. "I am the way and the truth and the life. No one comes to the Father except through me." (John 14:6).

What are you depending on to get you into heaven? Have you accepted the grace God freely offers you though Christ Jesus? How often do you share the good news of His grace with others? I often think of where I would be if no one had shared with me.

Help and Escape...Tuesday, September 10, 2013

Good morning. I hope I can be coherent for our time together. Not only is my body tired, but even my mind is tired. Yesterday, as I worked, it was more difficult than usual to keep my concentration on the task at hand, because of fatigue. However, I made it through the eight hours of work and the radiation treatment. Praise the Lord! Fatigue is still quite strong.

I still cannot seem to sleep enough to satisfy my body. I heard somewhere that when you are sleeping, your body is completing some of its best and deepest healing. My body sure needs that after five months of chemo and is trying to recover from systematic and controlled poisoning. And, now it is being hit with controlled radiation five days a week. As much as I don't like it, I should not be surprised by the fatigue and lousy feelings I suffer with. I continue to remind myself that it is what it is, and this too, with time, shall pass.

In this life, we are often in need of help. We are faced with trials and temptations, day in and day out. I have never been more keenly aware of my desperate need of help than in the past few years of my life. When I need help with the trials and temptations of life, where does it come from?

> I lift up my eyes to the hills–where does my help come from? My help comes from the Lord, the Maker of heaven and earth. (Psalm 121:1-2)

The Lord often uses other people and circumstances to bring His help to me. But, ultimately, my help comes from the Lord. The Lord made the heavens and the earth and all that is within them. He knows exactly how the universe works, how people think and act, and even what lies ahead of us. There is nothing the Lord does not know. When we realize that truth, why would we not go to Him for help? He loves us and constantly watches over us. He knows when we come and when we go (Psalm 121:8). My favorite part of the verse is the "both now and forevermore" part. It reminds us that there is never a time the Lord is not watching over us. He knows what temptations will come our way and makes sure that as we are tempted, He has made a way of escape for us.

> No temptation has seized you except what is common to man. And God is faithful; He will not let you be tempted beyond what you can bear. But when you are tempted, He will also provide a way out so that you can stand up under it. (I Corinthians 10:13)

Hmmm... are you and I taking the Lord's help and way out? Or, are we saying that the temptation is too great? God's Word clearly tells us we can stand firm when we rely on Him, taking the way out He has provided. There is nothing you or I face, or ever have or will face, that the Lord does not understand. To receive His mercy, grace and help, we can come to the Lord and He is faithful to provide the way out.

Anxious Anticipation... Wednesday, September 11, 2013

I had another morning to sleep in and I am relishing it. My favorite place to be, as of late, is in bed. My days are beginning to take on a new pattern, which is quiet time with the Lord and you, work, radiation treatment at the hospital, a long nap, rising for a short while, and then back to bed for the night. It is not my ideal for how I would order my day, but, I do not have much of a choice right now. I am anxiously anticipating when things will be different. The end of the cancer treatments seems much nearer. I am excited by that thought.

Have you ever noticed how much fun anxiously anticipating something is? Whether it be a vacation or a trip, the birth of a baby, a wedding, a party, a special event of some kind, acquiring a new item you have wanted for a while, or seeing a friend or family member you haven't seen for quite some time. Often, the time spent anticipating is almost as much fun as the event itself.

Hmmm... anticipation. Christians have much to anticipate, not only in this life, but after their days on this earth are done. They can anticipate the transformation the Lord works in them as He molds them into the image of His precious Son, Jesus. They can anticipate the blessings the Lord gives as they are obedient to His commands. They can anticipate the Lord working in and through them touching the hearts and lives of other people. They can anticipate answers to their prayers in God's perfect timing. They can anticipate the excitement of the future the Lord has for them.

I often ask myself, exactly what does the calling He has placed on my life look like in the future? Who will He allow me to touch, love, and to minister to as each day unfolds? Where will He lead me? What will I do when I get there? I get excited when I think about the God and Creator of the universe choosing to use me to accomplish His work in this world. I cannot help but wonder why He would choose me. I certainly wouldn't choose me. The more I know Him, the more I love Him. I can anticipate the eternal home the Lord has prepared for me and the ability to be with Him, face to face, for eternity in heaven. "And if I go and prepare a place for you, I will come back and take you to be with me that you also may be where I am." (John 14:3).

We can anxiously anticipate a home in heaven that is free from sin and pain, tears and sorrow. We will no longer be subject to the weaknesses of our flesh. As I think about heaven, there is a part of me which can hardly wait for the day the Lord takes me home.

Chosen and Honored... Thursday, September 12, 2013

Hey there. Yesterday was a nice day off. I enjoyed a little extra rest, washed the new vehicle again, brushed Ellie Mae to get rid of the loose hair, and I pushed myself to take a walk. I did better than I thought I would, considering the fatigue I have been dealing with. I was tired when I finished, but I made it. It has been several weeks since I have been able to do a short walk. After completing the chores around the house, I headed to the hospital for the daily radiation treatment. The nurses there are very helpful. It is, however, taking me longer to get to know them very well because I am so quickly in and out. Almost within fifteen minutes of walking in the hospital doors, I am walking back out again. And, I do not always have the same nurse setting me up for the treatment. I am sure after a few more times, I will start to get more names and faces put together.

In His infinite power, wisdom, and might, God esteems His children so greatly that He calls us to serve Him. He has work specifically prepared for us. He prepared it *in advance* for you and me. That means, He did not choose you because you were handy or because He didn't have any one else at the moment. He specifically prepared the work for you and for me. What an honor!

> For we are God's workmanship, created in Christ Jesus to do good works, which God prepared in advance for us to do. (Ephesians 2:10)

I am amazed that He would choose me, as I am sure most of you are amazed He would choose you. I would never pick myself to have the honor of being His servant. I know I do not have the ability. Since He chose us to serve Him, we can anticipate being given His power, wisdom, strength, and ability to accomplish whatever He has asks us to do

What Price Are You Willing to Pay? ...
Friday, September 13, 2013

Good morning. It is dark and early as I start my time with you. I am sad to say it, but I am already finding it difficult to keep the eyes open and I have a long day ahead of me. I work 6 a.m. to 2 p.m. today, then have my radiation treatment. I had hoped to have enough energy to go to my ladies Sunday school class get-together this evening but I am not sure I am going to have the "spit and vinegar" for it.

Yesterday I made it through work fine and my feet held out longer than usual before they felt like they were burning on the bottom. I had a special treat yesterday as I talked with a couple who are missionaries in the inner city of St. Louis and minister mostly to immigrants to the United States. In their ministry, many of the people they encounter come from Muslim backgrounds. I was blessed as I listened to them tell how they are able to share Jesus, leading some to faith in Christ. It was sad to hear how some were cast out of their families and suffered persecution at the hands of those closest to them simply because of their faith in Christ. It is hard for me to imagine that kind of rejection from people who once held you dear. Former Muslims pay a high price for their faith in Jesus Christ.

Hmmm... persecution. I have to ask myself, what price am I willing to pay for my faith? What about you? As Christians, we should not be surprised when we face those who hate us and persecute us. What is our response to be? First, we are to continue in faith and obedience to the Lord's commands. "Bless those who persecute you; bless and do not curse." (Romans 12:14).

What does blessing those who persecute you look like? He tells us in Matthew 5:44 that we are to love our enemies and pray for those who persecute us. We have no greater example of this than Christ on the cross. When He had been beaten, scourged, mocked, scorned, rejected and was nailed to the cross, bleeding and dying, He prayed for those who had done these terrible things to Him and asked the Father to forgive them.

> We are hard pressed on every side, but not crushed; perplexed, but not in despair; persecuted, but not abandoned; struck down, but not destroyed. (II Corinthians 4:8-9)

God will not abandon us in our times of persecution or any other time. There is nothing we face that He is unaware of and no time when He will not be with us once we make Jesus Savior and Lord of our lives. Am I ready to face persecution for my Lord? What about you? What price are you and I willing to pay for our faith?

God's Truth or Your Deception... Saturday, September 14, 2013

Hello. I feel a bit groggy this morning. Yesterday after work and the radiation treatment, I came home to decide if I was going to have the energy to go to my class get-together. I had an early dinner and decided to rest. The next thing I knew, it was 10:30 p.m. and my Mom was coming into my room to take Ellie Mae out for the night for me. So much for a walk and spending time with the ladies. It seems no matter how much I sleep or rest, my body is always craving more. I suppose it was wishful thinking on my part to think that once I got to the other side of chemo, I would feel better more quickly. It is easy to deceive yourself into thinking what you want to think and into doing what you want to do. Hmmm... deceive ourselves.

> Do not merely listen to the word, and so deceive yourselves. Do what it says. Anyone who listens to the word but does not do what it says is like a man who looks at his face in a mirror and, after looking at himself, goes away and immediately forgets what he looks like. But the man who looks intently into the perfect law that gives freedom, and continues to do this, not forgetting what he has heard, but doing it–he will be blessed in what he does. If anyone considers he is religious and yet does not keep a tight rein on his tongue, he deceives himself and his religion is worthless. (James 1:22-26)

What the Lord has me focused on, is how often we sit under the teaching and proclamation of His Word and truth, and then, conveniently forget that we are not striving to live up to the truth we hear. We convince ourselves we are fine because we have done our religious duty. We have gone to church. We have given an offering. We have been baptized, or whatever else we think is enough in our service to the Lord. Religious actions will not gain us God's freedom and blessing.

An example of what the Lord is teaching is about one who carries out their religious rituals or duties, yet does not do what the law says by "keeping a tight rein on his tongue." This could mean foul language, gossip, telling lies, cutting another with sharp words or critical comments, or other ways we do not control our tongues. When we do not keep an accurate view of ourselves and our actions, we are deceiving ourselves, making our religious actions worthless.

God wants to give His children blessing and freedom, freedom from sin, freedom from bondage, and freedom to live their lives becoming all that He so gloriously created them to be. Living by God's Word and applying it to our life gives us that freedom.

Suffering and Joy... Monday, September 16, 2013

Hey there. It is nice to have a taste of autumn. It was cool enough the last several mornings to cause me to put on my long, heavy robe when I took Ellie Mae outside. Ellie Mae has had an extra spring in her step. She always seems to gain energy when the weather cools. However, she has not been feeling her best. Her digestive tract is unsettled.

I think she and I have had sympathy pains for each other. My stomach is still not feeling right. When the alarm went off on Sunday, I felt fine till I sat up and the room all but spun on me. Ellie Mae needed out, so I got up to take her and almost fell as I lost my balance. I had to use the wall to steady myself. I was dizzy, lightheaded, shaky, and nauseous, tired, and had a headache. Yuck! I almost didn't go to church. I felt so rough I had a tear or two this morning in church. God knew I needed a little extra encouragement and sent a precious lady who she felt impressed the Lord wanted her to pray over me. She put her arms around me and prayed a wonderful prayer. It lifted my heart. As I headed to my Sunday school class, I ran into Carol, who has dealt with breast cancer herself. She offered lots of encouragement to me, too. That is just like the Lord to send His people to lift me when I am down.

As I think about pressing forward into another workday, and all the energy it has taken to persevere continuing to work, I am reminded of my pastor's sermon on perseverance. The Lord knows how tired I am and gave a message to Dr. McLain to encourage me. A definition he gave of perseverance was "a long obedience in the same direction." Hmmm... I find myself in need of the Lord's continued encouragement to persevere and the reminders of its benefits.

> Not only so, but we also rejoice in our sufferings, because we know that suffering produces perseverance; perseverance, character; and character, hope. (Romans 5:3-4)

Physically or emotionally, it is hard to remember a time when I suffered more than I have in this last year and a half. But, as I look to these verses, I am encouraged. I see God's truth reminding me, as I persevere through life's sufferings, trusting Him, He will continue to mold my character into Christ's likeness.

If I did not have the hope and promise of the Lord working in me to mature and complete me, it would be easy to allow depression and discouragement, wondering why the Lord would allow me to suffer. This truth does not make suffering easy, but it surely helps me to look at it from God's viewpoint. God wants me to trust and thank Him saying, "Lord, I know you have promised to use this for my good. I look forward with joy to all you will accomplish in this time."

Service, Gifts, and Glory... Tuesday, September 17, 2013

I am going to start our time together tonight, but will probably finish in the morning. I can feel my energy fading. I have good news concerning Ellie Mae. Her digestive tract is much better. Praise the Lord! I am so very fond of Ellie Mae. I hate to see her not feeling her best.

The Lord sent me lots of caring customers to encourage and love on me today. He knows just how to lift me. The Lord topped off His encouragement to me with a kind sister in Christ at the hospital. I had the blessing of sharing some time and conversation with her, and then driving her and the large box she was carrying to a distant parking lot where her car was parked. The Lord used her to add more joy to my day.

I could have very easily walked past her, ignoring the fact that she was struggling with a big box. Instead, the Lord prompted me to have a conversation with her, offering to drive her. The Lord reminded me that when I do something for others, in reality, I am doing it for Him. "The King will reply, I tell you the truth, whatever you did for one of the least of these brothers of mine, you did for Me." (Matthew 25:40).

A generous gentleman and his caring wife from my church family have graciously cut the grass all spring and summer, at the home where my husband and I formerly lived. Not only are they serving me, they are serving the Lord. (Thank you, Frank and Sharon! You bless me abundantly.)

In this season, I have been blessed by many who have served me in numerous ways. Some with gifts and financial support, some with words of encouragement, and others as mighty prayer warriors. I am grateful, and thank the Lord for each one of them.

Nothing Hidden... Wednesday, September 18, 2013

One of my favorite things to do, at the end of a day, is to think back over the day, remembering all the times I noticed God at work. It leaves me encouraged and lifted. Because I see Him in the details of the day, I am reminded how much He loves me. Dr. Porter has helped me learn to do this. One of his favorite questions is, "What is your greatest blessing of the last seven days?" He asks me that question almost every time I see him. Because I anticipate his asking, I began to train my mind to focus on my blessings so that I would always be prepared to answer. Well, now it comes easy. I automatically watch for the blessings and remember them more regularly.

Yesterday, I received many blessings and things to praise the Lord for. The divine appointments He gave me with my customers top the list. I had the opportunity to encourage several who are currently going through cancer treatments, and I met a new one who had been through breast cancer treatments about seven years ago. She was a fabulous blessing. I had the opportunity to encourage my radiation nurse. As she set me up for my treatment, the Lord gave me the opportunity to encourage her to find a church home. In the past, her family had been hurt by some folks in the church who were not acting very Christ-like. She has not had a church home since. The radiation machine we were using malfunctioned prolonging the time it took to complete the treatment. So, I had extra time with her today. The Lord is always good to give us the time we need to encourage another.

> ...His work will be shown for what it is, because the Day will bring it to light. It will be revealed with fire, and the fire will test the quality of each man's work. If what he has built survives, he will receive his reward. If it is burned up, he will suffer loss... (I Corinthians 3:13-15a)

The word originally used for *the Day* has also been translated as court, referring us back to the judgment. Our deeds will be judged. Each and every one of our deeds will be tested with the fire of God's truth and commands

Hmmm... what are you doing that the Lord might reward you? I want to receive all the rewards the Lord desires to give me, don't you?

Squeezing the Heart... Friday, September 20, 2013

Good morning. It sure was nice to visit with my aunt and uncle yesterday. It is rare for me to see them. Any opportunity to visit is too precious to miss. After a quick visit with my aunt in the morning I headed off to radiation and from there I proceeded to church for a day of counseling with Dr. Porter. My appointment for the radiation treatment started my morning with a great time with two of my nurses. God gave me the opportunity to share with them how precious they are to the Lord and how much He loves them. One of them opened her heart to me, sharing the pain of a tragic situation she was struggling with. It was a tender moment. It is always a precious time as we open our hearts to share with another.

As my two nurses and I talked, they told me how easy I was to set up and treat. I told them I knew they had a tough job because a number of the people they treat are physically hurting and sick. Beyond that, many are angry, bitter, and afraid because of the cancers in their bodies. They agreed. At this thought, I am reminded that whatever we have in our hearts will flow out of us through our words and actions, when the difficulties of life squeeze and put pressure on us. Hmmm... "For out of the overflow of the heart the mouth speaks." (Matthew 12:34b)

Hmmm...what comes out of your mouth is exactly what is in your heart. When you have anger, bitterness, resentment, unforgiveness or fear in your heart, those are the exact kinds of words that flow from your mouth. Nothing will come out of your mouth that is not already in your heart. Think about that. How often do you speak hurtful or ugly words? Do you excuse them saying, "I was just mad or frustrated for a moment, but I am better now?"

When pressure of any kind is placed on us and we are squeezed, we become just like a sponge. If we have sweet water in us, sweet water is released. If we have sour milk in us, sour milk is released. Hmmm... what am I storing up in my heart that will be released when I am squeezed?

> The good man brings good things out of the good stored up in his heart, and the evil man brings evil things out of the evil stored up in his heart... (Luke 6:45a)

When I am squeezed by the pressures of life, my words and actions will be the telltale sign of what I have chosen to store in my heart. Search your heart and allow the Lord to remove any evil He finds there, filling it with the fullness of His Holy Spirit (Psalm 139:23-24). You will never regret it. I want Him to squeeze my heart and fill it with Himself. What about you?

Always There... Saturday, September 21, 2013

Hi there. I do not feel my best. My stomach hurts and my digestive tract is upset. I took some medication, which seems to have alleviated some of the pain. Praise the Lord! I am grateful for any relief.

There is a reassuring reminder in Psalm 139:7-10 that no matter where we are, the Lord is there. We can go nowhere on this earth or in heavens around it where the Lord will not be present. Even an astronaut, in outer space, cannot escape the Lord's presence. His right hand will hold me fast wherever I am.

> Be strong and courageous. Do not be afraid or terrified, for the Lord your God goes with you; he will never leave you nor forsake you. (Deuteronomy 31:6)

When the Lord promised He would never leave us, He meant it. He is *always* there. No matter where "there" happens to be. What a comfort that is. There is no place, nor any situation we face, where our Lord will not guide nor hold His children firm. Take comfort in that truth today. Be grateful for His ever present Spirit.

Sufficient and abounding ... Monday, September 23, 2013

Good morning, dear friends. What a beautiful day Father gave us yesterday. Ellie Mae and I spent some time outside together. I even took a little time to pick pecans with Elmer, my neighbor. There are three pecan trees at the back of our yard. They will surely taste good when we get them cracked and picked out. Pecans are one of my favorite nuts.

I want to share a quick update. I skipped supper to keep from making my stomach hurt. Eating seems to make it hurt about an hour after the food goes down. A couple of years ago, when all the enzymes, probiotics and such were not balanced appropriately in my digestive tract, my doctor told me to take a specific probiotic supplement. The chemo drugs are out of my system and radiation does not cause digestive tract issues. Sometimes life seems like it goes from one complication to another. I am grateful to have discovered, no matter the complication, God's grace is sufficient for me.

The Lord has continued to solidify this truth in my heart and mind as each new challenge, difficulty, trial, or pain comes. He reminds and shows me just how sufficient His grace truly is. "But he said to me, my grace is sufficient for you for my power is made perfect in weakness." (II Corinthians 12:9).

My grace refers to God's favor, kindness, and blessing. No matter what we are going through, God's grace and strength will give us all we need.

God is able to make His grace abound "in all things at all times." Isn't that good news? God promises His sufficiency to us always. I will always have what I need. He even gives over and above what is needed. I love that about God. No matter what comes your way today, His grace is sufficient.

Baskets Full, More than Enough! ...
Tuesday, September 24, 2013

Hello friends. I am up and at it early this morning. I have another early work shift. I had been convinced that my stomach was on the mend, but then when I woke up this morning it was hurting again. I will make an appointment with the gastroenterologist.

I pray do not end up with any skin problems due to the radiation. The armpit on the treated side is now beginning to peel and there is another area that seems quite tender. I use all the special lotion they recommended, and give the area more "breathing" time when I am at home and can.

I want to share with you an interesting tidbit I learned. (Thanks, Mark!) Matthew 15 tells the story of the feeding of four thousand plus women and children with seven loaves and a few small fish with which to feed the large crowd. As the disciples were obedient, passing out the food to the crowd, God multiplied the loaves and fish satisfying the hunger of the whole crowd. Not only was the crowd's hunger satisfied, but here were so many leftovers that the disciples had to gather them. There were seven basketfuls of broken pieces left *after* feeding the large crowd.

The Lord used this story to really drive home the point that with God, even a little is more than enough. Think about this in the light of what I share with you next.

The baskets referred to in these passages had to be big baskets, sizeable enough to put a man in (Acts 9:25). That sheds more light on how many leftovers there were and how Father, when He does something does not do just the bare minimum, but exceedingly and abundantly more than all we could think or ask (Ephesians 3:20).

The Lord sank that truth deeper for me. I love when He does that. He takes what I already know and makes it bigger, brighter, deeper, stronger, better. I hope you will allow Him to do the same for you. Holy Spirit loves to shine light on truth for us. Ask the Lord for His wisdom, truth, provision and ability in your life, dear friends, then step out in the instruction He provides.

His Love... Wednesday, September 25, 2013

Hello there. The update today starts with a continued increase in tenderness in the area where the radiation treatments are focused. At least, I am over a third of the way through with radiation. I still have some digestive tract issues, but they are no worse, so that is a plus and a praise.

Hmmm... as I think of the love friends and family shower on me, I think of God's love for us as well. God's love is seen as affection, a love that attaches, tethers, or binds. It has a sense of joining together. His love is like the love of a dearly loved friend. It is a love that takes delight. Finally, His love is seen as a devoted love, a love of goodness, kindness, faithfulness, which is unchanging and unconditional.

I cannot help but see the correlation between His love for the Israelites and His love for me. First of all, He chose me, setting His love and devotion on me when He picked me as His child (Ephesians 1:4-5). The Lord redeemed the people from Egypt and brought them out. He did the same for me when He saved me. He brought me out from under the guilt and weight of my sin. He redeemed me as I placed my trust in Him and chose to follow Him (Psalm 103:4).

When Jesus paid the ultimate price for me, He gave His life, dying on the cross. I cannot imagine a deeper love than that. Lastly, His love and promises are unchanging. They will never fail. There will never come a day when the Lord decides He is tired of me and tosses me away. His love is faithful. He never changes. I can only thank Him and praise Him for loving me so deeply and completely.

Embracing the Truth, Rejecting the Lie... Thursday, September 26, 2013

Good morning. The biggest praise to share is that my digestive tract is back to working normally. Praise the Lord! The probiotics are regulating my digestive system and restoring balance to the good bacteria. I shared with a fellow cancer patient who shops where I work about them. He was having difficulty with pain in his digestive tract too. He was in yesterday and said they had also helped him feel much better.

Yesterday was a workday. The fatigue was pretty strong, but I made it through work and then to the hospital and radiation. The radiated spot continues to be tender. My nurse said that was normal, since when they radiate, cells are being killed all the way down into the breast. My armpit and underneath the radiated area are tender to the touch. I pray each time before they start radiation, asking the Lord to protect my skin, bones, organs, and good cells and to allow the radiation to kill any cells that are cancerous or could become cancerous.

After coming home from radiation, I planned a nap, but I think the fresh air and sunshine might have been better for me than a nap. I have surely missed all the time I normally spend outside in the summer. I am already looking forward to next year. I will be feeling better, walking and maybe a little jogging, too. Who knows what else? Next year is a new adventure waiting for me, just as the day ahead of me is. The Lord has divine appointments set for you and for me. He knows each and every step set before us and places many opportunities for us to minister to others and be blessed. I am excited about them. Aren't you?

Lately, Satan has been attacking me, trying to get me off track with frustration, fatigue, and impatience. If he can get me off track, he will rob me of the opportunities God has for me and the blessings as well. He knows how tired I am and wants to get me to complain and feel sorry for myself. He also knows how ready I am to complete the cancer treatments, sale of the house, and divorce. All three have yet to be completed and have been in the works for a year or more. He likes to tell me to be angry and bitter about it all, and that I deserve to be able to indulge in resentment and impatience. I am praising the Lord for teaching me better than that and freeing me from being angry, bitter, resentful, unforgiving and impatient. I do not want any of those things back in my life. Maybe you could use a reminder, just as I do. Satan is a liar! (John 8:44b)

He wants nothing more than to pull you and me as far away from the Lord as he possibly can. Only when we fully submit ourselves, body, soul, and spirit to the Lord can we resist Satan. The best part comes next. The Lord will draw near to us (James 4:7-8a).

Be diligent, dear friends, as you hear the voices and thoughts in your mind. Are they the encouraging and uplifting thoughts and words of Holy Spirit or are they the putting you down and making you feel bad about yourself and others, the discouraging lies of the devil? With Holy Spirit's help, you can discern the difference. It is imperative that you reject the devil's lies and embrace God's truth, if you are to live in the complete freedom Jesus died to give you.

Remember, Holy Spirit will never put you down nor discourage you. He will always draw you nearer to the Lord. That is where true peace is found.

Listening and Adjusting… Friday, September 27, 2013

Hi there. I am very glad to have a day off. I have some phone calls to make, errands to run, things to accomplish at home, as well as the daily hospital trip for radiation. After all those things are accomplished, I hope to be able to have time to take a walk with Ellie Mae and catch up on my Bible study homework.

It seems like there are always so many things to do, many of them attempt to draw me away from my time with the Lord. Some of them are good things and some are things that are a waste of my time even though they are not evil things. When I do that, I miss doing some of the more important things. It is of utmost importance in our daily lives that we listen for Holy Spirit's leading and promptings.

Holy Spirit is a Christian's indwelling guide (Galatians 5:16). "Living by the Spirit" is to continually make adjustments in your life as Holy Spirit prompts and directs you. Listening to and obeying Holy Spirit's instruction is the key to overcoming our sinful nature. When we give in to the flesh, we are dragged off into temptation and sin.

The adjustments and changes Holy Spirit encourages us to implement in our lives will protect us from the traps Satan lays for us. Holy Spirit can guide us safely around the darkness and destruction of the devil's snare and into the victory and the abundant life and peace the Lord has for us (Romans 8:6). What or who is controlling you? What do you have you mind focused on? Is it your sinful desires or the godly desires of the Spirit? What you choose to set your mind on is important.

> Those who live according to the sinful nature have their minds set on what that nature desires; but those who live in accordance with the Spirit have their minds set on what the Spirit desires. (Romans 8:5)

Hmmm…set your mind on the things of the Lord today and completely submit yourself to His Spirit's leadership. Only there will you find peace, victory, and life. Listen to hear Holy Spirit's voice leading you today. You won't regret it.

Encouraged and Rejoicing... Saturday, September 28, 2013

Good morning, dear friends. I had more energy than I have in a while. Praise the Lord for energy and strength.

As I start to hmmm the things the Lord would have me share with you today, I need to start our time by sharing something with you. The last week or so, Satan has been hitting me hard, trying to tempt me to feel sorry for myself and to get me to feel bitter and resentful.

I am physically tired. Even though I had more energy than usual yesterday, fatigue still weighs heavily on me as it has through the last several months. In the few months prior to the cancer diagnosis, as you know, I also faced bankruptcy, divorce, and losing my home. I was already emotionally tired when the cancer diagnosis hit. Of course, Satan knows all that. He is the one who laid the traps to put my husband and me in that ugly place. He continues to dig at me where he knows I am weakest. Satan will do the same to you.

The Lord knew I was in need of encouragement today, and sent me to a devotional book I have on my shelf. He used this verse to bless and encourage me: "Rejoice in the Lord always. I will say it again: Rejoice!" (Philippians 4:4).

The book of Philippians was written by Paul while he was in prison. This is evident in Philippians 1:13 where Paul writes, "It has become clear throughout the whole palace guard and to everyone else that I am in chains for Christ." Though he is in prison, he wrote to encourage the Philippians to stand firm in their faith in Christ, despite their difficulties or struggles. He is a great example for them to follow. He is in chains, yet he continues to stand firm in the truth of Christ. He exhorts them to be content, no matter their circumstances (Philippians 4:11). What gave him the ability to be content? It was God's continual strength. "I can do everything through Him who gives me strength." (Philippians 4:13).

God reminded me this morning that He knows exactly where I am, and exactly what I feel. He is there to give me His strength to persevere as I ask and trust Him for it. He also reminded me that there is never a time when He is not with me.

> Let us not become weary in doing good for at the proper time we will reap a harvest if we do not give up. (Galatians 6:9)

The Lord knows exactly what you are feeling and going through today. He wants to encourage you, just as He has me.

Remembering and Rejoicing... Monday, September 30, 2013

Hello. Each day always has something new we can learn and enjoy if we will watch for it. Looking to see what God is doing is fun. Looking forward to what He will do is exciting. Then, looking back to see what He has already done is encouraging. He had me spend a bit of time thinking back over His faithfulness to me, specifically in the last year.

I read back over some of the things I had written around the time my husband decided he no longer desired the marriage. It was a blessing and encouragement to see and remember how the Lord had His hand on me, sustaining me and lifting me.

As I read, I remembered the peace He gave me, despite the fact that my life seemed to be crumbling around me. I remembered the strength and the wisdom He gave me as I dealt with the things that come with separation and divorce. Then, I remembered the joy He gave me as He worked healing among the painful emotions.

> Give thanks to the Lord, call on His name; make known among the nations what He has done. Sing to Him, sing praise to Him; tell of all His wonderful acts. Glory in His holy name; let the hearts of those who seek the Lord rejoice. Look to the Lord and His strength; seek His face always. Remember the wonders He has done, His miracles, and the judgments He pronounced. (I Chronicles 16:8-12)

The Lord reminded me that I need to look back and "remember the wonders He has done" in my life. I have much to be thankful for. Take a little time to think back over the Lord's faithfulness to you. Thank Him. Take time to tell someone else of the wonderful things He has done for you. Praise Him and rejoice. He is worthy of all our praise, worship, and adoration.

Promises and Faithfulness... Tuesday, October 1, 2013

Just as an update, I am down to thirteen more radiation treatments. Praise the Lord! I am getting closer and closer to being done. At five days a week, they get knocked off a whole lot quicker than the chemo did at once a week. I cannot begin to tell you how much I am looking forward to being finished with all the regular trips to the hospital and the time when my body will finally be able to start healing from all the poisoning and radiation. The fatigue has been the most difficult side effect for me from the cancer treatments. One day at a time, then I will be finished and ready to start the upward climb to feeling normal again.

I am still dealing with most of the side effects. The swelling in my feet and ankles is less. Purple patches on my ankles still remain. I am hopeful those will go away with time. My toes still tingle and my feet still feel tired too quickly. However, since the swelling is better, I do not have to wear the compression socks and my feet are not experiencing the feeling of being on fire that the compression socks seemed to intensify. Praise the Lord! I do not get out of breath as easily as I did before. I have not experienced the dizziness and light-headedness that I was experiencing while singing at church. That is a big praise. The radiated area is developing more tenderness, and I still have mild headaches a lot. The digestive tract has improved, but it is not what it should be. There are other side effects that still bother me, but I do not want to focus on them. I would much rather focus on the Lord than the more negative things. "The Lord gives strength to his people; the Lord blesses his people with peace." (Psalm 29:11). This verse causes gratefulness to well up within me.

I look back and see clearly how the Lord has done this for me and still continues to. God is faithful to fulfill His promises. God is completely faithful and is not bound to human weaknesses as we are. God *always* delivers on His promises and does so in His perfect timing. The Lord will never fail us.

> Do not be afraid or discouraged, for the Lord God, my God is with you. He will not fail you or forsake you... (I Chronicles 1:20b

I encourage you to search your heart and your mind. What attributes are you consciously or subconsciously attributing to God, which are human frailties or weaknesses? The Lord is not now, nor ever will be, subject to frailty or weakness. Pray and ask Him to show you any misconceptions you have about Him. Ask Him to show you His heart and who He is in fullness and truth. It is His desire for you to know Him just as intimately as He knows you.

Suffering and Patience... Wednesday, October 2, 2013

Good morning. When I woke up my stomach was hurting. It looks to be a busy day for me. I work from 6 a.m. to 2 p.m. and then I head off to the hospital for radiation. I have only twelve treatments to go! Then, I have Bible study this evening and one counseling session to sit in on with Dr. Porter. I hope to make a stop, between hospital and church time, to do a little candy shopping to take to St. Luke's tomorrow for a visit with some of my friends there. I surely do miss them. They were all wonderful as I went through the surgeries and chemo treatments. The Lord used them to bless me abundantly.

He is doing the same with the nurses at St. Anthony's hospital as I go through radiation. It takes a special gifting to be a nurse and to do it well, especially dealing with cancer patients. Unfortunately, many cancer patients are depressed or angry and the nurse often gets the brunt of their unpleasant emotions.

How often have you expressed your frustration and anger over your suffering, unloading your negative emotions through harsh words on someone who may or may not have anything to do with your upset emotions?

As Christians, we are called to patience in our times of suffering. In James 5:7-11 we are encouraged to "be patient and stand firm, because the Lord's coming is near. Don't grumble against each other, brothers." This life will be filled with situations that are beyond our control and cause suffering. Though we cannot control them, we can, with Holy Spirit's help, determine how we react to them. He encourages us to approach His throne to seek the help and mercy we so desperately need.

His Reflection... Thursday, October 3, 2013

Hello there. I took extra time to sleep this morning since I was so tired yesterday. I will start the day with a trip to the hospital for a radiation treatment and then to church for counseling time with Dr. Porter. After that, we will visit our new friends at St. Luke's hospital.

For those interested in an update, my armpit is getting red and tenderer from the radiation. I find myself holding it away from the body as much as possible to keep it from rubbing. My digestive tract, while some better, is still not all it should be. I called and made an appointment with a gastroenterologist. I think it is probably gastritis that hasn't fully healed, caused by all the chemo. We shall see what the expert has to say.

Fatigue continues to give me the most difficulty. I talked with another breast cancer patient who is just a little ahead of me in her treatments. She said she could feel the energy difference within a week after she finished radiation. I am hoping that will also be the case for me. I am so very tired of being tired. I want to be able to go and do as I did before the cancer treatments started. It feels frustrating not to. But, as the Lord reminded me yesterday, I am to meet suffering with patience and trust Him

My focus is on the fact that we, as Christians, are to reflect God's glory. We are to love like Him, act like Him and think like Him. What we do, who we are, and how we think should, each day, be growing to be more and more like Jesus. We are to continue submitting ourselves to His Holy Spirit, who brings transformation to our lives.

Hmmm... God wants to transform each and every one of us to reflect His love, joy, peace, patience, kindness, goodness, faithfulness, gentleness and self- control. The only way we can do that is by developing a deeper and more intimate relationship with Him. Obedience is the key to unlocking the door to His transforming power.

Take a deep look and hmmm on these questions. Who do you look like when you look into the mirror of your heart? Is it reflecting more of the Lord than last time you looked? God is not concerned with your outer appearance. He is deeply concerned with the condition of your heart. He wants us to be reflections of Jesus in a world that is dying and desperately in need of the love and forgiveness He has to offer. Don't forget to check the mirror.

A Great Day and a Great Psalm... Friday, October 4, 2013

Happy morning. I want to tell you what a glorious day yesterday was. I had my radiation treatment, sit in on counseling sessions with Dr. Porter, and visited my friends at St. Luke's. You all know that watching the Lord work to free folks and encourage them in counseling times is one of my favorite things. Well, that blessing was joined by a precious moment with one of my radiation nurses. We were able to enjoy a heart to heart talk as she set me up to receive the treatment. Then, as we finished, I was able to snag a few pictures of some of my nurses at St. Anthony's.

The best part of the day was a fabulous visit with the folks at St. Luke's. I have missed them a lot, so going to visit blessed "my socks off." When Dr. Porter and I first arrived, we went to the lab to see Melinda and Charity. Unfortunately, Melinda had a sick day today, but we got to visit with and love on Charity. Before we left, Dr. Porter prayed for Melinda and Charity and we all enjoyed hugs. Of course, we left sweet treats of chocolate behind before heading up to the oncology department.

When we arrived there, it was lunch time for some of the ladies in the office, so we left little piles of candy by their computers as we worked our way back to the area where the patient examining rooms were, sharing candy with patients and their families and other workers along the way. We went back to the transfusion area. We were both greeted with happy hellos, loving hugs, encouraging words, and warm smiles. My heart leaped with joy as I had the pleasure of hugging and talking with my friends. It was so wonderful to see each and every one of them. Wow, I love those folks! While I visited with the folks who had taken such good care of me for many months, Dr. Porter made his way through the transfusion area, going from patient to patient, sharing the blessings of the Lord's joy, and candy with each one. After a heartwarming time with the folks in the transfusion area, one of them went to get Dr. Gill from her office so we could say hello. She came out for a quick visit, too. Yup, yesterday was a really pleasant day.

This Psalm has been great encouragement to me for many years. Let the words sink in and wash over you.

> I lift up my eyes to the hills—where does my help come from? My help comes from the Lord, the Maker of heaven and earth. He will not let your foot slip; He who watches over you will not slumber; indeed, He who watches over Israel will neither slumber nor sleep. The Lord watches over you; the Lord is your shade at your right hand; the sun will not harm you by day, nor the moon by night. The Lord will keep you from all harm – He will watch over your life; the Lord will watch over your coming and going both now and forevermore. (Psalm 121)

Always remember, the Lord is your ultimate help. I am grateful for the Lord's help and His ever watchful eye on me. I hope you are, too.

Revelations and Secrets... Saturday, October 5, 2013

Hello, my friends. I think I actually got almost nine hours of sleep last night. What a rare treat! Yesterday was spent counseling. During our time together, we discussed how the Lord tells us things and whether or not He tells us everything. As I was doing some reading this morning, I ran across verses in Daniel 12:8-9 that reminded me of that discussion.

God had been revealing things about the end of the age to Daniel. He did not fully understand them all, so He asked God to give Him further understanding. He wanted to know more about what the Lord had been revealing. However, the Lord declined. God tells us many things and reveals things that we could not know except that He reveals them.

> Call to me and I will answer you and tell you great and unsearchable things you do not know. (Jeremiah 33:3)

Even though He tells us unsearchable things, things that are not accessible to us except from Him, there are positively things He does not tell us, secret things. The things that are secret belong strictly to the Lord (Deuteronomy 29:29). Everything He has revealed belongs to us and future generations as well. God knows exactly what is needful and beneficial for us to know.

God wants us to know Him and to know that only He and He alone, is God. Allah is not God, Buddha is not God, Mother Earth is not God, nor is any other thing that man has chosen to exalt. Only the Lord is God. And He loves to reveal Himself to us, sharing with us things that we could not otherwise know. But when we ask Him to tell us "why, when or what about?" of life and He declines, we must know the answers are not beneficial to us.

If His Holy Spirit is not in you, you will not accept nor understand the things He reveals (I Corinthians 2:10, 14). If you have not yet put your trust in Jesus, it is my prayer that you will do so today. If you have, I hope you will thank the Lord for the wonderful revelations He has given us. Trust Him with the questions He leaves unanswered. He is faithful and knows what is best for you. He will always give you what you need.

Knows All... Second Guessing... Monday, October 7, 2013

Happy Monday! I started Sunday with the worship service and then lunch with Dr. Porter and Miss Linnie and my parents. It was a great time. After lunch, I had a short stop at home before going back to church for my ladies Bible study and the evening worship service. My, the day flew by. As the saying goes, "Time flies when you are having fun!"

The night went a little differently. I woke up a little after 1 a.m. with pain in my stomach that would not subside. Finally, around 3 a.m. I got up and took some Pepto-Bismol. An hour after taking it, the pain eased enough for me to go back to sleep. When the alarm went off this morning, I did not want to move. I still have discomfort, but not nearly as much as during the night. I am glad I made the G.I. doctor's appointment. I chose not to get up as soon as the alarm went off in order to rest a bit more, so my time to hmmm will be short. As I read my Bible this morning, these following two verses stood out.

> Who has understood the mind of the Lord, or instructed him as his counselor? Whom did the Lord consult to enlighten Him, and who taught Him the right way? Who was it that taught Him knowledge or showed Him the path of understanding? (Isaiah 40:13-14)

The Lord knows absolutely everything. He understands where you are, who you are, and why you are where you are in life. He also understands what it will take to get you where you need to be (Psalm 147:5). "His understanding has no limit."

Hmmm... have you ever second guessed God? Ever thought you knew more than He did or that He didn't really understand your situation? When Job suffered great hardship, the Lord reminded Job of all the things He had done, created, and controlled (Job 38-Job 41) and that he did not understand all the great mysteries of the Lord. When we do not understand the difficulties and mysteries of life, and have chosen to second guess the Lord, we should respond as Job did when he replied "I know that you can do all things."

I encourage you to come before Him, confess your sin of doubt and turn from it. He knows where you are and the difficulties you face. He is faithful to see you through whether you understand them or not.

Never Failing Compassions... Tuesday, October 8, 2013

Hello there. I awoke with stomach pain again, so I thought I might start our time together now. Maybe when I finish writing I will be able to get some sleep. Yesterday was a little tough. Fatigue and stomach discomfort persisted all day. But, the praise is that I made it through all day at work and then the radiation treatment, too.

Ellie Mae is a "cool weather girl." She is more lethargic in the hot months and when the fall starts to move in, it boosts her energy. It normally does mine, too. So far this year, it hasn't, but I am hoping after radiation is finished in a couple of weeks, energy will pick up. I asked the radiation oncologist when I saw him today how long after radiation it takes for the fatigue of radiation to go away. He said usually it takes about a month, but it depends on how much fatigue a person has left from chemo, too. (Sigh) Patience… Patience… Patience…

One of the nurses told me today that they are going to change the area where they treat with the radiation on Wednesday. I think they call it a "boost" if I remember right. That will require a longer appointment to realign the equipment. I suppose I may get "redrawn" with all the pretty blue body paint lines they put all over my chest, side and stomach. They will shrink the area they are treating in order to hit only the area where the tumor was and not the surrounding tissue as well. Hopefully that will mean they will no longer be hitting the armpit. It is the rawest area.

As I was reading, I ran across a couple of verses that lodged in my heart. They remind me of the sermon my pastor, Dr. McLain, gave Sunday evening. His sermon was on Jonah and how the Lord gave him a second chance to do what He had called him to do, rather than letting him drown when he disobeyed. The whole story can be found in the book of Jonah. The verses I read this morning are:

> Because of the Lord's great love we are not consumed, for His compassions never fail. They are new every morning; great is Your faithfulness. (Lamentations 3:22-23)

I think about how often I failed the Lord and chose to be rebellious, how often I turned a deaf ear to what I heard Him calling me to do, how often I looked the other way when He wanted to show me something that I was not sure I wanted to see, how often I backed off when I felt fear, even though

He assured me I had no reason to fear. These verses are a comfort to me because they remind me that the Lord loves you and me, and He continues to have compassion on us. "His compassions will never fail." Isn't that good news! We often fail, but God never will.

Hmmm... not only did Jonah fail the Lord by running from Him when he was called to go and preach in Nineveh, but Peter failed the Lord as well. Peter was one of Jesus' Twelve Disciples, who at a critical moment, when he could have stood for Jesus, denied Him three times. His fear, denial and failure grieved him so deeply that he went out and wept bitterly (Luke 22:54-62). Even though Peter denied the Lord, his own failure and denial, just as Jonah's, and ours, can never diminish God's love and compassion. He is faithful, even when we are not. Great is His faithfulness.

Have you failed the Lord? Do you need a second chance, or a third or fourth? The Lord is faithful. Run to Him in repentance. He will never fail you.

Her Many Sins Have Been Forgiven...
Wednesday, October 9, 2013

I slept all the way through last night and did not wake up once. Praise the Lord! After the last two nights of pain and little sleep, it was certainly needed. A second praise is, though my stomach is uncomfortable, it is not nearly as painful as it has been.

Yesterday's appointment with Dr. Sajid Zafar, the gastroenterologist resulted in scheduling an endoscope to be done. (For those of you who do not know what that is, it is when they run a scope down your throat to see what is going on in your stomach.) I also will have an abdominal ultrasound. Yesterday was busy. I ran from the time I got up till I crawled back in bed for the night. Work was followed by the doctor's appointment and then to the lab to have blood drawn for tests. I had to hurry through that and drive as fast as and maybe a little faster than the law allowed to get from St. Luke's to St. Anthony's to have my radiation treatment. By the time I got home, all I had time to do was to take Ellie Mae out, bring in the laundry that was hanging outside, and pack my lunch bag for today's work shift and then hit the bed. Whew! What a day.

Hmmm... the Lord reminded me, as I pondered this verse, that *my* sins have been forgiven (Luke 7:47a). There have been many. God promises to forgive our sins if we will confess them.

> If we confess our sins, He is faithful and just and will forgive us our sins and purify us from all unrighteousness. (I John 1:9)

Once we confess and turn away from our sins, no matter how numerous, we are forgiven. However, we must believe that they are forgiven. I had fallen prey to the devil's lies for many years and did not forgive myself, even though God had forgiven me. In allowing Satan to convince me of his lies rather than believing and standing on God's truth, I gave up the peace, comfort and contentment Jesus died to give me. By refusing God's truth, I lived in inner turmoil and misery. When Satan comes peddling his lies, point him to the truth of God's Word.

Thinking of Him... Thursday, October 10, 2013

I will start the morning with praise. I slept through last night again with no pain, no awake time, and no trips to the smallest room in the house. Hip-Hip Hooray! I am, and have been, very tired, so this is a huge praise. Today is planned to be another very busy day, so having rest was extremely important. I will start the day after my time with you by working the early shift and then I have to be at St. Anthony's for a radiation treatment followed by an appointment for an abdominal ultrasound at St. Luke's. I cannot eat or drink anything after 6:30 a.m. this morning, so I will try to stop writing early enough to have a decent breakfast before that time. The Lord knows how much I want to get all the medical issues settled.

When I went for my radiation treatment yesterday, I was on the table for much longer than usual so they could realign the equipment and redraw their markings for the new treatment area. I was there so long I fell asleep while they did some of their work. Whenever I get still for too long, I am quickly sound asleep. The radiation treated area is now smaller and more centralized. I had to laugh when I saw my body after they finished. Not only do I have the blue and purple lines from the first treatment area, but a whole lot of new green lines, squiggles, circles, and X's all over the place. I really do look like a kiddo had a field day scribbling all over half of my chest, side and belly.

I had hoped that the new treatment area would no longer hit my armpit where I am the rawest, but that will not be the case. However, the area underneath the breast that was irritated won't. That area was the second most irritated. When my nurse, Cathy, who was redrawing the lines, told me that the armpit was going to still be hit, I asked her about the second spot. When she said, no, it wouldn't be hit, I said, "Yea! That is a plus!" She grinned at me and told me she loved taking care of me because I always looked at the positive side of things. Life is better that way. If you choose to focus on the negative all the time, you will be miserable. And, I hate to be miserable.

Hmmm... your mind's focus is of utmost importance to your ability to keep a positive and upbeat attitude. God continues to remind us throughout scripture that the focus of our hearts and minds will be the steering wheel that guides our attitude. "For as he thinks in his heart, so is he." (Proverbs 23:7a).

Take some time to search your heart and mind. What are you spending your time thinking about? Are you a positive person or a negative one? Ask the Lord to help you keep your heart and mind focused on Him and to direct your thoughts. That will always keep your day on a positive and upbeat note.

Not My Will But Yours... Friday, October 11, 2013

Hi! It is me again. I have to be at the surgery center at 6 a.m. this morning, so I will be leaving the house a little after 5 a.m. The procedure today is an endoscopy. The good news is, the last couple of days, my stomach began feeling much better. I will be glad to get the assurance all is healing well or at least get on the path there. I got to the imaging center for the ultrasound a little early and thought I was going to have to wait for a while, but as soon as I sat down, they called me to get started. I had a pleasant technician to perform the procedure. We had a great opportunity to chat about the Lord and His faithfulness. It has been fun to watch how the Lord gives me opportunities to share Him with others in this season of life. He will do that for all of us, no matter the season, if we are willing.

The radiation treatment went well yesterday. I am thoroughly enjoying the nurses who take care of me. I am glad the treatments do not take a lot of time each day, but I would like to be able to hang out with the folks there just a little bit longer. The treatments, though now more centralized, are given with a stronger dose of radiation than I was receiving before. The skin is showing more and more discoloration. It is red and, for lack of a better word, tanned. The tan is not a pretty tan like the sun gives, but different somehow, maybe a bit grayish. It is hard to describe.

As I was writing an email to a friend of mine last night, I expressed the desire to have at least a brief reprieve from all the less than pleasant things I have been experiencing in the last year and a half. I was not complaining, but simply expressing the feeling of wanting a break from it all. The Lord reminded me that He was, is, and always will be faithful, no matter what I am experiencing. I positively don't doubt it. I know He has been, and is still, working patience and perseverance in me. Those are good things, and I want them, even though I desire a reprieve from it all. As I contemplated this line of thought, Holy Spirit reminded me of Jesus' prayer in the Garden of Gethsemane.

> Father, if you are willing, take this cup from me; yet not my will, but yours be done. And being in anguish, he prayed more earnestly, and His sweat was like drops of blood falling to the ground. (Luke 22:42, 44)

Holy Spirit reminded me that Jesus was not excited about having to face the horrific difficulty of the cross and his temporary separation from the Father; nevertheless He submitted His will to the Father in order to allow Him to bring about what He desired and knew was best. If Jesus had not gone to the cross, you and I would have no hope. We would have been lost to the consequences of our sin forever. Praise the Lord for His great plan to rescue us. Just as the Father had a perfect plan for Jesus' life, He has a perfect plan for your and my life as well. He is forever, completely, and undeniably faithful.

Worry and the Lord's Encouragement...
Saturday, October 12, 2013

Hello. I had another good night of sleep and enjoyed sleeping in this morning. I think the anesthesia took the "sap out of me" yesterday because most all the things I thought I was going to accomplish did not get done. I rested and napped, lying on the floor with Ellie Mae most of the day and evening.

The results of the endoscope showed no sign of any problems. Everything looked completely normal with the exception of the discovery of a very minor hiatus hernia. He said it would likely never give me any problems and that 60% of folks have one by the time they are 60 years old. When I asked what causes them, heavy lifting was a common cause.

As I think back over the last several years, I remember the heavy bales of hay I helped pick up and stack in the barn each summer, the bundles of t-posts and rolls of barbed-wire I would carry to the area of fencing we were working on, the stacks of boards as we built fencing and rebuilt stall dividers in the barns, stacks of tile I moved when the house was built, then there were all the heavy cases of product and wood pallets to stack when I worked the grocery department at Schnucks.

Hmmm... or, maybe it was the furniture I moved by myself from time to time or the sacks of grain that I would buy at the feed store and then stack in the barn. Those are only a few of the heavy things that came to mind after the nurse asked if I was a weight lifter. I told her that I was not a weight lifter when she asked. As I contemplate it now, maybe I was, but just not in the traditional sense. This last year, beyond moving all my things when my husband and I separated, and the things required at work, I have lifted very little with the exception of a sweet, ninety-plus pound Rottweiler who thinks she is a lap dog. I cannot complain about that, however, because I spoiled her to be that way.

As always, Father sends encouragement to lift me as I have need of it. I shared with Dr. Porter what I was feeling and how Satan was working to discourage me and trying to cause me to worry. He wrote me back confirming to me the truth that was already in my heart. His Words to me were, "It is the work of our enemy in these last five days of radiation trying one final time to bring you down. But you have come this far, Father will not let you falter now. Lean on Him strongly. He will lift you up tomorrow." (Thank you, Dr. Porter and Miss Linnie for your many prayers and encouragement.) Holy Spirit reminded me of this verse this morning.

> Therefore do not worry about tomorrow, for tomorrow will worry about itself. Each day has enough trouble of its own. (Matthew 6:34)

The Lord has taken care of me and all the trouble I faced. I have no need to worry about whatever trouble tomorrow might bring. He will walk with me in the future, too. I have no need to worry. God is absolutely sovereign. Worry on my end is futile. "Who of you by worrying can add a single hour to his life?" (Matthew 6:27).

God knows what we need and has the means, ability, and willingness to provide it. He promises to provide for all our needs. We have absolutely no need to worry.

Hmmm... are you worrying today? You are much more valuable to the Lord than all the other things He has created. You are so valuable that He gave the life of His one and only Son to reconcile you to Himself.

Praises and Psalm 23... Monday, October 14, 2013

Good morning. Yesterday was absolutely beautiful. It was sunny and bright with a bit of fall crispness in the morning and evening and warmth through the day. Hmmm... it is my favorite kind of day. I was blessed with the ability to hang out with my wonderful church family and worship. As you all know, Sunday is my favorite day of the week.

And I got an email from Dr. Gill to let me know there was nothing of concern in the results of the ultrasound test. Praise the Lord! I still think that the discomfort in the upper stomach area and digestive tract that is not totally happy is somehow tied to the side effects of the chemo. The body has a lot of healing and rebuilding to do after all the treatments.

As I write to you now, I can hardly keep my eyes open, even with a nap and a somewhat decent night of sleep it is hard to stay awake. Psalm 23 is one of my favorite psalms. It always brings peace, comfort, joy and thanksgiving. You will see that the Lord gives us: relationship, provision, rest, refreshment, healing, guidance, purpose, testing times, protection, courage, His presence, faithfulness, discipline, comfort, hope, satisfaction, honor, abundance, blessing, security, eternity and so much more.

> The Lord is my shepherd; I shall not be in want. He makes me lie down in green pastures, he leads me beside quiet waters, and he restores my soul. He guides me in paths of righteousness for his name's sake. Even though I walk through the valley of the shadow of death, I will fear no evil for you are with me; your rod and your staff, they comfort me. You prepare a table before me in the presence of my enemies. You anoint my head with oil; my cup overflows. Surely goodness and love will follow me all the days of my life, and I will dwell in the house of the Lord forever. (Psalm 23)

Thank the Lord for all the wonderful things He gives to you today and every day. He is more wonderful to us than words can express. His love for you and me never ceases to amaze me.

Blessed by His Sweet Assurances... Tuesday, October 15, 2013

Hi there! I am on the countdown. Only three more radiation treatments! Each day brings me one day closer to the end. I have been on this path so long that it almost seems surreal to be almost finished with the treatments. My skin continues to get pinker in some areas and browner in others with each radiation treatment. When I saw the doctor today, he said that I was still doing great. He did not expect that I would experience any major difficulties with my skin, even with the increased strength of the radiation. Praise the Lord!

I am continually amazed by the number of customers who are still sharing with me that they have been praying for me. Some, I do not even remember waiting on before. Even though I am sure that I have at some point. I just can't seem to remember all their faces. Other customers tell me how much they love my "haircut." It tickles me when they say that. Some of them truly do not realize the short hair is not a "cut", but regrowth, while others are just looking for something nice to say. It is considerate of them to engage in conversation with me, whatever the case. As I think about the hair that is steadily growing on my head, I am pleasantly pleased with the soft waves I see when it is wet. The longer it gets the more of them I see. I am currently putting some product on them to keep them from sticking up as they dry. They can be a bit unruly if I do not use a little bit of beauty shop help to keep them lying properly. Lots of folks keep asking if I am going to grow my hair out or keep it relatively short. The honest answer is: I have absolutely no idea. I am taking the hair growth just as I am my life, one day at a time.

I have been through a heap of life changes in a relatively short period of time. Some days they left my head feeling like it was spinning. When I went into the cancer treatments, they gave me a radical life change on top of the other recent changes of the marital separation and moving. Now, as I emerge from the cancer treatments and prepare to start a new chapter of life, I know more changes are coming. I am excited about them, yet, I feel a little disconcerted. There are more than a few "Okay, now what?" feelings swirling around inside. I know the Lord has it all under control. He knows what is coming next in my life. As I contemplate these feelings, the next verse is particularly comforting. "All the days ordained for me were written in your book before one of them came to be." (Psalm 139:16b).

The Lord knows exactly what is ahead for me. He ordained each and every day of my life before I was born. Nothing can take Him by surprise. That is a great comfort, because I have had many surprises. And, several have been decidedly unpleasant. The Lord already had His provision in place for me as each one arrived on the scene. None of my surprises were a surprise to Him. Even though I still face much uncertainty, I am excited because the Lord has assured my heart that there are many surprises yet to come and a large number of them are pleasant. He reminds me that He has a bright future for me that is full of hope.

> "For I know the plans I have for you," declares the Lord, "plans to prosper you and not to harm you, plans to give you hope and a future." (Jeremiah 29:11)

No matter where I go, no matter what my future holds, I have His assurance that His goodness and love will always follow me. Even if, in the future, I have to face days just as dark and difficult as the ones in the last year and a half, I have His promise to be with me, just as He is now.

In my younger years, I was bound by much fear, but the Lord set me free from it. He gave me His comfort and assurance that He would always be with me and I had nothing to fear. He knows just what I need and when I need it. As I seek Him, He always gives it. He will for you too, dear friends. He is always faithful and true to His Word.

Shall and Shall Not... Wednesday, October 16, 2013

The radiation count is now down to two, today and tomorrow. The nurses got me in early yesterday as they have done every day that I showed up early. They are so thoughtful to do that for me. On the days I work a 6 a.m. to 2 p.m. shift, I get to the hospital early and my appointment time is not until 3:15. But, because of their quick and effective work, I have always been leaving the hospital, finished with my daily treatment, by that time if not before. I have come to love these ladies just as I do the ones at St. Luke's. On my way home from the hospital, I bought the largest jar I could find and lots of assorted candies to fill it. I will take it to my new friends at St. Anthony's on my last treatment day, just to let them know how much I appreciate them.

When I stopped at the store to purchase my thank you gift for the staff in the radiation department, I ran into another lady who had gone through breast cancer and divorce within a short period of time, just as I have. We were able to stand and chat for a while, sharing the stories of our lives and praising the Lord for His faithfulness to us. It was a precious time with a fellow sister in Christ. She let me know that she had needed a bit of encouragement and that the Lord provided it through me. Praise the Lord that I could be His instrument of encouragement.

Today, I was reading in Deuteronomy 5, where the Ten Commandments are found. The Lord gives us important instructions there. He tells us things we are to do and things we must not do. Some folks seem to think God is some kind of "cosmic killjoy" because He sets laws and rules for us to follow. Nothing could be further from the truth. When the Lord tells us, "You shall not," He is showing us how to keep from unnecessary pain, trouble, and destruction in our lives.

> Oh, that their hearts would be inclined to fear Me and keep all My commands always, so that it might go well with them and their children forever! (Deuteronomy 5:29)

Have you ever stopped to realize that? He loves you deeply and gave His instruction so that "it might go well with you and your children." He is a loving Father, guiding His children to a place of safety and blessing. When the Lord tells us "You shall", He is telling us how to be happy and live prosperously.

> Honor your father and your mother, as the Lord your God has commanded you, so that you may live long and that it may go well with you in the land the Lord your God is giving you. (Deuteronomy 5:16)

Obedience, plainly and simply, is the way to joy and blessing. Disobedience brings pain, trouble, and destruction. We must be careful to take the Lord's instruction seriously. He does not speak nor give idle words, but words of life and truth. It is important for us to set our hearts and minds to obey the Lord's instructions.

Hmmm...the Lord wants to give us His best. He can only do so when we follow His commands. I want His best. How about you?

Last Radiation Treatment, Praise Him...
Thursday, October 17, 2013

The day is finally here. Today is the last official day of cancer treatments! It has been a long journey, but, it really has been a good journey. I met so many wonderful people and have been blessed with lots of neat experiences, too. I will contemplate more of those with you later. The best news is I know there are more great experiences yet to come. I will have one more stop to make after today. I am scheduled to have my final procedure, surgery to take the port out.

Yesterday was a good day. I worked in the morning then had a radiation treatment. I had three delightful nurse technicians with me: Brandy, Cathy, and Kasey. My spellings may be wrong of their names because I am always flat on my back when I get my chance to visit with them, so I never get a close look at their name badges. They line me up with the radiation equipment and draw on me with their pretty markers as we chat. After treatment, they all posed for a picture for me for my scrapbook. Before I left, I had a moment or two to talk with Brandy. She told me how much she would miss me and gave me a great big hug, making me promise to come back and see her when I had my follow up visit with the doctor in a month or so. I will have to make sure I do.

I am feeling, even more than usual, like praising the Lord. I feel particularly blessed this morning. As I started my time with you, the Lord brought me to some verses in Jeremiah that really spoke to my heart.

> But blessed is the man who trusts in the Lord, whose confidence is in Him. He will be like a tree planted by the water that sends out its roots by the stream. It does not fear when heat comes; its leaves are always green. It has no worries in a year of drought and never fails to bear fruit. (Jeremiah 17:7-8)

As I read these words, the Lord reminded me that I was able to walk this challenging path without great fear and with His peace because I trusted Him. As I continued to trust Him, He continued to bless me. He is so worthy of honor, praise, and thanksgiving.

> Heal me, O Lord, and I will be healed; save me and I will be saved, for You are the one I praise; …You are my refuge in the day of disaster. (Jeremiah 17:14, 17b)

The Lord heals me. I praise Him! The Lord saves me. I praise Him! The Lord is my refuge, no matter the storm. I praise Him! The Lord is always with me. I praise Him! He gives me peace and provision. I praise him! He gives me beauty for ashes. I praise Him! He turns my sorrow to joy. I praise Him! He lifts and encourages me. I praise Him! He is faithful. He is love. He is kind. I praise Him!

The Lord gave me a little extra time for reflecting on His goodness and grace this morning, as well as loving and praising Him. I hope you will do the same. Take time to look over your life. Praise the Lord for all the good things He is doing and has done. Thank Him in advance for the good things He will do in the future. He is so very worthy of all the praise, honor, and gratitude we can give.

Chapter 12

The End of Cancer Treatments

Final Days - The Port Comes Out
October 18, 2013 – October 23, 2013

No Trip to the Hospital….Friday, October 18, 2013

I am yawning and stretching after sleeping in this morning. What a wonderful treat. Shortly after waking, I remembered I would have **NO** trip to the hospital today. Praise the Lord! All my cancer treatments are finished. It seems very odd to see this chapter of life coming to a close. I have been on this journey for eight months. The appointments to find out what was wrong started back in February. Now I am heading into the latter part of October. While I was in the midst of all the treatments, it seemed so long. Now, it really does not seem so long after all. It is funny how life works. When we are anticipating something good, the good thing seems like it takes a long time in coming. But, when we finally get to what we are anticipating, it seems like time passes too quickly.

Our lives here on this earth are quickly passing. If you are like me, you want to make the most of your life. I received an email from Rick Mead, my playfully adopted "African Daddy." He said, "I believe you have found the secret to a victorious life. It is praise and thanksgiving always in all things to God the Father in the Name of our Lord Jesus Christ."

Hmmm… the secret to the victorious life. That prompted me to think about all the things that have helped me to live a life closer to the Lord, a life of more joy, more fulfillments, more purpose, more strength, more peace, and more love, a life of "more" of all the truly good things.

As I pondered this thought, I started going through my Bible and pulling out scriptures that the Lord has taught me and encouraged me to do. The list is not a final list by any means, but, these scriptures and are and have been a great blessing and encouragement to me as I live the life the Lord has given me. I pray they will be to you as well.

Give Him Praise and Thanksgiving.
> Enter his gates with thanksgiving and his courts with praise; give thanks to him and praise his name. (Psalm 100:4)

Pray always about Everything, Give Thanks always.
> Be joyful always; pray continually; give thanks in all circumstances, for this is God's will for you in Christ Jesus. (I Thessalonians 5:16-18)

Find your Joy in His Presence.
> You have made known to me the path of life; you will fill me with joy in your presence, with eternal pleasures at your right hand. (Psalm 16:11)

Trust Him, Delight in Him, Make Him Lord and Master, Wait Upon Him.
> Trust in the Lord and do good; dwell in the land and enjoy safe pasture. Delight yourself in the Lord and He will give you the desires of your heart. Commit your way to the Lord; trust in Him and He will do this: He will make your righteousness shine like the dawn, the justice of your cause like the noonday sun. Be still before the Lord and wait patiently for Him; do not fret when men succeed in their ways, when they carry out their wicked schemes. (Psalm 37:3-7)

Focus, Give Diligent, Consistent attention to His Word and Obey.
> But the man who looks intently into the perfect law that gives freedom, and continues to do this, not forgetting what he has heard, but doing it; he will be blessed in what he does. (James 1:25)

Always Abide in Him.
> If you remain in Me and My words remain in you, ask whatever you wish, and it will be given you. (John 15:7)

Confess Sin and Repent Immediately.
>If we confess our sins, He is faithful and just and will forgive us our sins and purify us from all unrighteousness. (I John 1:9)

Always Listen to and Obey Holy Spirit and Be Filled by Him.
>Do not put out the Spirit's fire... (I Thessalonians 5:19)
>...Instead, be filled with the Spirit. (Ephesians 5:18b)

Continually Renew Your Mind and Focus on Positive Things.
>Do not conform any longer to the pattern of this world, but be transformed by the renewing of your mind. Then you will be able to test and approve what God's will is, His good, pleasing and perfect will. (Romans 12:2)

>Finally, brothers, whatever is true, whatever is noble, whatever is right, whatever is pure, whatever is lovely, whatever is admirable, if anything is excellent or praiseworthy, think about such things. (Philippians 4:8)

When you Need Rest, Go to the Lord and Learn from Him.
>Come to me, all you who are weary and burdened, and I will give you rest. Take my yoke upon you and learn from Me, for I am gentle and humble in heart, and you will find rest for your souls. (Matthew 11:28-29)

Trust Jesus to Save You, Trust Him and Do Not Fear.
>Surely God is my salvation; I will trust and not be afraid. The Lord is my strength and my song; He has become my salvation. (Isaiah 12:2)

Find Strength and Courage in the Lord; Place Your Hope in Him.
>Be strong and take heart, all you who hope in the Lord. (Psalm 31:24)

Know and Always Remember, He Alone is God.
>Acknowledge and take to heart this day that the Lord is God in heaven above and on the earth below. There is no other. (Deuteronomy 4:39)

Submit Yourself to God, Resist the Devil, Draw Near to God
> Submit yourselves to God; resist the devil and he will flee from you. Come near to God and He will come near to you. (James 4:7-8a)

Remember you are in a Spiritual Battle, Fight with Spiritual Weapons. Trust the Lord to Free You from Strongholds.
Keep Your Mind Pure, Submit every Thought to Jesus.
> The weapons we fight with are not the weapons of the world. On the contrary, they have divine power to demolish strongholds. We demolish arguments and every pretension that sets itself up against the knowledge of God, and we take captive every thought to make it obedient to Christ. (II Corinthians 10:4-5)

Remember what the Lord has Done, Rejoice
in Him, And Seek His Face.
> Glory in his holy name; let the hearts of those who seek the Lord rejoice. Look to the Lord and his strength; seek his face always. Remember the wonders He has done, his miracles and the judgments He pronounced. (I Chronicles 16-10)

As I mentioned at the beginning of this list, it is not a comprehensive list by any means. They are simply scriptures of great help to me in my journey through this life. I hope you will take a little time today and in the next couple of days and hmmm a bit on each one. Search your heart and see how close you are to living as the Lord has instructed in each verse. May these verses encourage and lift you as they have me, many, many times.

Port Comes Out; Pain and Gain... Monday, October 21, 2013

Tomorrow is the last scheduled procedure to be done in conjunction with the cancer. I am to have my port removed at St. Luke's. When the hospital called to confirm the procedure this evening, I found out I will not have to go under anesthesia. Praise the Lord! It is an even more minor procedure than I thought it was. The person from the hospital told me from start to finish; the port removal should only take about fifteen minutes. Wow! That is much better than I could have imagined. Even more wonderful is the fact I can eat, drink, and take my vitamins in the morning. I do not have to fast after midnight. I can even drive myself to and from the hospital if I want to. I am not so sure I want to. It might be the last chance "Miss Daisy" has for "Hoke" to drive her for a while. Having my own personal chauffeur for chemo treatments was quite a treat.

As I sit here thinking about this being the last procedure in a long line of treatments, I have a swirling mixture of thoughts and emotions. They are a lot to process. Some are a feeling of relief… an end to all the treatments, the ability to get back on the road to feeling better, and the chance to regain normalcy in my life.

I have an excited anticipation for the future, but I also have sadness, too. I am already missing, and will miss, the folks who have cared for me at the hospitals. The thought of missing the regular times of sharing with them is a sad one. I have come to enjoy them so very much. In many ways, I am starting over again. I am beginning to readjust my life and starting new routines. I am very much a creature of habit. Changing habits is not usually easy for me.

The good part is that the Lord used the whole upset in my routines and the difficulties of my life, when things seemed out of control and nothing like I had hoped or expected, to teach me how to trust Him more completely. I am always happy to have Him teach me to trust Him more. Usually, the learning requires some pain on my part, but the pain is well worth the benefit gained. I love how the Lord works in that way. It gives a whole new perspective to the saying, "No pain; No gain!" Hmmm… that line of thinking reminds me of a verse.

> … but God is faithful, who will not allow you to be tempted beyond what you are able, but with the temptation will also make the way of escape, that you may be able to bear it. (I Corinthians 10:13b)

When difficult times come into our lives, we will always be faced with temptation. The temptation may be to run, quit, hide, get angry, lash out, or any other of a long list of negative and wrong responses. One of the worst responses to difficulty in our lives is the temptation to disbelieve God and what He says about us and the situation. Satan will always tempt us to disregard God and His truth, walking in fear rather than trusting the Lord.

God will never allow Satan to tempt us beyond the ability He will give us to withstand the temptation and/or escape it. God's promise is a promise of faithfulness. In the original language, *faithfulness* has connotations of reliability and trustworthiness. When God's children are facing difficult times and are weak, we can expect God to show Himself strong on our behalf. He is faithful to this promise.

> But he said to me, "My grace is sufficient for you, for my power is made perfect in weakness." Therefore I will boast all the more gladly about my weaknesses, so that Christ's power may rest on me. That is why, for Christ's sake, I delight in weaknesses, in insults, in hardships, in persecutions, in difficulties. For when I am weak, then I am strong. (II Corinthians 12:9-10)

It is important to remember, we must trust the Lord and have our hearts fully committed to Him. Our submission and commitment to Him are of utmost importance to our reception of His strength. "For the eyes of the Lord range throughout the earth to strengthen those whose hearts are fully committed to Him." (II Chronicles 16:9a).

Hmmm... what difficulties are you facing today? Do you believe the Lord for His strength to withstand the temptation to fear and distrust God and His Word? Do you truly trust Him? If not, is your heart fully committed to the Lord? God is looking for those whose hearts are fully committed to Him that He might strengthen them.

I am grateful for the Lord's faithfulness and work in my heart, growing me and teaching me how to trust Him more completely in these difficult months. I am grateful He made a way of escape from the many temptations Satan placed before me. I am also grateful for the strength He gave me to withstand them. The pain of this season has been well worth the gain. When we fully commit our hearts to Him and believe His Word, the pain will always be worth the gain.

Final Daily Update... Wednesday, October 23, 2013

Hello. It is me once again. The update is that I am now "port-less." Praise the Lord! The last procedure is complete. Mom and Dad went with me for the port removal. We arrived in plenty of time and all got sleepy while waiting for the procedure to begin. When I was taken to have the port removed, Dr. Limpert and I chatted the whole time she was removing it and sewing and gluing me back up. We discussed God's goodness to me in this season as well as many of the awesome things I have witnessed Him do.

She told me she has shared my story and testimony with her other patients and that it has proved to be an encouragement to them. Praise the Lord! What a heartwarming conversation it was.

Dr. Limpert was tickled with me when I asked if I could have my port after it was removed. I thought it would be a great memento and possibly something to put with my "Stones of Remembrance" scrapbook I plan to make. I was not allowed to keep it because of legal reasons, but she did clean it off and showed it to my parents and me. I snapped a picture or two of it instead of keeping it. Before she finished with me, she took a look at the area where the radiation had been done and told me how great it looked. She said I heal fast. Praise the Lord! He is the one who created these wonderful bodies of ours with the ability to heal.

After finishing with Dr. Limpert, the Lord prompted me to stop and see one of the ladies I have come to know at the hospital. I did, and found He had scheduled a divine appointment for me with her. She was dealing with a difficult situation in life and needed a bit of encouragement and love. I was blessed to be able to provide it. Praise the Lord! We hugged and chatted and shared tears. We prayed and asked the Lord to intervene and to show Himself strong on her behalf and give His wisdom. He loves to do those things for His children.

After my visit with her, my parents and I headed home to rest. I did very little in the afternoon except to rest. I even took a several hour nap. I crawled in bed shortly after lunch and a little bit of time in the back yard playing soccer with Mom and Ellie Mae. I did not rise again until almost 7 p.m. I think the rest was what I needed most. Praise the Lord for the ability to get it.

As I write to you today, I do so with a bit of sadness in my heart. Today will be the last of the daily updates. The cancer treatments are finished and the last procedure done. The cancer has been eradicated and all that is left is to continue to wait for the completed healing of the rest of the body from the side effects of the chemo and radiation and to start the work required to rebuild strength and muscle lost during treatment. I am excited by the thought of knowing I can work toward rebuilding the energy and no further treatments will back track me. Yea! The fatigue is on its way out and "spit and vinegar" are on their way back. Maybe it is not as fast as I would like, but I thank the Lord for His patience and strength as I deal with the fatigue.

I have enjoyed sharing this journey with you and have been so very blessed by those, who have prayed for, supported, provided, encouraged, helped, spoiled, comforted, and taken such very good care of me in so many ways. I have thanked the Lord more times than I can count. "I thank my God every time I remember you." (Philippians 1:3).

I cannot thank you enough for accompanying me on this journey. It has been an encouragement beyond what words can express just to know that you were there with me on the other end of the computer screen. I could feel the prayers lifted for me and was blessed beyond measure as I watched the Lord answer them in awesome ways. "Thank you" does not begin to describe the depth of what I feel in my heart as I think about you.

I am not sure what the Lord has ahead for me as I finish this season and step toward the next, but because of His promises to me, I can rest assured it will be good. I am not sure it is my "life verse," but the verse that the Lord has truly taken from head knowledge to heart knowledge for me in this season is:

> And we know that in all things God works for the good of those who love him, who have been called according to his purpose. (Romans 8:28)

I have watched the Lord take what, from a worldly perspective, was the ugliest year and half of my life, and use it for my good and His glory. He has grown me and given me a deeper understanding and knowing of who He is. He has given me a boldness and greater confidence in Him. He taught me how to rest in His peace even when my life is in chaos. He deepened my understanding of His love and increased my ability to share it with others. He taught me, no matter what things look like or feel like, what He has spoken is what is truth and I am to put my confidence and trust in Him and not what "appears" to be truth. *Only He is truth.* Dear friends, when you decide to wholeheartedly trust the Lord, He will take you through the dark and difficult journeys of this life in a way that you could never imagine possible. He is faithful, so completely faithful.

As I think about winding up our time together, the Lord reminded me of an old hymn I have sung many times. I will leave you with a part of it. If nothing else, I hope our time together has encouraged you to do these two things.

> Trust and Obey; For there's no other way;
> To be happy in Jesus; But to Trust and Obey.

I am excited about and anxiously anticipating the things that the Lord has ahead for me. He put in my heart the knowledge of good and happier days ahead. I have kept in my heart the words He spoke to me a short time prior to the cancer diagnosis. "There are harder days ahead, but there are days ahead filled with more joy and happiness than you have ever known. Trust Me."

He reminded me of that same thing this morning and put a knowing in my heart that the happier days are much closer now. Part of me feels like a little girl waiting for Christmas morning. I am anxiously awaiting the time to open the gift of the tomorrow the Lord has planned for me.

Thank you, dear friends. I love you all more than words can express. As I close our time together, I find myself praying for the Lord's blessing upon each and every one of you.

> The Lord bless you and keep you; the Lord make His face shine upon you and be gracious to you; the Lord turn His face toward you and give you peace. (Numbers 6:24-26)

Final Chapter in Kimberly's Life

During the months following her recovery of breast cancer, Kimberly worked full time at Schnucks Market, was active in church and the counseling ministry. She continued to experience fatigue and developed a persistent cough, but followed an exercise program to regain strength. While on the treadmill at the gym in October 2014, she experienced a seizure and was taken by ambulance to the hospital. After extensive tests, including CT scans and a MRI, it was determined that radical cells from the Infiltrating or Invasive Ductile Carcinoma (breast cancer) had migrated to the brain and lungs.

The assumption was that the brain cancer originated from the breast cancer. Dr. Gill speculated that a few radical cells had detached themselves from the breast and landed in the brain. The chemo would not have killed them because the brain has a natural defense system which keeps the chemo from being allowed into the brain to cause damage.

The medical team with Dr. Gill as lead oncologist determined that the plan was to begin with radiation treatments for the brain and steroids to help control the swelling in the brain and later to start chemo for treatment of the lungs. As a result of the radiation, she again lost her hair, but as always approached it with a positive attitude. She was most disappointed when the doctors advised that she could not drive for at least six months and would not be able to return to work. Kimberly loved being with her coworkers and customers and missed them. She shared the following with her friends and family:

> "Though my body is fragile and weak, just as a clay jar, His power is in me. It is His power that allows me to be in hard and difficult seasons of life and not be overtaken and crushed by them. I can stand strong in the Lord because He made His light to shine in me. His light shining in me is the knowledge that I have Jesus Christ

> as my Savior and His Holy Spirit living in me to be my constant guide and strength. I am never abandoned or alone. God's promise is that He will never leave me. I have no reason to fear or be discouraged. Knowing and sensing God's presence with me gives me the courage to face all that lies ahead without fear. I praise and thank the Lord for His encouragement and promises!"

In November after the last radiation treatment, she took a much anticipated trip to Denver to spend time with her brother, Mark and his family. It was a delightful and spiritually uplifting time for her.

In the following months, there were a number of emergency trips to the hospital and a prolonged stay of almost three weeks, many x-rays, blood tests, antibiotics to fight off infections, drains to remove fluid from her lungs. By the end of December she had again started chemo treatments, but in January 2015 due to blood clots in the lungs and leg she was in ICU for several days. Although she had planned to return to work in February, it became apparent that it would not be possible.

Kimberly though plagued with headaches, blood clots, coughing and fatigue continued to help Dr. Porter with counseling and with her parents had "chemo parties" on the chemo treatment days. In March she had a special surprise when the St. Luke's oncology infusion and radiation departments chose her as one of the patients who had been the most encouraging and inspiring patients. At the Awards ceremony, she was presented with a "Powered by Hope" medal. The Awards are a way to encourage, bring hope, and thank the patients who bring joy and encouragement to the staff and patients around them.

On Sunday evening, April 26, 2015, Kimberly's parents rushed her to the ER at St. Luke's Hospital in Chesterfield, Missouri (St. Louis area) as the result of a severe headache, nausea, vomiting, fatigue, coughing and unsteadiness, A few days later she sent an email with the results of the medical tests.

> "Dr. Julie Gill shared that the cancer at the base of my brain is continuing to grow, which she believes is causing the headaches, nausea and vomiting. There is nothing more, from a medical standpoint that can be done...no radiation, no surgery, and no chemo. Dr. Gill also informed us, from a medical standpoint, most patients have two to three months at this stage. How much time

on this earth I do or don't have is the Lord's. I am His, and was created for His good pleasure. And, if you want to get right down to it, I am tired of feeling lousy. That is not to say that I am asking for the Lord to take me home now, but heaven surely does sound more beautiful every day."

Only a few days later with her parents, Paul and Shirma Laughlin and Dr. Curtis Porter with her, she closed her eyes on earth and opened them in the presence of the Lord in heaven. Dr. Porter shared the following:

"After a week of suffering and pain at St. Luke's Hospital, one of the brightest lights in Heavenly Father's family experienced the greatest moment in her life at 5:15 pm Monday, May 4, 2015. As she left this earth to fly into the presence of her Heavenly Father and Loving Savior Jesus Christ, Kimberly McGary declared her readiness and eagerness to join her Christ in the home He has prepared for her. The doctors indicated that pneumonia was the final crushing blow to her body, filled with brain and lung cancer. As a chorus of praise and songs of victory were sung in her ears, she stopped struggling and released herself into the loving arms of Christ. There was no struggle, but rather instant perfect peace."

It has been my privilege and blessing to know Kimberly and to be a part of telling the story of her inspiring life.

Linnie G. Porter
Editor

Printed in the United States
By Bookmasters